'This book focuses on the impact of loss in couples and families where persistent grief leads to a chronic form of melancholic depression and sense of hopelessness, referred to diagnostically as complicated grief. Drawing on clinical and theoretical developments in couple and family psychoanalysis over the last several decades, this text, the first of its kind, provides the reader with a range of contemporary and innovative contributions concerning this clinical presentation, one hundred years after Freud's original text Mourning and Melancholia (1917). The extensive clinical experience of the internationally known authors has allowed them to develop and illustrate an integrated object relations and link theory framework, which opens new perspectives in the understanding of complicated grief as it, manifests in couples and families. The editors propose an original approach to the assessment of this problem and a short-term intervention model for its treatment, underpinned by this framework. Their clinical approach allows a questioning of the method, the metapsychology and the epistemological pedestal of contemporary psychoanalysis and in doing so, opens up a new field of research. This new way of listening to psychic suffering, which focuses on the inter-subjectivity of the couple relationship, also highlights the potential preventive mental health value of such an approach to diagnosis and treatment. From this vertex the book also examines the effects of the intergenerational transmission of un-mourned loss, which not only affects the couple (family) as a whole, but also has consequences for the broader social and cultural contexts in which they live. Moreover, the book addresses a clinical issue of immense contemporary relevance considering the suffering and adverse implication un-mourned loss can cause in individuals, couples and families and thus our world. The book, whose authors are recognised by the IPA and the IACFP, therefore represents a significant contribution to the field of couple and family psychoanalysis.'

*Rosa Jaitin President,*
*International Association of Couple and Family Psychoanalysis*

'Loss, grief and mourning are universal human experiences. Over the centuries, tradition, culture, religion, philosophy, direct interpersonal sensitivity, generosity and intergenerational wisdom have provided human beings help and support in facing these painful experiences. This book demonstrates, however, that when complicated grief occurs, such supports are often not enough and darkness and despair can dominate the internal psychic landscape. In these circumstances medication is often seen as the solution. The authors show how psychoanalysis can go deeper. In particular, they demonstrate how couple and family psychoanalytic interventions can help in facing and working through the immense loss of a family member and avoid the temptation of denial, disavowal, withdrawal or fixation to an impossible, omnipotent recovery, as in the myth of Orpheus and Euridices.

I highly recommend this seminal text on complicated grief, not only because it is scientifically valuable, but also because it is full of humanity. The book is both fascinating and touching, wide and deep and profoundly rooted in psychoanalytic theory and culture. It contains the best psychoanalysis can offer today about this crucial subject, thanks to the contributions of some of the most experienced and qualified clinicians from around the world, who represent cutting-edge thinking about couple and family psychoanalysis.'

*Stefano Bolognini, Immediate Past-President, International Psychoanalytical Association*

'How timely, following the publication just over 100 years ago of Freud's seminal paper, Mourning & Melancholia, that such a rich collection of perspectives on loss are explored in relation to the important field of couple and family relationships. Timothy Keogh and Cynthia Gregory Roberts have brought together their own creative thinking on working with loss in couples and families with a collection of astute clinical papers from highly acclaimed couple and family psychoanalytic therapists from around the world. All affirm that it is the unconscious meaning of loss that determines the capacity to mourn or fall into serious depression.

The editors are, both experienced clinicians in this area, have also produced a book that interweaves Object Relations theory with the concept of the link (el vinculo) creating an enriched understanding of the impact of unmourned loss on relationships, including intergenerationally on those in the present. The other contributors to the book highlight through closely observed clinical material or film, both the shockingly tangible losses that are nonetheless avoided and the less tangible losses such as the loss of an idealised relationship, that are harder to get hold off. They show that without being addressed, these have a destructive influence on relationships. We know that loss is an intrinsic part of human experience and the failure to mourn is detrimental to mental health. What this impressive book achieves, is to show how unrecognised and unmourned loss gets deeply embedded in the couple and family psyche, how, without being addressed, this impedes creative development. This excellent book will be of enormous value to all those working with couples and families, whether couple therapists, analysts or mental health practitioners, particularly for those wishing to expand their understanding of the more deeply unconscious aspects of loss and the impact on relationships.'

*Mary Morgan, Reader in Couple Psychoanalysis, Tavistock Relationships*

# Psychoanalytic Approaches to Loss

*Psychoanalytic Approaches to Loss: Mourning, Melancholia and Couples* applies psychoanalytic ideas to the clinically complex issue of loss in couples and families and outlines a new model for the assessment and treatment of associated unresolved grief. In line with contemporary approaches to couple and family psychoanalysis, this integrated object relations and link theory model provides a clear framework and approach for assessing and treating this clinical presentation.

The book brings together contributions from internationally known and respected clinicians and authors who focus on loss, including repeated pregnancy loss, the loss of a child or parent and the loss of a relationship itself. These psychoanalytic couple therapists take the reader inside their consulting rooms, enabling observation of their approaches to the treatment of couples experiencing loss and associated unresolved grief.

*Psychoanalytic Approaches to Loss: Mourning, Melancholia and Couples* will make an important contribution to the literature on grief and mourning and the application of psychoanalytic thinking to couples presenting with difficulties linked to unresolved grief, following loss. It represents an essential resource to psychotherapists, counsellors, family therapists, mental health professionals and many others supporting those experiencing loss.

**Timothy Keogh** is a training and supervising analyst and full member of the Australian Psychoanalytical Society. He is Honorary Senior Lecturer, Medical School, University of Sydney and a research fellow of the International Psychoanalytical Society.

**Cynthia Gregory-Roberts** is an individual, couple and family psychoanalytic psychotherapist in private practice in Sydney, Australia. She is a member of the Australian Association of Social Workers and College of Social Work and an accredited Mental Health Social Worker.

# Psychoanalytic Approaches to Loss

## Mourning, Melancholia and Couples

Edited by
Timothy Keogh and Cynthia Gregory-Roberts

Routledge
Taylor & Francis Group
LONDON AND NEW YORK

First published 2019
by Routledge
2 Park Square, Milton Park, Abingdon, Oxon OX14 4RN

and by Routledge
711 Third Avenue, New York, NY 10017

*Routledge is an imprint of the Taylor & Francis Group, an informa business*



*British Library Cataloguing in Publication Data*
A catalogue record for this book is available from the British Library

*Library of Congress Cataloging in Publication Data*
A catalog record has been requested for this book

ISBN: 978-1-138-31243-2 (hbk)
ISBN: 978-1-78220-548-7 (pbk)
ISBN: 978-0-429-45823-1 (ebk)

Typeset in Times New Roman
by Taylor & Francis Books

# Contents

*List of illustrations* ix
*Acknowledgements* x
*Editors* xii
*List of contributors* xiii
*Series Co-Editor's Foreword* xv
*Preface* xviii

Introduction 1
TIMOTHY KEOGH

**PART I**
**Theoretical understandings and clinical approaches to loss** 13

1 Psychoanalytic understandings of loss and their relevance to couples and families 15
TIMOTHY KEOGH

2 Link theory and object relations theory: an enriched approach to working with melancholic couples 34
ELIZABETH PALACIOS

3 Assessing and formulating issues of unresolved loss in couple functioning 45
CYNTHIA GREGORY-ROBERTS AND TIMOTHY KEOGH

4 A proposed theoretical framework and model for intervention 60
TIMOTHY KEOGH AND CYNTHIA GREGORY-ROBERTS

**PART II**
**Loss in couples and families: theory and practice** 75

5 The family's use of regressive defences as an avoidance of mourning 77
ANNA MARIA NICOLÒ AND STEFANIA TAMBONE

6 The lamp of tragedy past: traumatic intergenerational loss and the couple 87
JUDITH PICKERING

7 Some considerations regarding the impact of early parental loss on adult couple functioning 102
CATRIONA WROTTESLEY

8 Mourning and melancholia and the couple experience of a miscarriage 118
CARL BAGNINI

9 Loss in the everyday life of couples 129
MONICA VORCHHEIMER

Epilogue 140
TIMOTHY KEOGH AND CYNTHIA GREGORY-ROBERTS

*Author Index* 143
*Subject Index* 145

# Illustrations

## Figures

4.1 Dynamic developmental anxieties/link theory model of couple functioning 65
4.2 The Unresolved Grief Triad (UGT) 67

## Table

4.1 A grid depicting developmental anxiety, link and therapeutic focus 70

# Acknowledgements

The desire to produce this book arose from both clinical and personal experience. We acknowledge how deeply we are indebted to our patients (individuals, couples and families) from whom we have learnt so much. Moving from this experience to writing about it, however, has required significant support and encouragement. We thus wish to acknowledge those who introduced us to couple and family psychoanalytic work, those who trained us in this modality in Australia, and our peers who have helped us develop our clinical thinking.

We would also like to specifically thank David and Jill Scharff, who supported the ongoing development of couple and family psychoanalytic psychotherapy internationally, who have been a constant source of inspiration and guidance. We have also benefitted from the support of international colleagues (including some of the contributors to this book) through contact with the International Psychoanalytical Association's (IPA) Committee on Couple and Family Psychoanalysis and those we have met at IPA-sponsored International Couple and Family Psychoanalysis Conferences (Buenos Aires 2015 and Madrid 2017) that have allowed us to forge new professional alliances and supportive collegiate relationships.

We are particularly grateful for the encouragement we received from our South American colleagues (during our attendance at the Buenos Aires conference), especially Monica Vorchheimer, along with the generous reception to our ideas from internationally respected couples and family psychoanalysts, including Janine Puget and Roberto Losso.

Support and encouragement to present and write about our clinical experience have also come from colleagues we met through the International Association of Couple and Family Psychoanalysis, especially Rosa Jaitin; our Tavistock colleagues, especially Mary Morgan; our American colleagues including Caroline Sehon, Janine Wanlass, and Karen Proner; and European colleagues, particularly Anna Maria Nicolò, Diana Norsa, and Elizabeth Palacios. We also wish to acknowledge the encouragement that we have received from Molly Ludlam, Editor of *Couple and Family Psychoanalysis*.

We particularly wish to acknowledge Thomas Murphy for his extensive and comprehensive editorial support. We would also like to thank Toby Brunckhorst for his work on the figures in this book.

Finally, we acknowledge the quiet suffering of so many couples and families who have experienced unresolved grief and hope that this book will in some small way contribute to an increased awareness of their need for appropriate intervention.

# Editors

**Timothy Keogh, PhD** (Medicine) is a training and supervising analyst and full member of the Australian Psychoanalytical Society, a member of the IPA Committee for Couple and Family Psychoanalysis, a Board member of the International Association of Couple and Family Psychoanalysis and a member of the International Advisory Board for the journal *Couple and Family Psychoanalysis.* He is Honorary Senior Lecturer, Medical School, University of Sydney, and a research fellow of the International Psychoanalytical Society. He is author of *The Internal World of the Juvenile Sex Offender: Through a Glass Darkly then Face to Face* and has also authored and co-authored a number of journal articles and chapters on couple and family psychoanalysis.

**Cynthia Gregory-Roberts, MAASW(Acc), MACSW** is a clinical social worker and a couple and family psychoanalytic psychotherapist in private practice in Sydney, Australia. She is a member of the Australian Association of Social Workers and College of Social Work and an accredited Mental Health Social Worker. She is also a member of the International Association of of Couple and Family Psychoanalysis and the Couple, Child and Family Psychotherapy Association of Australasia. She has co-authored a number of journal articles and chapters on couple and family psychoanalytic psychotherapist. She has extensive experience as a teacher and supervisor of general practitioners and mental health professionals.

# Contributors

**Carl Bagnini, LCSW, BCD** is a founding member and a member of senior faculty at the International Psychotherapy Institute (IPI) in Washington, DC and Long Island, NY. He is a featured presenter in the IPI Masters and Couple Therapy Teleconference Training Programs. He also teaches in the IPI Child Psychotherapy Program and is a group facilitator in the Child Psychoanalysis Program. Carl is a member of the faculties of The Adelphi University Derner Advanced Programs in Psychoanalysis, Supervision and Couple Therapy, and St. John's University Post-Doctoral Program in Integrative Family Therapy, teaching family therapy and couple therapy. Carl has been a featured presenter and discussant at national and international conferences on a variety of object relations clinical topics, and has written and co-authored many book chapters and papers on psychoanalytic child, couple and family therapy, supervision, and clinical education. His book: *Keeping Couples in Treatment: Working from Surface to Depth* was published by Roman and Littlefield (Aronson) in 2012.

**Ana Maria Nicolo, M.D.**, President of Italian Society of Psychoanalysis (SPI) is a Training Analyst (SPI-IPA) and an IPA recognised expert on Children and Adolescents. She has been the Regional Representative (for Europe) on the Board of Representatives of the International Psychoanalytical Association (IPA). She is also a member of the Forum for the adolescence of the European Psychoanalytical Federation (FEP), a founding member of the Society for Psychoanalytic Psychotherapy for Children and Adolescents (SIPsIA), and a founding member of the International Association of Couple and Family Psychoanalysis (AIPCF). She is also Editor-in-Chief of *Interazioni* and the author of many books published in Italian, English, French, and Spanish and co-editor of *Families in Transformation*.

**Elizabeth Palacios, M.D.** is a psychiatrist, adult and child psychoanalyst with Madrid's Psychoanalytical Association, a member of the IPA, Founding member and president of Aragon's Society for the Research of Child and Adolescent Psychic Life (AAPIPNA). She is also a full member of the Spanish Federation of Associations of Psychotherapists, teacher of postgraduate studies in Child and Adolescent Psychoanalytical Psychotherapy and co-chair for the European region of the IPA Couple and Family Committee. She is the co-editor with David Scharff of *Couple and Family Psychoanalysis: A Global Perspective,* as well as an author and editor of several books on child and adolescent psychoanalysis and editor of the Spanish review *Pensamiento Psicoanalítico.*

**Judith Pickering, PhD** is a psychoanalytic psychotherapist, family and couple therapist working in private practice in Sydney. She is a supervisor and faculty member of the Australian and New Zealand Association of Psychotherapy and a Training Analyst with The Australian and New Zealand Association of Jungian Analysts. She is a member of The Couple, Child, and Family Psychotherapy Association of Australasia, the British Society of Couple Psychotherapists and Counsellors and the International Association for Analytical Psychology. She has published and lectured widely in Australia, USA, and Europe. She is the author of *Being in Love: Therapeutic Pathways Through Psychological Obstacles to Love* and forthcoming books, *The Meaning of Life: Psychotherapy as Spiritual Practice* and *Transformations in Love Beyond the Couple: An application of the clinical theory of Bion to Couple Therapy.*

**Stefania Tambone PhD** is a psychologist and child and adolescent psychotherapist who also specialises in couple and family psychoanalysis. She is the founder of a therapeutic community for maltreated children.

**Monica Vorchheimer** is a training and supervising analyst from the Buenos Aires Psychoanalytical Association (APdeBA), a full member of the IPA, member of the European Federation of Psychotherapy (FEAP), and honorary member of AAPPIPNA (Spain). She is Co-Chair for Latin America on the IPA Committee on Psychoanalysis with Families and Couples. She is a professor at the University Institute of Mental Health in Argentina. She has been awarded the Bleger (1998) and Storni (2001) prizes by the Argentine Psychoanalytic Association and the Liberman prize (1999) by the Buenos Aires Psychoanalytic Association. She has extensive experience treating individual patients, families and couples. Recently, she co-edited with David Scharff *Clinical Dialogues on Psychoanalysis with Families and Couples.*

**Catriona Wrottesley** is a couple psychoanalytic psychotherapist and individual psychotherapist registered with the British Psychoanalytic Council. She is Head of Studies at Tavistock Relationships, London (Head of the MA in Couple and Individual Psychodynamic Counselling and Psychotherapy, and Head of the MSc course in Psychosexual and Relationship Therapy). She is a member of the Editorial Board of the international journal *Couple and Family Psychoanalysis* and its Book Reviews Editor.

# Series Co-Editor's Foreword

Psychoanalytic couple psychotherapy has always been seen as derivative of psychoanalysis – perhaps a poor and somewhat closeted cousin, only distantly related to the pure gold of individual analysis. This characterisation does significant disservice to the psychoanalytic study and treatment of couples. Paradoxically, if we reverse our lens, we readily discover that individual psychoanalysis could equally be thought of as deriving from the study of couples in the sense that individual analysts refer frequently to "the analytic couple". It is as if they are implicitly stating that the analytic relationship derives its power from its likeness to the far more frequent image of emotional intimacy of marital couples and life partnerships.

Developmentally we are born from couples. Most children either live with couples who raise them, or long for a partner for their single parent. In the case of increasingly common single parent families, the child often forms an overly intimate partnership with the parent, and such child–parent partnerships then offer a poor substitute for an adult pair of parents for which the child longs. In such diverse ways, adult couples form the crucible in which children can grow while being securely nurtured. Writing this, I am aware of the cultural context of the Western cultural tradition that descends from the Judeo–Christian cradle. Many indigenous, Middle Eastern, or African cultures see families differently. But the prototype of a two-parent family is resilient in the West, and has, for instance, come to be the norm in China and elsewhere.

If you accept my thesis that the deep structure of Western thought now includes the unconscious construction of the foundation of the family as being a bond between two parents, then we might regard this as the starting place of any psychology. And in any event, biologically the starting place is the single cell couple of egg-and-sperm that are the beginning of each of us individually! In this biological sense at least, the individual is built on the foundation of a couple. This presents us with the philosophical conundrum of how to see individual self-investment – Freud's "primary narcissism" – once we consider the premise that we are each individually built on the biological and psychological foundation of the couple. Many or even most of us spend our lives searching to recreate the security of early couple relationships, and facing the threat that such a secure base may break down.

John Bowlby described falling in love as the emotion that attends the establishment of an attachment bond, and loss as the feeling attendant on the loss of that bond. In the perspective I am suggesting, we have all faced such losses in separating and individuating from our parents as we grow beyond the original love relationships that we are (hopefully) born into, whether with one parent, two parents, or even an extended loving family. These are of course the ordinary losses that are necessary to maturation into adolescence and adulthood, but they nevertheless form the foundational processes of mourning that allow not only for maturation, but also for processing the painful and unexpected losses that life inevitably brings.

This book offers multiple vectors for the study of the mourning of early losses and developmental trauma, and then explores their legacy in relationship to adult couples. It is the first book that I know of to explore the unique aspects of loss and mourning in the couple, and in doing so it provides a framework for the assessment of unresolved grief in the setting of couple therapy. It is not (and should not have been) a study of the mourning inherent in common, ordinary maturation. Not that unimpeded "ordinary maturation" is all that common! But, as I said, it is a truism that maturational experiences of loss and mourning form a foundation both for healthy development and for the vicissitudes of painful and traumatic losses of the kind that cripple later development. These early ubiquitous developmental losses are also losses within couple and triangular relationships – loss of the fact and of the illusion of being a life partner with one's parents, even in single-parent families – the disillusion inherent in finding that one's mother and father have other loves and partners. This and the many other wrinkles of developmental loss begin with loss of aspects of couple and family relationships. So when, as clinicians, we are faced with couples suffering from loss and the stunting of their capacities to mourn, with the shared melancholy of a legacy of trauma or early deprivation that is common in our consulting rooms, we see that this happens most often because they are not the first losses for these couples, but are repetitions of situations that were never completely overcome in earlier in life.

Each of the contributors to this volume has considered this situation from a different point of view. It is a particular strength of this book that the writers come from the four points of the globe, from Argentina to Australia, the United States, the United Kingdom, Italy and Spain. This rich mixture of sources brings with it a variety of starting places that we then have an opportunity to examine both in the authors' exposition of their theoretical assumptions, and in the vivid clinical examples that highlight each contribution.

Reading these chapters, each focusing on different aspects of loss and the vicissitudes of inhibited mourning, I was struck with the variety of foundational assumptions that paradoxically converge around important ideas. This happens because the editors have brought together colleagues who know each other through meetings at which they presented their ideas and clinical work, both to illustrate their varying ways of thinking, and to seek such convergences. We get to view couples through the shared lens of their difficulties in processing grief and mourning, but in each case from the standpoint of the contributors' varying theories and countries – and from the distance that separates four continents. Then this also allows us to focus on what they have in common. In this way, the book shows how different theoretical approaches to treating loss in couples and families can be brought together to represent a synthesis of cutting-edge contemporary approaches to loss and mourning.

We have in this volume contributions that use the varying perspectives of object relations theory, Freud, Bion, and link theory – all offered in order to enlarge our understanding of the central problem of loss, melancholy and blocked mourning in couples. These inhibited processes are at the bottom of depression and melancholy in people seen in individual psychoanalytic treatment, but they are just as central when we encounter troubled partnerships or struggling families.

This volume, a basic resource for the study of blocked mourning and depression in couples, is also a basis for new ways of seeing the origin of depression in all individuals. Patients who come, apparently by themselves, arrive in our offices accompanied internally by their bereft parents, the sad and lonely couples they carry inside, and very often actually accompanied by their life partners who sit in our waiting rooms while we meet with an individual who speaks for a couple's shared suffering. For this perspective, for the clear exposition of foundational theories, and for the vivid clinical illustrations, we can be grateful for the wisdom that awaits the reader in the pages that follow.

David E. Scharff, MD

# Preface

One of the creative outcomes of this book is its attempted integration of significant theoretical and clinical approaches across cultures, centred on the universal issue of loss. Chatwin (1998), discussing the Australian Aboriginal notion of "Dreaming", notes that "Aboriginal Creation myths tell of legendary totemic beings who had wandered over the continent in Dreamtime, singing out the name of everything that crossed their path – birds, animals, plants, rocks, waterholes – and so singing the world into existence". The author continues: "... each totemic ancestor, while travelling through the country, was thought to have scattered a trail of words and musical notes along the line of his footprints, and how these Dreaming-tracks lay over the land as 'ways' of communication between the most far-flung tribes .... In theory, at least, the whole of Australia could be read as a musical score". (Chatwin, 1998, p. 2; Hooke, 2016). Chatwin's words are an evocative metaphor which could be seen to represent some aspects of the psychoanalytic movement toward geographical new places and new places in the mind: "The wandering of the totemic beings ... The trail of words ... The footprints and the Dreaming tracks left as ways of communications between distant tribes ...".

Relevant to this book, we can imagine a map of the world where such dots and lines are marked and connections are created between psychoanalytic groups and cultures and the successive flourishing of psychoanalysis in new lands through the merging, combining, and intersection of cultures which gradually transform the psychoanalytic map as we know it. *Psychoanalytic Approaches to Loss: Mourning Melancholia and Couples* traverses a range of diverse clinical and theoretical approaches across wide geographical zones and opens up new scenarios and possibilities which resonate in many different ways.

One of these relates to the institutional aspect of international psychoanalysis, that is, the International Psychoanalytical Association (IPA) as a "container of diversities" and its role as a scientific organisation, a community of colleagues who come together to work on a project and a specific research and interest. Stefano Bolognini (2017) has noted that this does not happen by chance. He says, "This is not at all obvious; it is very difficult to conceive and to realise this kind of work without having actively co-participated in a wide

Hooke, M. T. (2016). Psychoanalysis in new places: the work of the International New Group. In: *Cartographies of the Unconscious*. Milano: Mimesis International.
Jullien, F. (1998). *Trattato sulla Efficacia*. Torino: Einaudi.
Magris, C. (2001). *Utopia e Disincanto*. Milano: Garzanti.
Mitchell, S. (2002). *Can Love Last? The Fate of Romance Over Time*. New York, NY: Norton.

institutional scientific group." He further highlights the function of the IPA Family and Couple Committee as "the natural base and frame that provides a number of researchers with regular international and inter regional contacts and exchanges that generate an enriching cross fertilization which would be impossible to achieve, not only individually, but also within a single scientific group or local society."

Of course, functioning as a "container of diversities" is not a given and, like the *depressive position,* it is something that is constantly lost and regained; as the history of psychoanalysis shows us, the acceptance of developments in new countries and of new ideas has not been without pain. The encounter with "the other" in new cultures or new theoretical schools inevitably raises the dread of the unknown: a dialogue is possible only if each is open to confrontation and to review and reflect on its own assumptions and beliefs (Jullien, 1998).

This remarkable and innovative book shows us that such an integration of diversities is possible. It brings together in a creative conjunction object relations theory and link theory (where *teoria del vinculo*, "el vinculo" as a noun has a more powerful resonance in the Latin languages). Further, it develops an important new approach and intervention for couples and families who have experienced loss. In doing so, it opens an area of great clinical and social relevance in the contemporary world. Here, I am also thinking about the opening of psychoanalysis in new countries which have suffered massive historical traumas and where the losses may not even be recognised and are "suffered" instead in the body. I am also thinking of the losses encountered by the increasing number of refugees and migrants leaving their own countries and extended families, as well as colonised indigenous populations.

This cross-fertilisation, this blending of multiple theoretical clinical sources in new creative ways found in the book, represents not only a geographical and theoretical dimension, but also a temporal one. It continues the theoretical line of Abraham, Freud, and Klein on the psychology of loss and mourning and connects it with the contribution of Pichon Rivière and the rich Latin American psychoanalytic tradition, that is, with the notion of both internal and external social bonds. Here we see how the development of psychoanalytic ideas works when an institution functions as a "container of diversities". Ideas can be built upon and similar ideas occurring to more than one person can be brought together, allowing insights to arise not from a vacuum, but from hard won, shared experience and cooperative clinical work. The year the book was written, being the one hundredth anniversary of Freud's *Mourning and Melancholia,* makes its publication particularly poignant.

There is also a further aspect of this book to consider: its value not only for clinicians, but also for policy makers and for the wider community, namely its social value. I see four strands to this issue. Firstly, its potential to influence public policies relevant to the nature of mental health services that could be offered to the community. Secondly, its potential to contribute to education and training of psychoanalysts. Our field has a very rich tradition in the so-called applied psychoanalysis; psychoanalysts have been pioneers in organisational work, group work, and more recently on studies on violence, trauma and transgenerational transmission of trauma. Such work has not translated into the inclusion in psychoanalytic training. The very recent addition to the training of Child and Adolescent Psychoanalysis, through an Integrated Model, could be taken as a template for a future, much-needed inclusion in our training of group analysis and family/couple analysis.

A further strand is the book's potential for raising awareness in the community about losses in families and couples as an inevitable and normal part of life and of the human experience, and with it, the entitlement to suffer them, so opening the way to mourning. I mean the "normalisation" of loss which this book goes a long way in doing in a very real and practical way. That is the idea that with help, such suffering can be understood, worked through and let go.

This last point refers to the modern western culture of idealisation of love and romance, and what Monica Vorchheimer says in this book about ordinary, everyday losses which challenge the life of couples and their shared "idealised representation of togetherness" and sameness. A similar concept was explored by Stephen Mitchell in his book *Can Love Last? The Fate of Romance over Time* (Mitchell, 2002). These important and helpful views about "the other side of romance" are not part of the current social discourse and one wonders if and how they could be part, for example, of sexual education in high schools, and have a voice in the media, and in women's magazines.

All this may sound like Utopia, yet as Claudio Magris (2001), an Italian contemporary writer has suggested, the word *Utopia* represents an unreachable ideal, which nevertheless allows men to dream of a better world. He sees the absence of illusions and the disenchantment which brings us back to reality, limiting our dreams, as something which could correct the Utopia, and reinforce its fundamental element: hope.

I think the psychoanalytic ideas and clinical examples in the chapters that follow leave us with hope: the hope that this new psychoanalytic approach could contribute to alleviate the personal suffering inherent in unresolved grief, and raise our collective awareness about the social consequences of un-mourned losses.

Maria Teresa Savio Hooke
Past President, Australian Psychoanalytical Society
Past Chair, International Psychoanalytical Association's International New Groups (ING) Committee

## References

Bolognini, S. (2017). Preface. *Family and Couples Psychoanalysis.* London: Karnac.
Chatwin, B. (1998). *The Songlines.* London: Vintage Books.

# Introduction

*Timothy Keogh*

Loss of a loved one through death is one of the most miserable of all human experiences. This is particularly the case when instead of normal mourning a more serious psychological reaction to loss ensues. This has been referred to diagnostically as Complicated Grief or a Prolonged Grief Disorder (Stroebe & Schut, 2006; Lobb, Kristjanson, Aoun & Monterosso, 2006; Hall, 2011; Maciejewski, Maercker, Boelen & Prigerson, 2016; Kristensen, Dyregrov & Dyregrov, 2017).

Grief, which can be considered as intense sorrow, sadness, or anguish, is itself a part of normal mourning and is considered pathological only when it becomes unremitting with adverse consequences on day-to-day functioning. Complicated grief refers to grief which is unremitting six to 12 months after the loss, and also encompasses a failure to accept the reality of loss, self-reproach, persistent yearning for the deceased, and preoccupation with the events of the death. This type of unremitting grief is often severe and can result in self-injurious behaviour and suicidal ideation (Latham & Prigerson, 2004; Stroebe, Stroebe, & Abakoumkin, 2005). Stroebe and Schut (2001) have noted that reactions to traumatic death, especially of someone with whom there is a strong attachment often leads to such sustained melancholic grief. Prolonged grief disorder is considered to be a common form of complicated grief which has unique characteristics (Maciejewski et al., 2016; Kristensen et al., 2017). In particular, it is characterised by what is referred to in the proposed diagnostic criteria for ICD-10 (International Statistical Classification of Diseases and Related Health Problems 10th Revision, 2004) as "separation distress, which refers to an intense longing for, or persistent preoccupation with, the deceased person" (Kristensen et al., 2017, p. 538). In this book we will refer to the concept of unresolved grief, acknowledging that one or both of the partners in a couple may manifest features of complicated or prolonged grief disorder.

The criteria for complicated grief disorder have been widely researched (e.g., Prigerson et al., 1995; Horowitz et al., 1997; Lichtenthal, Cruess, & Prigerson, 2004), resulting in an argument in favour of it being established as a separate diagnostic entity. Complicated grief has been found to occur in about 10–20% of the normal population (Kristjanson, Lobb Aoun, & Monterosso, 2006). As mentioned above, a case has also been made for a distinct diagnostic category for prolonged grief disorder (Maciejewski et al., 2016). The Fifth Revision of the *Diagnostic and Statistical Manual of Mental Disorders (DSM-5)* (American Psychiatric Association, 2013) already includes a diagnostic code corresponding to prolonged grief disorder in the section – Other Specified Trauma- and Stressor-Related Disorder, listed as Persistent Complex Bereavement Disorder (PCBD) – with criteria for this diagnosis contained in the section of the manual devoted to conditions needing further study.

Not surprisingly, insecure attachment status (connected to internalised working models of relationship [Bowlby, 1969]) has been noted to be a significant risk factor for an individual to develop a melancholic reaction, given that insecure attachment renders one vulnerable to psychopathology as a result of a poor adjustment capacity to stressors (Shear & Shair, 2005; Lobb et al., 2006). Moreover, Stroebe, Schut and Stroebe (2005) have shown that it is an ambivalent attachment style in particular which renders a bereaved person to becoming pre-occupied and ruminative about their loss. Other factors that are seen to predispose one to an adverse reaction to loss include a history of childhood abuse and serious neglect, separation anxiety, close kinship relationship to the deceased, marital closeness, the level of support gained from, and the dependency on, the person lost.

In normal grieving, the individual gradually develops the ability to accept loss. This is usually achieved by being able to confront and manage a myriad of different circumstances which confront one with the reality of the loss. Dream content often reveals a shift in the level of acceptance of a loss. When the loss, however, cannot be faced or worked through, the individual is left feeling persecuted and tormented. Such a reaction not only impacts on one's view of oneself and (especially intimate) others, but ultimately also on one's hope about the future.

Whilst complicated grief in an individual can present a treatment challenge for the clinician, its manifestation in couple relationships represents unique challenges, as well as special opportunities for resolution.

The concept of *melancholy,* as a commonly used term to describe an adverse reaction to loss, has had a long history linked to its etymological origins. Melancholy is a Latin translation of a Greek word that denoted a serious mental condition involving a form of chronic depression linked to loss. The term was originally linked to the notion of Black Bile: a core concept of the Hippocratic corpus that defined the approach to medicine until the nineteenth century, which was detailed, according to Aristotle, by Polybus (the son-in-law of Hippocrates) in the publication *Nature of Man* (Jones, 1931). According to Humoural Theory, disease could be accounted for by four elements of bodily fluids: blood, yellow bile, black bile, and phlegm. These fluids were seen to account for different types of temperaments: phlegmatic, choleric, sanguine, and melancholic. By the seventeenth and eighteenth centuries, the term "melancholic" was in common use as a term to describe "a disease" involving states of dejection. Later in the nineteenth century, depression became the term used to describe conditions that encompassed melancholia (Jackson, 1986). As mentioned above, contemporary diagnostic systems now distinguish clinical depression (especially Major Depressive Disorder from a complicated grief reaction, the latter of which is seen to be linked to underlying adjustment difficulties (Ogrodniczuk et al., 2003).

Freud (1917) was the first theorist to use psychoanalytic theory to conceptualise melancholia, describe its underpinning psycho-dynamics, and differentiate it from normal grieving. In his journey of understanding the concept of loss from a psychoanalytic perspective, he noted in his paper, *On Transience* (Freud, 1916), that a failure to face the pain of mourning (the basis of a melancholic reaction) results in an interference in one's ability to experience beauty and live in the experience of the moment. He later noted that holding onto the (libidinal) *attachment* to a lost loved object is central in this interference. In this writing, in which he was beginning to think psychoanalytically about loss, he pondered:

> Why it is that this detachment of libido from its objects should be such a painful process is a mystery to us and why we have not hitherto been able to frame any hypothesis to account for it. We see that libido clings to its objects and will not renounce those that are lost, even when a substitute lies readily to hand. (Freud, 1916, p. 12)

Supporting the qualitative difference between normal mourning and melancholia that Freud described, contemporary neuroscientists (e.g., O'Connor & Arizmendi, 2014) have also shown that in individuals who have a prolonged experience of such distress: "The neural mechanisms distinguishing complicated grief from non-complicated grief are unclear ... *but* ... in complicated grief, reminders of the deceased activate neural reward activity, which may interfere with adapting to loss in the present" (p. 3).

Contemporary psychoanalysts also understand that an individual's psychological maladaptive response to loss varies not only with the nature and timing of the loss, but also in accordance with an individual's pre-existing level of psychological adjustment, in particular and as noted above, that individual's attachment status and his related psychological incapacity to mourn.

Psychoanalytical understandings about loss are based on the heritage of the psychoanalytical understandings of Freud and object relations theorists who developed these ideas further (see Chapter 1). These theorists viewed the response to loss as ultimately linked to how one navigated the first prototypical experience of loss in one's relationship with a primary attachment figure. That is, with an ever-increasing awareness of reality, the baby's necessarily omnipotent view of her early world gradually dissolves, as the loss of the perceived ideal mother has to be managed. A successful resolution of this challenge paves the way for the development of a sense of self as separate from the attachment figure on whom one originally depended and was felt to be inseparable.

As Lemma (2016) notes:

> Freud, the bearer of bad news, starkly reminded us that we simply cannot have it all our own way. The hard lessons begin at birth. As reality impinges upon us, the experiences of frustration, disappointment, loss, and longing make their entry into the chronicles of our existence … (*and if all goes well with our development*) … our capacity to delay gratification, to withstand absence and loss are hard won lessons that challenge our omnipotent feelings, whilst also reassuring us that we can face reality, without being overwhelmed by the enormity of the task. (Lemma, 2016, p. 6, *italics added*)

Such understandings not only form the basis of the psychoanalytical treatment of loss, but also disorders of the self, such as narcissistic and borderline disorders, which are characterised by an unstable sense of self linked to a failure to manage developmental challenges whose resolution would otherwise favour a capacity to mourn.

Having a means of understanding and working therapeutically with loss is important when we consider not only the number of people who experience a form of complicated grief, but also because of the prevalence of loss. There are, for example, 824 deaths per 100,000 people in the US each year (Kochanek, Murphy, Xu, & Tejada-Vera, 2016). In indigenous populations, such as in Australia, loss is more commonly associated with infant mortality, suicide, accidental death, and homicide. Along with other factors, especially poor health status, it has led to a shocking age-standardised death rate of 9.6 per 1,000 persons for the Australian indigenous people, which is 1.7 times the rate of their non-indigenous counterparts (Australian Bureau of Statistics, 2016). The loss of either a child for a parent, or of a parent for a child, are amongst the most challenging experiences of loss. In this regard, surveys of Western societies have revealed that more than one million children will lose a parent before 15 years of age (Kliman, 1979). Other studies (e.g., Owens, 2008) have shown that 5% of children aged 15 years or younger will lose one or both parents, often suffering significant adverse psychological impacts as a consequence (Weller, Weller, Fristad, & Bowes, 1991). Again, these rates are higher in disadvantaged groups, including indigenous populations. The numbers of parents who lose children is also significant, with the mortality rate of children in the US at 54 per 100,000 and the infant mortality rate at 6.2 per 100,000 (Kochanek et al., 2016).

The loss of a child also frequently leads to a complicated grief disorder (Prigerson et al., 1999). In terms of psychological reactions to loss in parents, Rogers, Floyd, Seltzer, Greenberg, and Hong (2008) found parents who experienced non-normal grief reactions reported more depressive symptoms, poorer well-being, and more health problems than a comparison group. Loss through miscarriage, which is a particularly distressing form of loss, can also lead to a variety of adverse mental health outcomes (see also Chapter 8).

Miscarriage rates have been estimated to occur in 15% of all pregnancies, with Recurrent Pregnancy Loss (RPL) defined as three consecutive pregnancy losses under 20 weeks at 1–2%, with women who experienced miscarriages or stillbirths having a significantly greater hazard of their relationship ending, compared with women whose pregnancies ended in live births (Ford & Schust, 2009).

These statistics all refer to the loss of someone with whom there is a significant emotional attachment. Loss of such attachment, especially where the attachment has involved ambivalence, has been shown to have the most significant psychological impact. It cannot only impact on an individual's cognitive functioning (O'Connor & Arizmendi, 2014), but also on relationships with significant others and the capacity to maintain these relationships (Najman et al., 1993; Enguidanos, Calle, Valero, & Dominguez-Rojas, 2002; Rogers et al., 2008).

Given unresolved grief can lead to couple breakdown and divorce, it can also lead to related developmental impacts on children in affected families, which can lead to a cycle of relationship breakdown as loss reverberates intergenerationally. In addition to the emotional and psychological costs, there are also direct financial costs such as those associated with divorce and custody proceedings, as well as indirect costs such as loss of productivity, impacts on physical health, and other morbidity costs. Many of these impacts can be reduced when families at risk are identified and where appropriately timed intervention is provided (Rosner, Kruse, & Hagl, 2005; Rosner, Pfoh, & Kotoucova, 2011).

Research has addressed the issue of the appropriate timing of intervention such that it does not interfere with, or over-pathologise, the process of normal mourning (Simon, 2013). This research indicates that an individual normally begins to demonstrate some adjustment to loss within six to twelve months. When this adjustment fails to occur, an assessment for the need for intervention is indicated.

Given this, there is clearly a strong case to be made, not only for appropriately timed intervention with at-risk individuals, but also with at-risk couples and families. Intervention in couples and families enables the longer-term benefit of stemming the inter-generational transmission and effect of unresolved grief.

In terms of intervention, through our collaboration with our international colleagues, we have come to view a psychoanalytic theoretical framework wherein object relations theory is integrated with link theory to represent a cutting-edge approach to contemporary couple and family psychoanalysis and psychoanalytic psychotherapy (Scharff & Palacios, 2017; Scharff & Vorchheimer, 2017). We consider that such an approach expands the benefits of an object relations/developmental anxiety account and is helpful in assessing and developing clinical interventions to deal with melancholic reactions to loss in couples and families. This arises out of the inter-subjective (subject-subject) perspective that link theory identifies. This is a perspective of intersubjectivity that has built upon the original view of it by Husserl (1931) which goes beyond the notion of putting oneself in the shoes of the other to being shaped by him. An approach to working with couples and families underpinned by such a theoretical framework emphasises the central relevance of object relations and their related developmental anxieties. It also highlights the nature of the dyadic link that the couple has co-constructed (Käes, 2016). Moreover, it focuses on the level of integration in the personality (Fairbairn, 1952; Klein, 1946) and the extent to which there is a mind capable of autonomous functioning (Bion, 1962; Caper, 1997).

Consequently, in its clinical application, a framework that integrates object relations and link theories firstly focuses on ways of working with internalised templates of relationship (self-object relations) or "internal links" that make loss difficult to manage. Secondly, it focuses on how the subject-subject link can act as a potentially transformative "interference" to the attempt, on the part of the couple or partner, to project these internal links onto the analyst or partner. The framework can assist in highlighting the impact of intergenerational loss (disruptive "vertical links") (Faimberg, 2005) and the pressures within couples to evade mourning (disruptive "horizontal links") (see Chapter 2).

When under the aegis of growth-stymieing links, reaction to loss in couples and families can disrupt a capacity to mourn loss and also encourage regressions to levels of functioning and their associated developmental level-related anxieties (Keogh & Enfield, 2013). These can render an individual or couple incapable of normal day-to-day functioning and, as noted above, prone to self-blaming and self-loathing and, in extreme circumstances, susceptibility to ideas of suicide. This regression can sometimes also encompass anxieties associated with primitive mental states (Ogden, 1989) and psychotic links amongst family members (see Chapter 6).

In attempting to integrate and illustrate these concepts, this book is intended as a useful guide to clinicians involved in providing interventions for couples and families who are suffering the effects of a complicated form of grief. It rests on a uniquely psychoanalytic framework from which to approach the issue of loss in couples (a commonly occurring but complex clinical presentation). In particular, it proposes a theoretical framework for assessment and intervention for couples who react to loss in this melancholic way or become carriers of an unmourned loss from a previous generation. It also looks at the consequences of particular experiences of loss in a couple or family, and contemporary psychoanalytic approaches to such complex and prolonged grief responses to loss. As such, it highlights the value and importance of understanding the *internal world* of such couples and the nature of the "links" (see Chapter 2) that couples form with each other.

The book contains contributions from well-known psychoanalysts and psychoanalytic psychotherapists in the field of couple and family psychoanalysis from a variety of cultural contexts around the world including Europe, the United Kingdom, Australia, the United States, and South America. It therefore seeks to provide a significant cross-cultural perspective. Such a perspective is important in that even though we view loss and grief as universal experiences, we also acknowledge that there are cultural differences in the manner in which these are expressed, both in the internal and in the external world. That is, culture is a link that shapes us all.

In terms of the structure of the book, Chapters 1 and 2 outline the background to the psychoanalytical framework of loss espoused in this book. Chapter 1 necessarily begins with the seminal contribution of Freud (1917) and traces how his thoughts on mourning and melancholia developed. It then examines the progression of Freud's ideas, noting the collaborative exchange of ideas between Abraham and Freud and Abraham's unique perspective. It subsequently focuses on the development of object relations theory as articulated by both Klein and Fairbairn. It is noted that in its Kleinian form, object relations theory provided a bridge from Freud's instinctual view of man (which it incorporated) to a more relational view and, as Fairbairn articulated it, a view of human beings motivated by a need for relationship. The chapter also looks at the contributions of post-Kleinian/object relations theorists, notably Bion (see also Chapter 6) and other contemporary theorists, who have espoused an inter-subjectivist clinical perspective to the development of an individual mind. The chapter pays particular attention to the psychic (projective and introjective) processes identified, primarily by Klein (1946), that occur within couples as a means of dealing with unwanted aspects of the self, in particular the parts of the self that are split off and projected into others, which can result in a projective gridlock (Morgan, 1995).

Chapter 2 introduces link theory and explains, by revisiting some of the concepts of object relations theory, how its integration can enrich our approach to work with couples. The chapter considers the limitation of this theory, especially in terms of its focus on the ego's relationship with only internal objects and not encompassing the nature of the subject-subject relationship. In reviewing the development of theories that have looked at the clinical implications of this dimension of the therapeutic relationship, the value of the concept of link is made clear. Through the use of case vignettes, it is shown how in the clinical situation the other can act as an "imposition" which has the potential to disrupt the replay in the external relationships – an internal self-object link. Link theory is subsequently referred to, in the discussion of couple interactions in the context of loss, within a number of chapters that follow in the book.

In Chapter 3 a model of assessment of pathological reactions to loss in couples and families is proposed. This model consists of a theoretical framework which pays attention to the regression level of couples and families and their associated defensive strategies, and also links this with a particular approach to psychoanalytic assessment and the articulation of what we believe are some particularly helpful tools. Tools such as tracking affect, the importance of matching interventions with the level of psychic development, the use of countertransference, and the interpretation of play (in family sessions) are explained. In addition, the utilisation of co-therapy, specialist techniques of co-therapy, and countertransference-based exploratory interpretation in assessment are also discussed. The chapter also focuses on the issue of the assessment and relevance of internal links/object relations and couple or family links. The concept of the psychodynamic formulation is also presented in relation to couples and their experience of loss. A case vignette is used to illustrate the value of the psychodynamic formulation in couple therapy.

In the final chapter of the first part of the book (Chapter 4), a framework for working with melancholic reactions to loss in couples is offered. This framework highlights the importance of anxieties related to the regression points found in couples, including those associated with the autistic–contiguous, paranoid–schizoid, and depressive modes of psychic functioning and the relevance of working *parri passu* with links. Acknowledging that assessment is itself a part of an intervention, the chapter outlines basic phases of therapy and the challenges of these phases of couple and family psychotherapy. This includes an articulation of the engagement phase with couples and families and the role of "containment" and the development of a therapeutic alliance. It also considers the particular and unique role of interpretation in assessment. A schematic outline of a proposed short-term intervention model for couples presenting with melancholic reactions to loss is then provided. In this outline the essential aspects of the assessment/engagement, working-through, and termination phases are described.

In the second part of the book a number of particular clinical situations of loss that couples and families can face are considered, along with suggestions about specific clinical issues that demand attention with such presentations.

Chapter 5 describes a melancholic reaction to loss in a family. The case study highlights how unresolved loss in a family can contribute to psychotic manifestations in members of the family. The chapter also highlights the value of family therapy when a child member of the family is presented as the identified problem. The chapter takes up particular psychoanalytic concepts that the authors find useful, especially those emanating from link theory. In this case example the value of understanding the vertical (intergenerational) link (which in this family concerned unresolved intergenerational loss) is highlighted.

In Chapter 6 the theme of intergenerational loss is further explored, in this instance through a Bionian lens, detailed in the case of Aya and Joe, which encompasses an intergenerational holocaust history. Although not discussed explicitly from the lens of link theory, the relevance of the vertical link connected with unacknowledged intergenerational loss is once again highlighted by this case. The chapter illustrates in particular the utility of Bion's concept of the selected fact, which the author elaborates into a concept of a conjoint selected fact, as she explains how, through the use of her countertransference, she and the couple come to realise the un-mourned losses that have been limiting this couple's ability to develop intimacy.

Chapter 7 next addresses how the often unacknowledged experience of unresolved grief related to the loss of a parent can impact on couple relationships and on the development of a child within a family. The cases presented in this chapter illustrate how the combination of the early loss of the mother combined with the inability of the father to provide an emotionally compensatory experience, shapes the melancholic reaction to the early loss of a mother. In turn, it highlights how it creates and maintains a barrier to future intimacy. The chapter also describes the use of a particular application of Green's concept of the "dead mother" to help understand the intrapsychic state (of internal self-object links) and how this manifests as couple difficulties.

In Chapter 8 the special therapeutic challenges associated with the issue of adjustment difficulties related to miscarriage (or Repeated Pregnancy Loss [RPL]) are considered. It is noted that a couple's capacity to stay together is often challenged in response to the loss of a pregnancy. Unprocessed emotions, particularly those related to childhood trauma can erupt, resulting in aggressive blaming or distancing and withdrawal within the couple. An important issue highlighted in this chapter is the relevance of loss through miscarriage on an individual's unconscious destructive feelings and the moderation of these by the creative act of producing a child. It is suggested that a therapeutic focus on destructiveness and reparation is particularly helpful when intervening with such couples.

In Chapter 9 the focus is on the experience of loss suffered by couples in everyday life. It addresses the types of difficulties that couples with a narcissistic style of relating face when life crises challenge their defensive structure. The movie *45 Years* is used to illustrate such dynamics with the aid of link theory, which the author demonstrates as an important explanatory concept in dealing with melancholic reactions to loss in couples. The chapter provides an insight into how narcissism can underpin a particular type of "link" by which the couple is bound into a relationship based on the notion of perfection, which is achieved by denying any differences between the two individuals.

The book concludes with some thoughts about the centrality of mourning to all psycho-therapeutic endeavours and highlights the value of addressing such issues in couple therapy where the dynamics that are dealt with in individual therapy can be seen, identified, and worked with, as they occur in the relationship with the couple in the session.

In an era when many outdated criticisms about psychoanalysis are being addressed, particularly those concerning its treatment efficacy (Shedler, 2010; Leuzinger-Bohleber & Kächele, 2015), we believe that psychoanalytic interventions with couples (and families) who are struggling with the pain of unresolved grief, as defined in this book, represent an important therapeutic resource to the community. We also believe that these psychoanalytic interventions warrant a place in the suite of mental health services that should be made available within the public health system.

In conclusion, we hope that in some small way this book may help to alleviate the chronic psychological pain with which many couples and families suffer following loss.

## References

AmericanPsychiatricAssociation. (2013). *Diagnostic and Statistical Manual of Mental Disorders* (5th edn). Arlington, VA: American Psychiatric Publishing.

Australian BureauofStatistics. (2016). Report 3303.0 – Causes of Death, Australia, 2016. Retrieved from www.abs.gov.au/ausstats/abs@.nsf/mf/3302.0

Bion, W. R. (1962). *Learning from Experience*. New York: Basic Books.

Bowlby, J. (1969). *Attachment and Loss. Vol. 1. Loss*. New York: Basic Books.

Caper, R. (1997). A mind of one's own. *International Journal of Psychoanalysis*, 78: 265–278.

Enguidanos, A. G., Calle, M. E., Valero, J., & Dominguez-Rojas, V. (2002). Risk factors in miscarriage: A review. *European Journal of Obstetrics & Gynecology and Reproductive Biology*, 102(2): 111–119.

Faimberg, H. (2005). *The Telescoping of Generations: Listening to the Narcissistic Links Between Generations*. London: Karnac.

Fairbairn, W. R. D. (1952). *Psychoanalytic Studies of the Personality*. London: Routledge.

Ford, H. B., & Schust, D. J. (2009). Recurrent pregnancy loss: Etiology, diagnosis, and therapy. *Review of Obstetrics and Gynecology*, 2(2): 76–83.

Freud, S. (1916). On Transience. *S.E.*, 14: 305–308.

Freud, S. (1917). Mourning and Melancholia. *S.E.*, 14: 239–258.

Hall, C. (2011). Beyond Kubler-Ross: Recent developments in our understanding of grief and bereavement. *Inpsych*, 33(6): 7–12.

Horowitz, M. J., Siegel, B., Hole, A., Bonanno, G. A., Milbrath, C., & Stinson, C. H. (1997). Diagnostic criteria for complicated grief disorder. *American Journal of Psychiatry*, 154(7): 904–910.

Husserl, E. (1931). *Cartesian Meditations*, D. Cairns (Trans.). Dordrecht: Kluwer, 1988.

ICD-10 (2004). *International Statistical Classification of Diseases and Related Health Problems* (10th Revision, 2nd edn). Geneva: World Health Organization.

Jackson, S. W. (1986). *Melancholia and Depression: From Hippocratic Times to Modern Times*. New Haven, CT: Yale University Press.

Jones, W. H. S. (1931). *Nature of Man. Regimen in Health. Humors. Aphorisms. Regimen 1–3. Hippocrates*, Volume IV. Loeb Classical Library, 150. Cambridge, MA: Harvard University Press.

Käes, R. (2016). Link and the transference within three interfering psychic spaces. *Couple and Family Psychoanalysis*, 6(2): 81–193.

Keogh, T., & Enfield, S. (2013). From regression to recovery: Tracking developmental anxieties in couple therapy. *Couple and Family Psychoanalysis*, 3: 28–46.

Klein, M. (1946). Notes on some schizoid mechanisms. *International Journal of Psycho-Analysis*, 27: 99–110.

Kliman, G. (1979). Childhood mourning: A taboo within a taboo. In: I. Gerber, A. Wiener, A. Kutscher, D. Battin, A. Arkin & I. Goldberg (Eds.), *Perspectives on Bereavement*. New York: Arno Press.

Kochanek, K. D., Murphy, S. L., Xu, J., & Tejada-Vera, B. (2016). Deaths: Final data for 2014. *National Vital Statistics Report*, 65(4). Atlanta, GA: Centre For Disease Control.

Kristensen, P., Dyregrov, K., & Dyregrov, A. (2017). What distinguishes prolonged grief disorder from depression? *Tidsskr Nor Legeforen*, 137: 538–539.

Kristjanson, L. J., Lobb, E., Aoun, S., & Monterosso, L. (2006). *A Systematic Review of the Literature on Complicated Grief*. Canberra: Edith Cowan University and Commonwealth of Australia.

Latham, A., & Prigerson, H. (2004). Suicidality and bereavement: Complicated grief as psychiatric disorder presenting greatest risk for suicidality. *Suicide Life Threat Behavior*, 34(4): 350–362.

Lemma, A. (2016). *Introduction to the Practice of Psychoanalytic Psychotherapy*. Hoboken, NJ: Wiley-Blackwell.

Leuzinger-Bohleber, M., & Kächele, H. (2015). *An Open Door Review of Outcome and Process in Psychoanalysis*. London: International Psychoanalytical Association.

Lichtenthal, W. G., Cruess, D. G., & Prigerson, H. G. (2004). A case for establishing complicated grief as a distinct mental disorder in the DSM-V. *Clinical Psychology Review*, 24: 637–662.

Lobb, E. A., Kristjanson, L., Aoun, S., & Monterosso, L. (2006). An overview of complicated grief terminology and diagnostic criteria. *Grief Matters: The Australian Journal of Grief and Bereavement*, 9(2): 28–32.

Maciejewski, P., Maercker, A., Boelen, P. A., & Prigerson, H. G. (2016). "Prolonged grief disorder" and "persistent complex bereavement disorder", but not "complicated grief", are one and the same diagnostic entity: An analysis of data from the Yale Bereavement Study. *World Psychiatry*, 15(3): 266–275.

Morgan, M. (1995). *The Projective Gridlock: A Form of Projective Identification in Couple Relationships*. London: Karnac.

Najman, J. M., Vance, J. C., Boyle, F., Embleton, G., Foster, B., & Thearle, J. (1993). The impact of a child death on marital adjustment. *Social Science and Medicine*, 37: 1005–1010.

O'Connor, M. F., & Arizmendi, B. (2014). Neuropsychological correlates of complicated grief in older spousally bereaved adults. *Journal of Gerontology: Psychological Sciences*, 69B: 12–18.

Ogden, T. (1989). On the concept of the autistic-contiguous position. *International Journal of Psychoanalysis*, 70: 127–141.

Ogrodniczuk, J. S., Piper, W. E., Joyce, A. S., Weideman, R., McCallum, M., Azim, H. F. & Rosie, J. S. (2003). Differentiating symptoms of complicated grief and depression among psychiatric outpatients. *Canadian Journal of Psychiatry*, 48: 87–93.

Owens, D. (2008). Recognizing the needs of bereaved children in palliative care. *Journal of Hospice & Palliative Nursing*, 10: 1.

Prigerson, H. G., Frank, E., Kasl, S. V., Reynolds, C. F., Anderson, B., Zubenko, G. S., Houck, P. R., George, C. J., & Kupfer, D. J. (1995). Complicated grief and bereavement-related depression as distinct disorders: Preliminary empirical validation in elderly bereaved spouses. *American Journal of Psychiatry*, 152: 22–30.

Prigerson, H. G., Shear, M. K., Jacobs, S. C., Reynolds, C. F., III, Maciejewski, P. K., Davidson, J. R., Rosenheck, R., Pilkonis, P. A., Wortman, C. B., Williams, J. B.,

Widiger, T. A., Frank, E., Kupfer, D. J., & Zisook, S. (1999). Consensus criteria for traumatic grief: A preliminary empirical test. *British Journal of Psychiatry*, 174: 67–73.

Rogers, C. H., Floyd, F. J., Seltzer, M. M., Greenberg, J. S., & Hong, J. (2008). Long term effects of the death of a child on parents adjustment in midlife. *Journal of Family Psychology*, 22: 203–211.

Rosner, R., Kruse, J., & Hagl, M. (2005). Quantitative and qualitative review of interventions for the bereaved; Stockholm. Paper presented at the 9th European Conference on Traumatic Stress (ECOTS).

Rosner, R., Pfoh, G., & Kotoucova, M. (2011). Treatment of complicated grief. *European Journal of Psychotraumatology*, 2: 79–95.

Scharff, D. E., & Palacios, E. (2017). *Couple and Family Psychoanalysis: Global Perspectives*. London: Karnac.

Scharff, D. E., & Vorchheimer, M. (2017). *Clinical Dialogues on Couple and Family Psychoanalysis*. London: Karnac.

Shear, M. K., & Shair, H. (2005). Attachment, loss and complicated grief. *Developmental Psychobiology*, 47: 253–267.

Shedler, J. (2010). The efficacy of psychodynamic psychotherapy. *American Psychologist*, 65(2): 98–109.

Simon, N. M. (2013). Treating complicated grief. *Journal of the American Medical Association*, 310(4): 416–423.

Stroebe, M., & Schut, H. (2006). Complicated grief: A conceptual analysis of the field. *Omega: The Journal of Death and Dying*, 52: 53–70.

Stroebe, M., Schut, H., & Stroebe, W. (2005). Attachment in coping with bereavement: A theoretical integration. *Review of General Psychology*, 9(1): 48–66.

Stroebe, M., Stroebe, W., & Abakoumkin, G. (2005). The broken heart: Suicidal ideation in bereavement. *American Journal of Psychiatry*, 162: 2178–2180.

Stroebe, W., & Schut, H. (2001). Risk factors in bereavement outcome: A methodological and empirical review. In: M. S. Stroebe, W. Stroebe, & R. O. Hansson (Eds.), *Handbook of Bereavement: Theory, Research, and Intervention* (pp. 349–371). Cambridge: Cambridge University Press.

Weller, R. A., Weller, E. B., Fristad, M.A., & Bowes, J. M. (1991). Depression in recently bereaved prepubertal children. *American Journal of Psychiatry*, 148(11): 1536–1540.

# Part I

# Theoretical understandings and clinical approaches to loss

Chapter 1

# Psychoanalytic understandings of loss and their relevance to couples and families

*Timothy Keogh*

## Introduction

The development of psychoanalytic understandings of loss are to be found in the writings of Freud, Abrahams and the object relations theorists who followed, notably Klein and Fairbairn. Their theoretical ideas and concepts concerning loss have had an enduring value and have been elaborated further by contemporary theorists. The value of integrating link theory with these understandings of loss is discussed separately in Chapter 2.

In order to contemplate the value of these ideas to contemporary clinical presentations, firstly consider the case of Melissa and Peter, who attended therapy at the suggestion of their general practitioner after a series of increasingly hostile arguments. Although they were previously a happy and seemingly well-functioning couple, during a recent argument Melissa said that she felt she could no longer stay in the marriage. About ten months previously, they had lost their only baby daughter, Felicity, as a result of a cot death. The couple were initially extremely distressed, yet appeared to manage to get on with their daily lives. Their family were supportive, but no one seemed to want to talk about their loss once the funeral was over.

Some months after the funeral, Melissa cut herself by accident as she was making breakfast and at first could not stop the bleeding. She was distressed about the thought of the unstoppable bleeding. Alone at the time, she had accused herself of stupidity in doing such a thing. She had also started to feel she could not do anything right, doubted her competency at work and questioned her capacity to drive safely. When considering a further pregnancy, she thought that perhaps God did not want her to be a mother. Initially, Peter appeared to grieve the loss of their baby and resume his normal level of functioning. Despite this he had begun complaining to his brother about Melissa becoming more critical of him. About 9 months after the death of Felicity, Peter's boss had told him that he was concerned about Peter's lack of productivity. Peter increasingly felt that he was not what the company needed – that he was not an asset for his employer.

The couple only mentioned Felicity occasionally. At these times Melissa's eyes would fill with tears. Peter felt that he was upsetting her by talking about Felicity and so stopped referring to her. Friends also avoided talking about the death with the couple. Melissa subsequently became more critical of Peter, even somewhat unreasonably suggesting that his absence from home, associated with the demands of his job, was related to the loss of Felicity. This hurt and shocked him. He ultimately felt he could do nothing right in her eyes. He found it hard to understand why she had become so unreasonable. The combination of the problems at home and the felt pressure at work saw Peter lose his job. This led to further criticisms from Melissa, who held him responsible for everything that was going wrong. Neither of them had classic signs of clinical depression, but their general practitioner, noting the history of loss and the self/other recriminatory features in their way of relating, referred them for couple therapy.

One can see in this couple the manifestations of a melancholic-type reaction to the loss of their daughter, where the self-recrimination attendant on the loss, was experienced in the form of the couple's increasing arguments, where blaming the other was pre-dominant. The impoverished ego functioning was a salient feature of both parties, as was the splitting and projection. With this case vignette in mind, let us now review the development of psychoanalytic concepts concerning mourning and melancholia.

## The development of psychoanalytic theories of mourning and melancholia

Psychoanalytical understandings concerning the dynamics of melancholic reactions, of the type described above, draw on a rich history of documented accounts of distressing reactions to loss, which have attracted a varied terminology over time (Jackson, 1986). What all of these accounts have in common is the description of states of dejection and self-blame, where the sufferer sees himself as central in the personal narrative of loss.

The melancholic-type reaction to loss, where the self is narcissistically identified with the lost object with which one is attached, is also common in those who suffer an experience of loss, other than an actual death (see Chapter 9). Whilst Freud's (1917) writings focused on the significant loss of a loved one through death, he also noted that mourning would result after "the loss of some abstraction which has taken the place of one, such as fatherland, liberty, an ideal or so on" (p. 243). This might include the loss of a relationship or a loss associated with different life stages, such as old age (McGinley & Varchevker, 2010). A common instance of loss not involving death is where a young person experiences the end of a first romantic relationship. Those with a melancholic tendency are hit hard and struggle to recover and lose their capacity to function. Consider the plight of Werther in Goethe's classic, *The Sorrows of Young Werther* (Goethe, 1774). Werther is plunged into a serious melancholic state as a result of the loss of his love, Lotte, who he discovers is betrothed to another. He asks:

> Must it ever be thus – that the source of our happiness must also be the fountain of our misery? The full and ardent sentiment which animated my heart with the love of nature, overwhelming me with a torrent of delight, and which brought all paradise before me, has now become an insupportable torment, a demon which perpetually pursues and harasses me. (Goethe, 1774)

Importantly, the personality of Werther, as Auden (1971) has suggested, was burdened with an excess of narcissism and arguably (attachment) insecurity, which rendered him vulnerable to feeling responsible for so much of his own unhappiness.

## Freud's contribution

Accounts of melancholia and melancholic-type reactions can be found throughout recorded history. It was, however, Freud (1917), in his seminal paper *Mourning and Melancholia*, who researched accounts of melancholia and compared and contrasted them to normal mourning, in order to understand the underlying psychodynamics in the former. He saw that melancholia, in contrast to normal mourning, could result in unremitting emotional suffering and misery and in extreme cases could (where there were substantial unconscious sadistic impulses towards the lost loved object) encompass the risk of suicide. Relatedly, it is not uncommon in couples who exhibit manifestations of complicated grief, for one partner to feel so (unreasonably) responsible for the death of a child that the verdict of that partner's internal judge (harsh superego) is that he does not deserve to live.

Freud wrote about melancholia at a time when he was developing his overall *Magnum Opus*, his theory of psychoanalysis. The development of his theory was characterised by a progression of thought which led initially to his topographic model wherein he accounted for unconscious, pre-conscious, and conscious states, to a structural (and more widely known) model by which he explained psychological conflicts and psychopathology. On the basis of his structural model he described the *id* as an instinctual reservoir of strivings and impulses; the *ego*, that which negotiated these with the demands of reality; and the *superego*, which he saw as the basis of conscience (Schimmel, 2014). In melancholia, he saw this last sub-structure as taking on an exaggerated role (like the internal judge referred to in the vignette above), which shaped it (the superego) into an agency, which instead of being supportive and helpful becomes something by which an individual can feel driven, compelled, and persecuted. Freud saw it forming an accusatory relationship with an ego, such that the latter feels impaired and inferior, as in the case of the experience of both Peter and Melissa.

Freud's *Mourning and Melancholia* was written as the fifth in a series of papers, which helped to redefine Freud's theory of psychoanalysis. It followed his paper, *On Narcissism* (Freud, 1916), where he had outlined the importance of identificatory psychic mechanisms and, in particular, narcissistic identifications in the determination of certain forms of psychopathology. It was a time of prolific output for Freud who, at 61 years of age, was dealing with his own losses. His half-brother Emanuel, with whom he had a close relationship, had died in 1914; at the same age Freud's father had died. Freud was also left in a state of loneliness and uncertainty as his three sons had gone off to fight in the war (Gay, 1995).

Importantly, Freud, in his 1917 paper, noted that for the mourner it is the loss of the object that is at the centre of the experience, whereas in melancholia it is the loss of a part of oneself, due to a narcissistic identification. Couples who lose children in whom they have been narcissistically invested, often feel that it is impossible to continue as a couple, as their lost child has previously defined them and they experience a loss of that sense of definition with the loss of their child. Frequently, such couples often make an unwise decision to rush into becoming pregnant again as a solution to their psychic pain.

Freud had originally talked about mourning from a cultural perspective in *Totem and Taboo* (Freud, 1913). Here he noted that there could be ambivalent feelings towards the dead that made their spirits feel potentially demonic and frightening. In *Mourning and Melancholia,* he showed how such processes could operate intrapsychically. He not only emphasised the role of narcissism in this, but also the roles of ambivalence (towards the lost object) and sadism, which he saw as factors in taking loss reactions into the direction of melancholia.

Freud was essentially arguing that the self-recriminations and reproaches that the patient with melancholic reaction experiences, are in fact accusations against the lost love-object that have been transferred onto herself, or her ego. Freud (1917), in explaining these phenomena for the first time, also indicated that the ego could split and aspects of the self could be projected onto an "other" with whom she is unconsciously identified. As Scharff and Scharff (1991) have noted, the couple dyad provides an ideal vehicle for the maintenance of such splitting and projection. Link theorists, notably Pichon Rivière (2017), also described how "the link", which is co-constructed by the couple, is the means through which such a pathological exchange of projective and introjective processes occurs and can either maintain or interfere with these processes.

In terms of splitting of the ego Freud noted how a bad self (part of the ego) could also become victim to a primitive and more brutal version of the superego, when he noted: "The shadow of the object fell upon the ego, so that the latter could henceforth be criticised by a special mental faculty like an object, like the forsaken object" (p. 249).

Ogden (2009) notes,

> The shadow metaphor suggests the melancholic's experience of identifying with the abandoned object has a thin, two-dimensional quality as opposed to a lively robust feeling tone. The painful experience of loss is short-circuited by the melancholic's identification with the object, *thus denying the separateness of the object*: the object is I and I am the object. There is no loss; an external object (the abandoned object) is omnipotently replaced by an internal one (the ego-identified-with-the-object). (p. 131, italics added)

In such a narcissistic internal world, the lost object therefore becomes transformed into a lost (split-off) part of the self/ego. It then becomes subject to the grievances about the lost object. This is linked to Freud's characterisation of all negative feelings that the patient experiences about himself as being those which he felt towards the lost object. As highlighted in relation to the story of young Werther, Freud also noted the role of sadism in melancholia. In this regard he pointed to the "indubitably pleasurable self-torment of melancholia" (Freud, 1917, p. 211). Perhaps it is only when this element of sadism is fully appreciated that we can realise how such sadism (and relatedly masochism), as part of the displacement of negativity away from the lost love-object, can also push an individual in the direction of suicide (see also the Introduction).

Freud's views on many subjects, including mourning and melancholia, were of course strongly challenged. In this regard, in the only audio recording Freud ever made, he noted:

> I started my professional activity as a neurologist trying to bring relief to my neurotic patients. Under the influence of an older friend and by my own efforts, I discovered some important new facts about the unconscious in psychic life, the role of instinctual urges, and so on. Out of these findings grew a new science, psychoanalysis, a part of psychology, and a new method of treatment of the neuroses. I had to pay heavily for this bit of good luck. People did not believe in my facts and thought my theories unsavory. Resistance was strong and unrelenting … the struggle is not yet over. (Freud, 1938)

Freud's understanding about melancholia has, however, stood the test of time and matched up well to subsequent research concerning loss and bereavement, his ideas on the subject thus providing a valuable legacy.

## Abraham's views on melancholia

We are also indebted to other psychoanalytic theorists who developed Freud's ideas. Abraham (1915) is one such theorist who was also thinking about the subjects of mourning and melancholia at the same time as Freud. Indeed, *Mourning and Melancholia* was a paper that was much influenced by Freud's communications with Abraham, who was researching depressive psychosis as Freud was writing his paper. Abraham thought of depressive psychosis as a condition of unresolved mourning. Abraham and Freud, in studying the normal and pathological variants of mourning, agreed that normal mourning was a natural and required psychological reaction to loss and, even though it involved a departure from a normal attitude towards life, it should not be treated as an illness.

As an example of the influence they had on each other's ideas, consider the following part of a letter Abraham (1915) sent to Freud well before the publication of *Mourning and Melancholia:*

> Even though I do not yet see that the melancholic displaces onto himself all the reproaches that are aimed at his love-object and that serve to denigrate it, all that you say about identification with the love-object is perfectly clear to me. Perhaps I could not fully grasp this because of the compression of your arguments. With my patients it appeared to me as if the melancholic, incapable of loving as he is, desperately tries to get possession of a love-object. In my experience, he does in fact identify with his love-object, cannot tolerate its loss, and is hyper-sensitive to the slightest unfriendliness, etc. from that side. He often allows himself to be tormented by the loved person in masochistic self-punishment. He reproaches himself for this instead of reproaching the loved person, because unconsciously he has done far greater harm to that person (omnipotence of thought). That is how I deduced it in my analyses. (p. 303)

Abraham (1924a) therefore, also concurred with Freud about the relevance of sadism in making sense of the self-reproach of the melancholic. He felt that the dejected state emanated from repressed hostile feelings towards the love-object. His thoughts about melancholia were also based on the presence of several etiological factors, which he saw as fundamental in its genesis. First was his notion of a developmental fixation-point, which he linked to his theory that children developed through five stages of psychosexual development (oral, anal, phallic, latency, and finally, genital). He maintained that a fixation at any one of these stages impacted adversely on the development of a child into a psychologically healthy adult. He attributed melancholia to a fixation at the oral stage, in particular an oral sadistic stage. Another factor, which he thought was of fundamental importance in the development of melancholia, was a history of relationship disappointments in early life, in particular those likely to have occurred at a pre-Oedipal stage and similar losses occurring later in life. This is why, when assessing couples and making a psychodynamic formulation, one listens for indications of any unresolved earlier losses.

Like Freud, Abraham believed that it was narcissism that accounted for the omnipotent belief in the sufferer, which was the cause and the source of the suffering about the loss (as a result of destructive impulses) of the loved object. He saw that it followed, that the subject felt a need to be tormented by the lost loved object and that this was in fact at the centre of the need for the self-punishment, seen in the melancholic reaction. According to Abraham (1924b), it was this process that is at the heart of melancholic self-punishment. He thus suggested that the melancholic reaction was essentially driven by two factors, on the one hand the identification with a hated object and on the other, the related belief that one is the cause of the suffering of the loved object.

Freud's later ideas, as expressed in his meta-psychology (Freud, 1922), also laid down the foundations for subsequent theorists to develop a conceptualisation of human behaviour seen to be motivated in large part by the need for attachment or relationship. In particular, it paved the way for understanding that, on the basis of our early attachments and our phantasies about these, we internalise templates about our relationships with others. The elaboration of this theory became known as *Object Relations Theory*. As developed by Klein (1945), her theory retained vestiges of Freud's instinct theory, whilst its iteration developed by Fairbairn (1952), which represented the so-called "British Independent Group", eschewed the need to incorporate instinct theory and saw the need for relationship as the primary motivator.

## Klein's contribution regarding mourning

Klein helpfully elaborated not only the notion of the importance of relationship as a key motivator for human beings, but as a key organiser of their psychic lives. In doing so she was able to enlarge our understanding of the mourning process. She proposed on the basis of her clinical work that there was a universal developmental path and structuring that occurs with mental life. She claimed that a baby is initially in a state of un-integration and comes to a state of integration painfully, by experiences with an object (other) that is initially seen to be part of itself, but from which it is gradually able to separate. Winnicott (1969) importantly provided us with an insight into how this process involves a shift from *relating to an object* to *using an object* which, he suggested, involved in a particular sense, the destruction of the real object (Ogden, 2016).

The major signposts of a dynamic, non-linear mental development, according to Klein, were psychic positions or modes of psychic experience from which even integrated, healthy individuals could temporarily regress when under stress. The first developmental mode of experience she described as *the paranoid–schizoid position*. She suggested that in order to deal with the frustrations associated with psychic development, especially those linked to its primary attachment object (usually its mother), the infant needs to split its object into two psychic representations: one good and one bad. These become internalised objects and are seen as identical to the external object (mother). In this sense one can see how important the quality of the actual mothering is, in the process of structuring such representations. Here Klein echoed the observations of Freud in *Mourning and Melancholia* that, at the same time as the object is split, so too is the ego (self). For Klein, the conclusion was that there are consequently split parts of the self in relation to split parts of the object. This is the basis of object relations theory.

The splitting of the object to which Freud had originally alluded, now more fully articulated by Klein, enabled a comprehensive understanding of the challenges of the normal mourning process. Klein highlighted that in order to achieve the other major position of psychic development, *the depressive position*, the necessarily split ego and object had to ultimately become integrated. This meant that the good and bad representations had to come together. Klein claimed that this was a painful psychic process as it entailed recognition that the loved and hated objects were one and the same. One consequence of this developmental stage (the depressive position) is the anxiety generated by the belief that one's hatred (sadistic impulses) towards the loved object *must have damaged it*. In this regard she noted:

> The baby experiences depressive feelings which reach a climax just before, during and after weaning. This is the state of mind in the baby that I termed the "depressive position", and I suggested that it is a melancholia in *statu nascendi*. The object which is being mourned is the mother's breast and all that the breast and the milk have come to stand for in the infant's mind: namely, love, goodness and security. All these are felt by the baby to be lost, and lost as a result of his own uncontrollable greedy and destructive phantasies and impulses against his mother's breasts. Further distress about impending loss (this time of both parents) arises out of the Oedipus situation, which sets in so early and is in such close connection with breast frustrations that in its beginnings it is dominated by oral impulses and fears. The circle of loved objects who are attacked in phantasy and whose loss is therefore feared, widens owing to the child's ambivalent relations to his brothers and sisters. The aggression against phantasised brothers and sisters, who are attacked inside the mother's body, also gives rise to feelings of guilt and loss. (Klein, 1940, p. 125)

Klein saw that if worked through, this painful process generated a template for normal mourning. She noted that the child is more likely to be able to manage this process (the integration of the split self and object) if there has been a loving relationship with the actual caregiver, which has strengthened the good object in relation to the bad one – in other words, a psychic situation where love is able to contain hate. This has important consequences for the couple's sexual relationship, as if this containment is not optimal, the sexual relationship can feel lacking in passion, persecutory, or even frightening (Kernberg, 1998). It is therefore not surprising (and important to one's assessment) that a characteristic of couples who present with features of unresolved grief, is that their sexual relationship is often of poor quality or even ceases following a loss.

Klein noted that if the good object is weak, instead of achieving integration, there is a resort to omnipotent (narcissistic) control, with attempts to keep the good and bad objects separate. The resolution of depressive anxieties where it is achieved, however, leads to a relinquishment of narcissism and fosters separation and individuation, with significant implications for being able to manage loss. The loss of the other is more manageable because it does not involve an experience of losing a part of oneself. Manic attempts to deal with loss, which might include sexual acting out, are important behaviours to understand in relation to melancholic reactions to loss. Such manic attempts at dealing with loss are important indicators that need to be canvassed in the assessment of couples presenting with unresolved loss.

Klein thus ultimately provided a much more comprehensive account of the mechanisms involved in achieving an internalised template for *normal mourning* and for those underpinning melancholic-type reactions. In couples when depressive anxieties are felt to be unbearable and there is a regression to a paranoid–schizoid mode of experience, the unwanted aspects of the self, as well as aspects of the other by whom one feels persecuted, are often projected into the partner, resulting in considerable blaming and hostility.

This dynamism and associated regression in psychic functioning also has implications for the capacity to represent painful experience. In a regressed couple one often observes a regressive type of thinking, which becomes very concrete. As Segal (1957) points out:

> When this *(depressive)* stage of development has been achieved, it is of course not irreversible. If the anxieties are too strong, a regression to a paranoid–schizoid position can occur at any stage of the individual's development and projective identification may be resorted to as a defence against anxiety. Then symbols, which have been developed and have been functioning as symbols in sublimation, revert to concrete symbolic equations. This is mainly due to the fact that in massive projective identification the ego becomes again confused with the object, the symbol becomes confused with the thing symbolized and therefore turns into an equation. (p. 394)

## Fairbairn's theoretical vertex on loss

Fairbairn (1941), as the other notable object relations theorist, developed a remarkably similar view of psychic development and loss. In his model of object relations he privileged human relationships as key motivators, rather than instincts. He noted:

> It would appear as if the point had now been reached at which, in the interests of progress, the classic libido theory would have to be transformed into a theory of development based essentially upon object-relationships ... [He continues] ... the great limitation of the present libido theory as an explanatory system resides in the fact that it confers the status of libidinal attitudes upon various manifestations which turn out to be merely techniques for regulating the object-relationships of the ego. (Fairbairn, 1941, p. 253)

Fairbairn's (1944, 1952) model of psychic development and functioning uses some different terminology to that of Klein, but nonetheless (and writing at the same time) he described a process of development beginning with a state of infantile dependence, which moves towards a state of mature dependence (what he called a "capacity for inter-dependence"). He claimed that what differentiated these states was the level of identification with the other. In the state of mature dependence (by which he meant a state of mutual inter-dependence), the notion of a psychological separation and individuation from the other (object) is implicit.

The process of psychological maturation, in Fairbairn's schema of the movement from infantile to mature dependence, consists of the gradual "abandonment of relationships based on primary identification, in favour of relationships with differentiated objects" (1952, p. 42). He saw that what is required is a progressive differentiation of the object from the self. In the earlier stages of development, he also described the need for the splitting of the self and the object in order to cope with the frustrations of development, in a similar way to Klein. His understanding of the way this splitting occurs is described in his *Endopsychic Model* (Fairbairn, 1944). Scharff and Scharff (1991) applied this model to couple therapy as a useful lens through which to view dyadic manifestations of splitting and projection. This elaboration is extremely valuable in understanding failed mourning and its counterpart melancholic reactions in couples dealing with loss.

Ogden (2010) has offered some insights, from a close reading of Fairbairn, that are also particularly relevant to understanding both failed mourning in couples and how this becomes manifest in a couple dyad. He notes, for example, that it is:

> ... the notion that the infant's unceasing efforts to transform the internalized relationship with the unloving mother [*Rejecting Object*] into a loving relationship – thus reversing the effect on his mother of his (imagined) "toxic love" – is the single most important motivation sustaining the structure of the internal object world ... [and that] ... the idea that attacks on oneself for the way one loves, while self-destructive, contain a glimmer of insight into one's own self-hatred and shame regarding one's endless, futile attempts to change oneself (or the rejecting object

[*Fairbairn's term for the mental representation of the bad object*]) into a different person. (p. 101, italics added)

The state of mature dependence to which Fairbairn refers involves recognition of the separateness of individuals, which coexist with intimate and interdependent relating. Such a sense of separateness is built upon an ability to recognise the existence of the agency of the other. This capacity to recognise the other as separate, whilst relating to the other, fosters personal responsibility and autonomy. One can therefore see that, from a Fairbairnian perspective, loss for someone who is at a stage of development that entails primary identification (with the lost object) will necessarily result in melancholic type reaction.

In terms of object relations theory, the post-Kleinian theoretical developments that Bion (e.g., 1962, 1963) fostered, formed the beginnings of a more inter-subjective viewpoint (see also Chapter 6).

## Bion and loss

Bion's inter-subjective view of the development of the psyche (the mind) further highlighted the notion that we need the help of another mind in order to develop our own. In particular he was referring to a functioning mind capable of containing hard-to-manage experiences (which he referred to as beta-elements). He stressed the importance of the mechanism of projective identification (a term originally coined by Klein) in this process. Bion (1963) noted that its function could be viewed more expansively, not just as a defence mechanism, but also as a means of communicating for those whose psychic development was at a pre-individuated stage, where the other was still seen as a part of the self.

Moreover, Bion felt that some experiences (truths), such as separateness, were unbearable at such early stages of development and that mechanisms, such as those that he described as "attacks of linking", are employed against thoughts that would result in knowing (what he denoted as a "K-Link"). It is important to note that Bion used the concept of link in a particular sense, which is different to how it is articulated in link theory. Reliance on psychic strategies that involve *not* thinking, that which he denoted as –*K*, he saw as resulting in a persecutory state of mind, or "nameless dread". From this vertex one can see such processes in un-individuated couples wherein there is still a dependence on projective identification and where the loss of the object cannot be contemplated, as it feels unbearable.

Bion's elaboration of how the mind develops also provided insight into what fosters the psychic conditions, which result in not being able to bear mental pain. Melancholia from the Bionian perspective can thus be seen as a state in which the pain of being separated from the object cannot be tolerated and in place of which omnipotent psychic mechanisms are brought into play.

A further elaboration of the relevance of Bion's ideas to loss and melancholia is provided in Chapter 6.

Following in the direction of a more inter-subjective position of psychoanalysis, Ogden's (2004) views about psychic development offer a further important perspective on how loss is perceived through the lens of primitive mental states.

## Ogden's vision of primitive mental states and loss

An adequate account of psychic development encompassing the emergence of a sense of self as separate from one's object also needs to include Ogden's addition of what he termed the "autistic–contiguous mode of experience" (Ogden, 1989). In terms of couples and reactions to loss, it accounts for a reaction entailing more primitive levels of regression and anxieties, which can be regarded as an *Anxious Melancholic Reaction.*

Here the regression attendant on the crisis of loss is to such a primitive level of development that it is largely dependent on the (lost) other for a basic sense of self. In such a psychic context the other is felt to be a part of the self, in a highly specific sense. The other in this psychic situation serves as a type of sensuous boundary, a type of psychic skin that provides a sense of a boundary between the self and other that would not otherwise exist. At such a primitive stage of psychic development a relationship with the other is essential in order to avoid the experience of catastrophic type anxieties. In such cases the loss of the other, experienced as the loss of what Ogden calls an "autistic object", is experienced with more primitive anxieties (see also Chapter 4).

The loss can result in an experience where one feels emotionally ripped open and in fear of spilling out and falling into nothingness: phobic-type experiences. In couples with this level of psychic functioning the loss of a child precipitates anxiety in the form of phobic responses which, when extreme, can disrupt daily activities such as being unable to leave the house or result in compulsive behaviour such as the problematic use of internet pornography. In this instance, the behaviour represents an attempt to restore a sense of self. As is often the case, one member of the couple in this context will exhibit the disturbing behaviour that often results in an individual referral, with the important couple dynamic (and hidden difficulties with the partner) left untreated.

## Bowlby and attachment theory

Bowlby's ideas concerning loss, though departing somewhat from traditional object relations-oriented theory, are worthy of consideration as they have as a basic referent the notion of internalised templates of relationship experience, what he referred to as "Internal Working Models" (Bowlby, 1969).

Bowlby was originally thought of as something of a heretic in psychoanalytic circles, yet his theorising, and writings, led to an impressive and widely referenced trilogy concerning attachment, separation, and loss (Bowlby, 1969, 1973, 1980). From his theoretical perspective he saw reactions to loss as akin to those involved in a traumatic separation. Working with James Robertson at the Tavistock Clinic in London (Bowlby & Robertson, 1952), he studied reactions to separations of children from their parents. Bowlby (1969) pointed out that loss of a significant attachment involves a type of searching for the lost object until the verdict of its loss is accepted. In discussing four main variations of reactions to loss, Bowlby (1963) noted,

> An unconscious urge to recover the lost object is a dynamic that probably is present or at least latent in all the other pathological variants of mourning but, because more deeply repressed, is more difficult to see. Moreover, little attention hitherto seems to have been directed to it, and much in my thesis rests on a clear understanding of its role. (p. 500)

In discussing the difference between normal mourning and a melancholic reaction, Bowlby's observations were closely linked to those of Freud. Bowlby (1963) noted, for example:

> … in addition to perseveration of thought, feeling, and behavior oriented toward the lost partner, are two main features: the first is weeping, and the second aggressive thought and action. Both it seemed had as their function the recovery of the object. When in fact the object is only temporarily lost responses of these kinds are useful and this, it was suggested, accounts in large part of their being so regularly the initial reaction to loss. When, however, the object proves to be permanently lost they are no longer useful; in due course, therefore, they may be expected to diminish and disappear. In healthy mourning this is what occurs, and the second and third phases of mourning duly follow: despair and disorganization are succeeded by reorganization and hope. In pathological mourning, on the other hand (or at least in some of its commonest forms), they persist, albeit in disguised forms. The bereaved person remains preoccupied in thought and action with the lost object, not only organizing his life as though it were still recoverable, but continuing to weep for it and commonly also to display dissatisfaction and ill temper with his friends and himself. (p. 504)

Given that Bowlby's attachment theory encompassed the notion that there are internalised working models (akin to object relations) that provide a template for how relationships are viewed, Shear et al (2007) note that:

> Attachment theory rests on two fundamental principles: (1) a well functioning attachment relationship affords a secure base that serves to

> optimize autonomy and goal strivings, as well as provide support and comfort under stress, and (2) attachment relationships are internalized in the form of working models that subsume many of the secure base functions. Attachment figures can be reliably identified as individuals to whom we seek proximity, from whom we resist separation, to whom we turn when in distress, and from whom we garner support and encouragement as we explore the world, engage in meaningful activities and strive to master new challenges. Loss of such a person creates a great disruption that is easily recognized as acute grief. Resolution of acute grief requires successful adjustment to far reaching effects of the loss, both practical and psychological. (p. 459)

Unresolved grief can be seen to occur when such a resolution is impeded. Related to this, Bowlby's attachment theory particularly highlighted the role of the mother/primary caretaker in the formation (creation of an internalised template) of a secure sense of self that could determine later reactions to loss. The four primary attachment styles in adults: Secure, Pre-occupied, Dismissive, and Unresolved, that were articulated from Bowlby's original ideas, provide a useful compass for clinicians to assess the basic psychic terrain in which they find themselves with couples in terms of their likely reactions to loss (Clulow, 2001). Each of these attachment styles entails either a positive or negative view of self and other in the unresolved category (where there is a negative view of self and other): an insecure attachment style that is seen to derive from traumatic and/or unresolved losses. Such an attachment style would predict a poor reaction to loss. An assessment of attachment style in a couple can be a very useful first step in understanding likely reactions to loss, in advance of a more in-depth understanding of the unique objects relations in the couple and the nature of the "couple link".

Colin Parkes, a researcher interested in mourning and grief, joined Bowlby at the Tavistock Centre in 1972. Parkes set out to study a non-clinical group of widows in their homes to chart the course of nominal adult grief, about which little was known at the time. The findings led to a joint paper (Bowlby & Parkes, 1970) in which the phases of separation response, delineated by Robertson for young children, were elaborated into four stages of grief during adult life. These were numbness, yearning and protest, disorganisation and despair, and reorganisation (see also Parkes, 1972). Parkes (1972) and Parkes and Weiss (1983) built on Bowlby's attachment theory and developed a stage model of grief, as did Kubler-Ross (1970). The approach that Parkes took also encompassed the relevance of the patient's unique history and particular relationship with the deceased.

## Postmodernist thinking about loss

Postmodern theorists (e.g., Neimeyer, 2002, 2008) have placed less emphasis on the loss of the attachment with the lost object and the idea of stages of grief, focusing more on the notion of the restoration of a sense of conscious meaning in the world, following loss.

Research supports this notion that difficulty in finding meaning following the loss of a significant attachment object, particularly where there is a problem of making sense of the loss, has been shown to be linked to prolonged grief disorder. At an unconscious level this is more likely to be the case where the sense of self is linked to the lost object. In such an instance there is likely to be a prolonged period of trying to make sense of the loss, which becomes (at least unconsciously) self-referenced. Research suggests that such types of reactions are more common with losses that are unexpected, such as the loss of a child (Rogers, Floyd, Seltzer, Greenberg, & Hong, 2008).

Coming to terms with loss, through being able to find meaning, involves both making sense of the loss and in some way finding benefits from the loss. Sense making and benefit finding appear, however, to be two distinct processes representing two distinguishable psychological issues. The benefit from the first seems to derive from becoming less focused on the loss event, whilst the second benefit can build with time (Davis, Nolen-Hoeksema, & Larson, 1998).

## Contemporary post-Kleinian contributions

In terms of the more contemporary psychoanalytic contributions to understanding melancholic reactions, Alvarez (2010) has identified the enduring value of a number of concepts arising from the work of Freud and Abraham particularly as Klein had elaborated them, which underpin our contemporary understanding of melancholia. These include: (1) the paranoid state of mind which involves split-off aspects of oneself which become the source of persecution (self-reproach); (2) the manic contempt of devalued objects and narcissism (which conspire to generate contempt of the self); and (3) perverse chuntering (which links to the sado-masochistic aspect of melancholia) and the value of the early development of identifications with, and internalisation of, the good object, in enabling the capacity to mourn. She notes that the explication of this last development was largely Klein's accomplishment. Chuntering, a form of moaning misery, was a concept developed by Joseph (1982) and describes a way of nurturing of misery which gives rise to a perverse-type of sexual satisfaction. This idea, as Alvarez notes, is linked to Freud and Abraham's original notions about the perversely pleasurable aspect of self-recrimination.

Alvarez (2010) also suggested that reactions to loss, in children in particular, can vary in terms of where the lost object is not *devalued,* but *unvalued.* She refers to cases where the external object is perceived to be weak and fragile and has to be protected from one's aggression and in melancholic reactions where this aggression is turned upon oneself. She cites alcoholic and depressed parents who have not been overtly abusive, as the external objects that are conducive to the development of such fragile and weak internal objects. This has clear implications for what could be thought of as a double knot that has to be unpicked in the treatment of such presentations.

All of these rich psychoanalytic understandings bring into the foreground the value of the object relations theory approach to melancholia, which highlights the relationship between internal and external objects and how the loss of the external object gives rise to anxiety about the loss of the internal one.

With these psychoanalytic ideas in mind, we are now ready to think about how they can inform our interventions with couples facing loss. In this regard, the first step is the application to assessment and the psychodynamic formulation. These involve an assessment of the level of couple functioning, especially in terms of levels of individuation and separation. Further, it involves the assessment of the couple's suitability for a psychodynamic intervention, especially a brief intervention that has a specific focus. The following chapters will also look at the way such theoretical understandings are used to deal with specific clinical challenges associated with loss.

Mindful of the criticisms (e.g., Clewell, 2004) of Freud's original psychodynamic formulations and those involving the notion of stages of grief (e.g., Parkes, 1972), one is nonetheless aware, as was Alvarez, of the enduring value of the overarching psychoanalytic model of loss. This model views the ultimate recovery from grief as involving *the restoration of the lost object* internally, a relation to which provides the reason to go on living. This, as we shall see in the following chapters, becomes our therapeutic task.

In recent years and especially as a result of international collaboration with our colleagues in South America and Europe (through organisations such as the International Psychoanalytical Association's Committee on Couple and Family Psychoanalysis and the International Association for Couple and Family Psychoanalysis), we have come to value link theory in understanding the impact of culture and intergenerational influences (particularly unprocessed trauma) on couples and families suffering unresolved loss.

Link theory, whose theoretical ancestry derives in large part from the writings of Pichon Rivière (2017), has been made accessible to English-speaking couple therapists through the research and scholarship of David Scharff who, with South American colleagues (Losso, de-Setton, & Scharff, 2017), have made this theory and its origins available in a landmark English language text. Although an emerging area, we endorse the view that an approach to couple and family psychoanalytic therapy that integrates a focus on link theory with object relations theory, significantly enrich the therapeutic work. Consequently, a brief account of link theory follows. This account illuminates an understanding of the interpersonal and transpersonal dimensions of psychoanalytic work with couples and families.

## References

Abraham, K. (1915). Letter from Karl Abraham to Sigmund Freud, March 31, 1915. In: *The Complete Correspondence of Sigmund Freud and Karl Abraham 1907–1925* (pp. 303–306). Classic Books. Retrieved from www.pep-web.org

Abraham, K. (1924a). A short study of the development of the libido. Part I. Manic depressive states and the pre-genital level of the libido. II. The process of introjection in melancholia: Two stages of the oral phase of the libido. In: *Selected Papers on Psychoanalysis: Selected Papers of Karl Abraham M.D.* (pp. 442–452). London: Karnac, 1988.

Abraham, K. (1924b). A short study of the development of the libido. Part I. Manic depressive states and the pre-genital level of the libido. IV. Notes on the psychogenesis of melancholia. In: *Selected Papers on Psychoanalysis: Selected Papers of Karl Abraham M.D.* (pp. 453–463). London: Karnac, 1988.

Alvarez, A. (2010). Melancholia and mourning in childhood and adolescence: Some reflections on the role of the internal object. In: E. McGinley & A. Varchevker (Eds.), *Enduring Loss: Mourning, Depression and Narcissism Throughout the Lifecycle* (pp. 3–18). London: Karnac.

Auden, W. H. (1971). Foreword. In: E. Mayer & L. Bogan (Ed. & Trans.), *The Sorrows of Young Werther: And Novella*. London: Random House, 1971.

Bion, W. R. (1962). *Learning from Experience*. New York: Basic Books.

Bion, W. R. (1963). *Elements of Psycho-Analysis*. London: Heinemann.

Bowlby, J. (1963). Pathological mourning and childhood mourning. *Journal of the American Psychoanalytical Association*, 11: 500–541.

Bowlby, J. (1969). *Attachment and Loss, Vol. 1: Attachment*. New York: Basic Books.

Bowlby, J. (1973). *Attachment and Loss, Vol. 2: Separation*. New York: Basic Books.

Bowlby, J. (1980). *Attachment and Loss, Vol. 3: Loss, Sadness and Depression*. New York: Basic Books.

Bowlby, J., & Parkes, C. M. (1970). Separation and loss within the family. In: E. J. Anthony & C. Koupernik (Eds.), *The Child in his Family: International Yearbook of Child Psychiatry and Allied Professions* (pp. 197–216). New York: Wiley.

Bowlby, J., & Robertson, J. (1952). A two-year-old goes to hospital. *Proceedings of the Royal Society of Medicine*, 46: 425–427.

Boylan, R. D. (2002). *The Sorrows of Young Werther (Dover Thrift Editions)*. UK: Dover Publications, 1902.

Clewell, T. (2004). Mourning beyond melancholia: Freud's psychoanalysis of loss. *Journal of the American Psychoanalytical Association*, 52: 42–67.

Clulow, C. (2001). *Adult Attachment and Couple Psychotherapy: The 'Secure Base' in Practice and Research*. London: Routledge.

Davis, C. G., Nolen-Hoeksema, S., & Larson, J. (1998). Making sense of loss and benefiting from the experience: Two construals of meaning. *Journal of Personality and Social Psychology*, 75(2): 561–574.

Fairbairn, W. R. D. (1941). A revised psychopathology of the psychoses and psychoneuroses. *International Journal of Psycho-Analysis*, 22: 250–279.

Fairbairn, W. R. D. (1944). Endopsychic structure considered in terms of object-relationships. *International Journal of Psycho-Analysis*, 25: 70–92.

Fairbairn, W. R. D. (1952). *Psychoanalytic Studies of the Personality*. London: Routledge and Kegan Paul, 1981.

Freud, S. (1913). Totem and Taboo. *S.E.*, 13: 1–161.

Freud, S. (1916). On Narcissism. *S.E.*, 14: 305–308.

Freud, S. (1917). Mourning and Melancholia. *S.E.*, 14: 239–258.

Freud, S. (1922). *Beyond the Pleasure Principle*, J. Strachey (Ed.). New York: Norton & Co., 1961.

Freud, S. (1938). Audio recording. London: British Broadcasting Commission (BBC).

Gay, P. (1995). *Freud: A Life for Our Time*. London: Papermac.

Goethe, J. W. von (1774). *The Sorrows of Young Werther*. Retrieved from www.gutenberg.org/files/2527/2527-h/2527-h.htm

Jackson, S. W. (1986). *Melancholia and Depression: From Hippocratic Times to Modern Times*. New Haven, CT: Yale University Press.

Joseph, B. (1982). Addiction to near-death. *International Journal of Psycho-Analysis*, 63: 449–456.

Kernberg, O. (1998). *Love Relations: Normality and Pathology*. New Haven, CT: Yale University Press.

Klein, M. (1940). Mourning and its relation to manic-depressive states. *International Journal of Psycho-Analysis*, 21: 125–153.

Klein, M. (1945). *Love, Guilt and Reparation*. London: The Hogarth Press.

Kubler-Ross, E. (1970). *On Death and Dying*. London: Tavistock.

Losso, R., de Setton, L. S., & Scharff, D. (2017). *The Linked Self in Psychoanalysis: The Pioneering Work of Enrique Pichon Rivière*. London: Karnac.

McGinley, E., & Varchevker, A. (2010). *Enduring Loss: Mourning, Depression and Narcissism Throughout the Lifecycle*. London: Karnac.

Neimeyer, R. A. (2002). Traumatic loss and the reconstruction of meaning. *Journal of Palliative Medicine*, 5(6): 935–942.

Neimeyer, R. A. (2008). Prolonged grief disorder. In: C. Bryant & D. Peck (Eds.), *Encyclopedia of Death and the Human Experience*. Thousand Oaks, CA: Sage.

Ogden, T. H. (1989). On the concept of the autistic-contiguous position. *International Journal of Psychoanalysis*, 70: 127–141.

Ogden, T. H. (2004). The analytic third: implications for psychoanalytic theory and technique. *Psychoanalytic Quarterly*, 73(1): 167–195.

Ogden, T. (2009). A new reading of the origins of object relations theory. In: L. G. Fiorini, T. Bokanowski & S. Lewkowicz (Eds.), *On Freud's "Mourning and Melancholia"*. London: Routledge.

Ogden, T. H. (2010). Why read Fairbairn? *International Journal of Psycho-Analysis*, 91: 101–118.

Ogden, T. H. (2016). Psychoanalytic theory and technique destruction reconceived: On Winnicott's 'The Use of an Object and Relating through Identifications'. *International Journal of Psychoanalysis*, 97(5): 1243–1262.

Parkes, C. (1972). *Bereavement: Studies of Grief in Adult Life*. London: Tavistock.

Parkes, C. M., & Weiss, R. S. (1983). *Recovery from Bereavement*. New York: Basic Books.

Pichon Rivière, E. (2017). The theory of the link. In: R. Losso, L. S. de Setton, & D. Scharff (Eds.), *The Linked Self in Psychoanalysis: The Pioneering Work of Enrique Pichon Rivière* (Chapter 5). London: Karnac.

Rogers, C. H., Floyd, F. J., Seltzer, M. M., Greenberg, J. S., & Hong, J. (2008). Long term effects of the death of a child on parents adjustment in midlife. *Journal of Family Psychology*, 22: 203–211.

Scharff, D., & Scharff, J. S. (1991). *Object Relations Couple Therapy*. London: Jason Aronson.
Schimmel, P. (2014). *Sigmund Freud's Discovery of Psychoanalysis: Conquistador and Thinker*. London & New York: Routledge.
Segal, H. (1957). Notes on symbol formation. *International Journal of Psychoanalysis*, 38: 391–405.
Shear, K., Monk, T., Houck, P., Medhem, N., Frank, E., Reynolds, C., & Sillowash, R. (2007). An attachment based model of complicated grief including the role of avoidance. *European Archives of Psychiatry and Clinical Neuroscience*, 257(8): 453–461.
Winnicott, D. W. (1969). The use of an object. *International Journal of Psychoanalysis*, 50: 711–716.

Chapter 2

# Link theory and object relations theory: an enriched approach to working with melancholic couples

*Elizabeth Palacios*

## Introduction

Psychoanalytic theory has historically viewed couple relationships from the vertex of self-object relations (internal links) motivated either by drives or the need for attachment. Contemporary approaches also consider that what happens in the relationship between subjects can not only be considered from this internal link or object relations perspective, but also from an external link perspective. This is because in the intersubjective world the presence of the *other* needs to be considered, not as an accessory, but as a presence that cannot be cloaked completely by the projective–introjective mechanisms. The *other* appears as an object of *imposition* (Berenstein & Puget, 2004) forcing the other ego to undergo some psychic processing to deal with this presence. The link theory *(el vínculo)* is a theoretical approach that tries to explain and cast further light on the theoretical field of couple and family psychoanalysis from a different perspective. In the text that follows these theoretical approaches will be addressed in an attempt to explain what each of them adds to our knowledge of human interactions.

## Working with couples in psychoanalysis

Working with couples in psychoanalysis creates opportunities for thinking theoretically about how to address the difficulties shown in the interaction between the individuals that compose it. The type of couple link that the two members can create, their psychopathology, and how psychic change can take place is the work of the assessment and treatment phase of psychoanalytic couple therapy. Integrating link theory into couples and family psychoanalysis provides us with new ways of thinking about couple difficulties. These contemporary theoretical concepts, however, need to be thoroughly understood in order to build a more substantial theoretical and methodological corpus of knowledge and practice.

This chapter will address not only the way in which these different theoretical models aim to explain the dynamic of a couple relationship and links with the other, but also how they can enrich each other.

Couple and family psychoanalysts such as Dicks (1967), Pincus and Dare (1978), Scharff and Scharff (1977), and Ruszczynski (1993), inspired by the writings of Klein, Rosenfeld, and post-Kleinian authors, hold a particular view of how unconscious selection of partners is made. Another group of mostly Argentinean authors have also applied the notion of "the link" in their clinical work and writing (Berenstein, 2001a, b, 2004, 2007; Pichon Rivière, 1985; Berenstein & Puget, 1997), following a mostly French conceptualisation of "the subject" and the constitution of subjectivity.

As mentioned in Chapter 1 an embryonic notion of "object relation" first appeared in Freud's papers on identification, with a fuller elaboration in his meta-psychological work *Mourning and Melancholia* (Freud, 1917). His ideas in this writing are linked to those published in 1914, *On Narcissism: An Introduction*. He compares melancholia to the process of mourning. During mourning, the mind needs to incorporate the loss of an object separate to itself as a result of required psychic work. Mourning is therefore described as a reaction to a loss, be it a loved person or some other abstraction (homeland, freedom, ideal, or others), which triggers a psychic response in which the person recognises the absent or lost object. In this case the reality is acknowledged. Initially the person turns away from reality and is unable to love. Inhibition takes hold of him. The work of mourning deals with the painful memories and, as time goes by, the ego does significant psychic work, finally finding new objects to replace the lost one and to restore it in an internalised form. Melancholia entails more uncertainty. As loss of the object in reality is denied, there is a loss of self involved. As Freud points out: "… in mourning the world becomes impoverished and empty, during melancholia it is the ego itself …" (p. 246).

In melancholia, the libido withdraws into the ego and identifies with the lost object which is, at the same time, a loved and a hated object. That is, there is an ambivalent relationship with the object whereby it is felt to be both lost and present. This is related to the fact that the nature of the self-object choice is narcissistic.

Psychoanalysis broadened its theoretical knowledge shifting away from Freud's drive theory towards a new way of considering psychic functioning in which object relations theory gained space. The concept of "object relation" was next referred to by Abraham (1924) in his work *A Short Study of the Development of the Libido, Viewed in the Light of Mental Disorders* and finally acquires its actual conceptualisation in Klein's work.

As noted in Chapter 1 the work of Melanie Klein and her ideas on loss and mourning became one of the great contributions to psychoanalytical thinking. The reaction to loss was focused on clinical observation and this had effect in the construction of a new way of thinking about the mind and its mechanisms. Klein stressed the importance of the early introjection processes which underlie melancholia, highlighting the importance of the ego structure and the integrated nature of the objects within the infant's mind. She declared in "A contribution to the psychogenesis of manic-depressive states": "... not until the object is loved as a whole, can this loss be felt as a whole" (1935, p. 264).

Klein felt that unconscious phantasies also played an important role in determining how one deals with separation and loss because the introjection of self-object relations are very much shaped by them. The ego develops out of the turmoil of phantasies associated with the paranoid–schizoid position involving the struggle between aggression and destructiveness and thereafter, if all goes well, the forces of love and reparation associated with achievement of the depressive position (Klein, 1940, 1946).

From the Kleinian point of view, all psychic activity follows such unconscious phantasies with experience connected to the resulting object relationships. That is, *the existence of an internal object implies the internalisation of experience with external objects in a personal way.* The unconscious phantasy establishes a logical structure that organises and codifies experience. As mentioned above, the code followed within the internal world goes from a paranoid–schizoid to a depressive position. Conflicts can help us understand the status of this internal object and its tendencies to integrate or disintegrate. This internal object is the foundation of psychic reality. Interpretations of the external world will always come from this internal source and the type of relationship that the ego will have to external objects depends on this.

The sense of life comes from this inner world. Each subject lives inside different characters in an internal family and interprets outer world experiences in the light of internal object relations. Objects can be considered independent and be felt to have their own existence as part of an external world, after the depressive position has been achieved. However, these objects are then at risk of being lost or damaged.

From other theoretical perspectives (Berenstein, 2001a, 2001b, 2004, 2007; Berenstein & Puget, 1997), the theory of object relations is open to question, since it may be considered to be solipsistically focused on the ego's relationship with only internal objects. That is, the notion of an object relation names the relationship that the ego has with an internal object and thus external objects are considered as conjectures, as if they were just a hypothesis or a speculation and as if they were not exerting effects *due to their unavoidable presence in relation to others.* According to the potential that each subject has of dealing with his own anxieties, he will, or will not, be able to conceive the external objects as independent, as unknown, and develop the desire and the need to gain knowledge about them. This is something that also happens to each of us, as subjects, within our own self. We also need to use conjecture to develop a sense of our self which otherwise remains unknown. This idea will be addressed later in this chapter.

## The concept of "link"

The concept of "link" offers a closer view of the phenomena which are addressed in this book. Link structures can be considered as having their origins within the organisation of a group in primary bonds. Meeting the difference present in others is intrinsic to being a member of a group (Palacios & Monserrat, 2017). This notion is highly polysemic in psychoanalytical theory, meaning different things according to the psychoanalytical context in which it is formulated.

There is a need for all of us who use the concept to be clear about what we mean by the notion of "link". The conceptualisation of the link became significant in the history of psychoanalytical ideas at a time when the need to understand how another mind plays a role in the development of a new mind, could not be explained with the terminology analysts had at that time, which was shown to be insufficient. Bion's (1962, 1967) and Winnicott's (1965) theories attempted to address this need.

Bion (1962, 1963, 1965) described the presence of another mind as necessary to receive and metabolise the infant's emotions, so that they could be turned into psychic material that can help the new mind to think and dream. His formulation meant that the new mind will not only incorporate those metabolised emotions, but that a link (in a particular sense that Bion used the term) is mandatory in acquiring the capacity to deal with emotions. The notion of links became a central axis of the theory posed by Bion. Bion describes what happens in the relationship between an object and the type of bond a mother can have with a baby, a field in which the capacity for thought is developed. He describes a particular series of links as love, hate, and knowledge, that reveal the emotional quality of bonds and the reciprocal way in which objects nurture or destroy one another. His ideas on the symbolisation of the missing object and the role of the link with the mother in this process are original notions.

Winnicott's (1971) hypothesis on transitional objects and transitional phenomena gave way to one of the most important discoveries in psychoanalysis: exploring how the infant acquires the concept of "not me". Relevant to link theory, the concept of transitional objects and transitional space refer to an intermediate area of human experience. Between the inner reality and the external reality, he envisaged a new subjective experience "between the thumb and the teddy bear, between the oral erotism and the true object relationship" (p. 1), that is, between the child's illusion of creation and the projection of what has been introjected.

Several authors have studied the suffering everyone must undergo through the involvement in shared links. "Suffering in the link" (e.g., Berenstein & Puget, 1997) is a notion that attempts to describe the psychic pain or distress that results from being part of shared links in couples or families. Many authors, from both within and outside of psychoanalysis, have tried to investigate and explain how an individual person is shaped by the group to which he belongs (Pichon Rivière, 1985; Berenstein & Puget, 1997; Berenstein, 2001b, 2004, 2007). Initially, they used this as an axis for their thinking about the notion of the third and thirdness, types of transference, and ideas derived from Lévi-Strauss's conceptualisations of links and laws of exchange (expounded in *The Elementary Structures of Kinship* (1969) and *Structural Anthropology* (1963)).

Some of these authors (e.g., Berenstein, 2007; Käes, 1987, 2007) have pointed out that we should not forget that subjects live in several worlds: an inner world with its representations, an intersubjective world in which the ego participates with others in intimate relationship experiencing emotions, and a third trans-subjective or socio-cultural world of belonging that determines our social identifications.

## The concept of subject in psychoanalysis

The above-mentioned authors use the concept of "the subject". This means that they are thinking about a link between subjects. This concept, however, requires some further explanation in order to understand what is meant by this notion.

Some decades ago psychoanalysts began to talk about the subject and the subjectivity. Freud had not used these terms in his writings. Before these concepts came into use analysts talked about the self, the identity, or the constitution of the psychic apparatus (e.g., Guntrip, 1968; Khan, 1996; Kohut, 1971). The concept of the psychic subject began to be used as a sort of synonym for the psychic apparatus. The subject was a term used in other areas of knowledge, such as philosophy or psychology. One of the most important contributions Freud articulated in his topographical model was that the human mind and thinking are radically divided or split, in terms of conscious awareness. This is an idea totally different to how this was thought about since the French philosopher, René Descartes, in his *Discourse on Method and Meditations* (Descartes, 1637) defined what he considered the starting point for existence: "I think, therefore I am" (*cogito ergo sum*). Freud describes a divided subject: a conscious subject and an unconscious one.

Objects and subjects can also be split. Whenever we talk about the object in psychoanalysis, we are referring to a construction that we make as human beings due to the use of our senses, which allows us to have the first level of representation of the world in our inner world. The concept of the subject, as used in psychoanalysis, refers to the specificity of each human being, which makes him totally different to any other human being, with a personal history that provides him with a radical difference, which can be studied in the transference in the analytical field. This is the subjectivity with which psychoanalysis deals.

Lacan (1966), inspired by the theory of interpretation and the methodology of philosophical interpretation, expounded by the German philosopher Martin Heidegger (1927) and the Swiss linguist and semiotician, Ferdinand de Saussure (1913), suggested a "return to the meaning of Freud". He returns to the Freudian conception of the process by which the subject is constituted. This process is dialectical in nature and involves the notion that the subject is created and sustained through a dialectical interplay between the unconsciousness and the consciousness. The contribution of psychoanalysis to a theory of subjectivity encompasses the formation of a concept of the subject in which neither the consciousness nor the unconsciousness holds a privileged position in relation to the other; the two of them coexist and, at the same time, foster and deny the relationship to one another.

When we use the term "link" to name a relationship between two subjects, it implies that we consider that an unconscious organisation is taking place between them both. It is essential for both members of that link to experience a sense of belonging to the structure they are building together. There is an area of this structure that they share in which a narcissistic investment takes place and there is an area of content which is not shared and cannot be shared. There are cases in which a need for fusion is present, with an illusion of being one with the other (see Chapter 5). When disillusionment appears, it may not be welcomed. The process of disillusionment within the link is fundamental for the couple's wellbeing. This enables each member of the couple to recognise that the other is different from himself.

Projection makes what is internal to be felt as external, as a continuity of oneself, based in being unable to register the other as radically different. The term "imposition" is used by these authors (Berenstein, 2001a, b; Berenstcin & Puget, 1997) to designate the impact the subject has on the other member in the link. The effect of the imposition of one member of the couple upon the other member, and *vice versa*, implies that each member of the couple has to do some psychic work within himself in order to accept the presence of the "other". We refer to the "other" as a subject which has an unyielding difference; he is an alien and we talk about this phenomenon as "the alienness of the other" (Berenstein, 2004, 2007). This is totally different to a character in a dream or in an unconscious fantasy (which is an internal object). If we understand the other as a subject and the link as a structure within which two member subjects, with their radical differences present, both need to engage in the psychic work previously mentioned in order to recognise the presence of this other. These two members have to build up a new subjectivity in order to be part of this link. This is known as "the subject's link" (Berenstein, 2001a). The effect of the presence of the other modifies each subject of that link. It can be said then that each subject is inhabited by object relations and by links with others (in the sense underlined by this theoretical approach). The difference between one subject and the other is not avoidable and, due to being members of that couple, both will need to build a different subjectivity in order to inhabit that particular link.

## The relationship with others

In terms of clinical practice many psychoanalysts now use such concepts to try to understand what is happening in the relationships with others, from the perspective of this link. This runs counter to the idea of an inner world in which the ego, with its object representations, pays little attention to the presence of others, as though they were incidental, are seen only through the screen of our minds, and are confused at different levels with our inner world. If we consider the intersubjective world, as seen through the lens of the link, the presence of the other is inevitable and determines how the ego constitutes itself and obtains its shape as a subject. The other is a foreigner and, in this sense, cannot be incorporated into the ego. At the same time, the other contributes to the makeup of the ego. As a subject, we need to do something with the other's presence because, as mentioned above, the other behaves as an object of imposition (Berenstein & Puget, 1997; Berenstein, 2001a, 2004). The presence of the other is thus an important agent, along with psychic phantasy, in modifying developmental anxieties (Keogh & Enfield, 2013). As this is a totally different mechanism from that of projection and introjection, the concept of the link is different, yet complementary and enriching, to that of object relations theory.

From this perspective, one can see that the subject has no permanent state. Subjects change according to age, and subjectivity evolves continuously with age. The changes that social realities impose on a person impact on his subjectivity. Therefore, we are what we are able to do with others. Subjectivity is what is derived from "our doing with others" (Berenstein, 2007).

Some analysts think that their interpretations can convey a version of what has taken place in a session. Others believe that their interpretation communicates a new meaning that is embodied in the interpretation, something that is created between patient and analyst. *We are all thus inhabited by both object relations and by links with others.* The analyst represents an internal object, and he or she also exerts the effect of a new presence, one that produces a difference. If there is any possibility of a new experience, it will be an outcome of the relationship between the patient and the analyst (Berenstein & Puget, 1997).

It has frequently been considered that couple and family links are determined by the individual psychic reality of each member of a link as, for example, in pathological mourning following the death of a father. Taking a new perspective, however, these group or couple links do not depend solely on individual psychic realities. Transference also has an impact on the actual situation; the effect of its presence causes "interference".

## A clinical vignette

Antonio, aged 39, and his wife María, aged 37, presented their 12-year-old daughter as the problem. She had significant difficulties in her relationship with peers. The assessment revealed that Antonio was the middle son of a couple with three sons, and María was the middle daughter of a family with three daughters. Antonio's father died one year before the assessment, due to heart failure. The couple worked together in a family shop and Antonio spent a great part of his free time with his wife's family. It appeared that he was jealous of María's relationship with her family and of her relationship with their daughter. Both were undergoing individual psychoanalytical treatment. It seemed that both had a total lack of awareness of the implication of their functioning on their daughter's difficulties, as well as on the family's problematic functioning.

The nature of their couple link is illustrated in the following vignette.

MARÍA: I don't really know why we have to come here. I don't have any problems with my daughter. My big problems are with my husband. My daughter and I are very close. She does exactly what I tell her to do and everything goes smoothly. I am the most important person in her life. But with Antonio it's totally different. He started his therapy because I insisted he should do so. He has lots of unsolved problems that cause problems between us. But his treatment is not helping him in any way and I'm repentant that he started it, because this treatment is not helping us. I deal with everything in our family life; every decision is taken by me. He asks me everything, but when he comes out from his treatment he is changed, as if he has been brain washed. He wants to do things his own way and I can't stand it.

ANTONIO: I feel much better. I have my own opinions now, but Maria thinks this is no good.

ANALYST: It looks as if there is a need of holding on to just one way of solving family life issues and, if this is not so, fury erupts between you.

MARÍA: This was how things were with my parents and how they've always been. Antonio does what he wants. I want everything to go back to its original state, if not I can't stand it and I feel furious.

ANALYST: It sounds as if there can't be different ways of addressing issues in family life, and you get anxious because of this. Antonio feels better having his own opinions and your daughter needs both a father and a mother.

What María wants is not what Antonio wants; both of you are different and difference is not easily tolerated.

MARÍA: It has always been like this. I have always been the centre. For your information (looking at the analyst), last year we had a big problem. We adopted a child from an African country and it turned out to be a complete disaster. We had to send him back, but it was me who took the decision. I feel guilty for this.

ANALYST: Why was it you who had to take the decision? It looks like too heavy a burden to be the one who takes decisions and feels responsible for them. It looks like an impossible place to be in.

ANTONIO: I told María that this shouldn't be so. I didn't want the boy to go …Antonio is interrupted violently by María.

MARÍA: Shouldn't be so, shouldn't be so (in a mocking tone). Antonio shrugged his shoulders and stayed sitting, without talking.

ANALYST: Antonio, you couldn't go on with what you had started to say. María, you seem to get furious when Antonio brings in the idea that he thinks you don't need to carry such a burden all by yourself and when he tries to bring in his perceptions and feelings.

## Commentary

In this type of link, the other is seen as part of the psychic world. If the other is taken into account with its real presence and not as an extension of one's inner world, that presence cannot possibly be assimilated by the ego. Each member of the couple will have to go into some sort of psychic work, in order to do something with this "presence". The other is involved in projective mechanisms, but also provides an effect of presence bringing conflict into the couple's relationship. When both members face the impossibility of maintaining the feeling of being "one with the other" in everyday life, violence inevitability erupts within the couple's functioning. In such a context a psychic space for new subjectivities (children) is not possible. If the phantasy of collusion is not given up, the feeling of not having a separate existence is blamed on the other partner. One of them tries to control the other with omnipotence, imposing his own view of reality as if there could be a unique version of it. The confusion of ego boundaries and the evidence that the other is different at an emotional level are felt as persecutory, with a need to deny the difference. There is no space for the mourning processes that needs to be taking place in response to the loss of Antonio's father, the relinquishment of the boy they had adopted to his country of origin, and the loss of their daughter as a child as she moves towards adolescence.

## Conclusion

In this chapter, the nature of link theory, and the multiple ways in which the link can be addressed from different theoretical perspectives, gives the therapist the possibility to add an enriching focus to her clinical work with couples and families. In some families and couples, the melancholic reactions to loss may be due to the effect of interference. The presence of a partner in the couple or others in a family may contribute to pathological links, that is, links that can stand in the way of the mourning process. Moreover, it speaks to recognition on the part of the therapist of the importance of her presence as a therapeutic agent.

## References

Abraham, K. (1924). Un breve estudio de la evolución de la libido considerada a la luz de los trastornos mentales [A Short Study on the Development of the Libido,

Viewed in the Light of Mental Disorders]. In: *Psicoanálisis Clínico*. Buenos Aires: Hormé.
Berenstein, I. (2001a). *El sujeto y el Otro* [*The Subject and the Other*]. Buenos Aires: Paidós.
Berenstein, I. (2001b). *Clínica familiar psicoanalítica. Estructura y acontecimiento* [*Family Clinical Work. Structure and Event*]. Buenos Aires: Paidós.
Berenstein, I. (2004). *Devenir otro con otro(s): ajenidad, presencia, interferencia*. Buenos Aires: Paidós.
Berenstein, I. (2007). *Del ser al hacer. Curso sobre vincularidad*. Buenos Aires: Paidós.
Berenstein, I., & Puget, J. (1997). *Lo Vincular* [*Working Psychonalytically*]. Buenos Aires: Paidós.
Berenstein, I., & Puget, J. (2004). "Implications and interferences in link clinical work" encounter with Janine Puget and Isidoro Berenstein. AUPCV, Uruguay: APU.
Bion, W. R. (1962). *Learning from Experience*. London: William Heinemann.
Bion, W. R. (1963). *Elements of Psycho-Analysis*. London: Heinemann.
Bion, W. R. (1965). *Transformations: Change from Learning to Growth*. London: Heinemann.
Bion, W. R. (1967). *Second Thoughts*. London: Karnac.
De Saussure, F. (1913). *Course of General Linguistics*. Paris: Ed. Payot.
Descartes, R. (1637). *Discourse on Method and Meditations*, L. J. Lafleur (Trans.). New York: The Liberal Arts Press.
Dicks, H. (1967). *Marital Tensions*. New York: Basic Books.
Freud, S. (1914). On Narcissism: An Introduction. *S.E.*, 14: 67–102.
Freud, S. (1917). Mourning and Melancholia. *S.E.*, 14: 239–258.
Guntrip, H. (1968). *Schizoid Phenomena. Object Relations and the Self*. New York: International University Press.
Heidegger, M. (1927). *Being and Time*. New York: Harper Perennial.
Kaës, R. (1987). Pacto denegativo en los conjuntos trans-subjetivos. *En: Lo Negativo. Figuras y Modalidades [*Denegative pact in trans-subjective groups. In: *The Negative. Figures and Modalities]*. Buenos Aires: Amorrortu Editores.
Kaës, R. (2007). *Linking, Alliances, and Shared Space*. London: The International Psychoanalytic Association.
Keogh, T., & Enfield, S. (2013). From regression to recovery: Tracking developmental anxieties in couple therapy. *Couple and Family Psychoanalysis Review*, 3(1): 28–46.
Khan, M. M. R. (1996). *The Privacy of the Self*. London: Karnac.
Klein, M. (1935). A contribution to the psychogenesis of manic-depressive states. In: *Love, Guilt and Reparation and Other Works 1921–1945. The Writings of Melanie Klein, Volume I*. London: Hogarth Press.
Klein, M. (1940). Mourning and its relation to manic depressive states. In: R. Money-Kyrle, B. Joseph, E. O'Shaughnessy, & H. Segal (Eds.), *The Writings of Melanie Klein*. London: Hogarth Press.
Klein, M. (1946). Notes on some schizoid mechanisms. In: R. Money-Kyrle, B. Joseph, E. O'Shaughnessy, & H. Segal (Eds.), *The Writings of Melanie Klein*. London: Hogarth Press.
Kohut, H. (1971). *The Analysis of the Self: A Systematic Approach to the Psychoanalytic Treatment of Narcissistic Personality Disorders*. New York: International Universities Press.
Lacan, J. (1966). *Écrits*. Paris: Les Editions du Seuil.

Lévi-Strauss, C. (1963). *Antropología Estructural* [*Structural Anthropology*]. Buenos Aires: EUDEBA.
Lévi-Strauss, C. (1969). *Las Estructuras Elementales del Parentesco* [*The Elementary Structures of Kinship*]. Barcelona: Paidós.
Palacios, E., & Monserrat, A. (2017). Contribution to the Link Perspective in Interactions with Families: Theoretical and Technical Aspects and Clinical Applications. In: D. Scharff, & E. Palacios (Eds.), *Couple and Family Psychoanalysis: A Global Perspective*. London: Karnac.
Pichon Rivière, E. (1985). *Teoría del Vínculo*. Buenos Aires: Nueva Visión.
Pincus, L. & Dare, C. (1978). *Secrets in the Family*. London: Faber & Faber.
Ruszczynski, S. (1993). *Psychotherapy with Couples: Theory and Practice at the Tavistock Institute of Marital Studies*. London: Karnac.
Scharff, D., & Scharff, J. (1977). *Object Relations. Family Therapy*. Maryland: Rowman &Littlefield.
Winnicott, D. W. (1965). *Family and the Individual Development*. London: Tavistock Publications.
Winnicott, D. W. (1971). *Playing and Reality*. London: Tavistock Publications.

Chapter 3

# Assessing and formulating issues of unresolved loss in couple functioning

*Cynthia Gregory-Roberts and Timothy Keogh*

## Introduction

In this chapter the essential features of a psychoanalytic approach to assessing couples are reiterated as a basis for explicating our model of assessing manifestations of unresolved grief and its impact on couple functioning. Object relations theory, integrated with an understanding of link theory, is seen to be a uniquely valuable framework by which to assess couples dealing with unresolved loss following a death. This is because it describes an internalised view of the relationship one has with one's objects (that is, others with whom one has had a significant emotional attachment) and how these internal links become transformed and modified through external (especially couple) links.

We see the couple relationship as the externalised *version* of internal self-object relations that are influenced primarily by the imposition represented by the other. It is also influenced by other intergenerational (vertical) links and cultural (horizontal) links. In the consulting room, we observe two sets of self-object relations influenced by both of these horizontal and vertical links as they are played out in the couple relationship.

For couples facing loss as the result of the death of an attachment figure, there is both the loss of an external attachment and its related internal object. It is only the internal object that can be restored. In unresolved grief reactions involving ambivalence towards the lost object, the self becomes impoverished due to the self-reproach it experiences. This is often manifested in a projected form as a part of the externalised difficulties with which the couple (or family) presents (see also Chapter 5). In the couple relationship unwanted projections of the self, prone to the harsh reproaches of a primitive superego, contribute to the disharmony. That is, in the couple dyad, the "other" can have projected into him unwanted and unacknowledged aspects of the partner's self, associated with the other's melancholic reaction to the loss. The couple may also carry (individually or jointly) unmetabolised intergenerational loss (via vertical links) that impinge upon the couple's capacity for mourning.

The uniqueness of the object relations approach integrated with link theory, as applied to assessment, lies not only in its attention to the unconscious aspects of mental life, but the requirement on the clinician to be subjected to these processes as a figure of transference and as an object that creates an "imposition" to these processes. It is ultimately the psychoanalytic psychotherapist's capacity to reflect on her countertransference which sheds light on these processes in a way that assists the couple to emerge from their difficulties.

Moreover, building on the importance of the ability to use oneself as a therapeutic instrument, an important part of a psychoanalytic assessment involves conveying to the couple that, as an analytically-oriented clinician, one is interested in relating to the unconscious aspects of his experience, as well as being a new (challenging) figure in a therapeutic link, helping to shape their internal self-object relations. It is also helpful if the therapist can convey to the couple that their difficulties, while perplexing to them, can be seen to have another meaning in need of discovery. Such understanding can be developed by means of a series of iterative interpretations to help the couple understand how they have come to function in the manner in which they do (Keogh & Gregory-Roberts, 2017a).

To facilitate the unfolding of the unconscious meaning of the couple's difficulties, the psychoanalytic psychotherapist firstly needs to establish an *analytic setting* in which the couple can feel held and safe. Within such a setting, the therapist begins to develop a communication with the couple that conveys an interest in understanding them. This emphasis refers to the need to develop a (positive) transference relationship with the couple as part of developing a *therapeutic alliance*. In turn, these achievements depend on the crucial issue of the *analytic stance/analytic attitude* of the couple therapist. It is therefore important to understand these core concepts, as they apply to couple therapy, before we can specifically look at the issue of assessing melancholic reactions in couples.

## Assessing the couple: the psychodynamic essentials

Whilst it is important to understand the internal world of each of the couple, the ultimate task of the couple psychoanalytic psychotherapist is to see how an individual's dynamics influence the functioning or malfunctioning of the couple as an entity. This implies the importance of approaching the task of assessment while holding a "couple state of mind" (Morgan, 2005). In this regard Morgan notes that in a couple state of mind:

> The therapist is thinking about what kind of relationship the partners are creating and what unconscious phantasies and beliefs they have about being a couple. The therapist tries to hold a neutral position in which, despite pressure from the partners to take sides and sometimes a real sense that she is more sympathetic to one or the other, she is working

> with a relationship as a dynamic whole, an unconscious system in which each partner carries aspects for the other. This aspect can easily shift between them. (p. 125)

We believe this also requires the clinician to adopt what we suggest is a "linked state of mind" which implies that she adopt a therapeutic stance that allows her to consider the nature of the couple link and how it assists or stymies psychological growth. The nature of the link is available for understanding by the therapist as she observes the couple relating.

It is further proposed that a preliminary interpretation is also an essential part of the assessment process, but that in this context it has a special role. If one considers interpretation to be an iterative process, then there is a need to begin to make psychoanalytic sense of the presenting problems of the couple by this means. To this end the therapist may begin with interpretations that are simply about noting or highlighting correlations between events. It may also be valuable to use interpretations as a means of assessing the couple's ability to use the psychoanalytic process. It is only as the therapeutic work with the couple progresses and following the processing of countertransference responses that significant mutative interpretations develop. In individual work the concept of a mutative interpretation is one that links archaic intra-psychic issues and their manifestation in the transference to bring about change. We also refer to a *mutative couple interpretation* (Keogh & Gregory-Roberts, 2017a) as one that takes the *individual* archaic psychic issues of each of the couple and connects them to their presenting problem. In doing so, it makes conscious underpinning couple dynamics as a means of achieving a psychic transformation in couple functioning. Such interpretations can also be facilitated in conjoint couple therapy by means of a "reflective couple interpretation" between the two therapists (Keogh & Gregory-Roberts, 2017b). This technique can be particularly helpful where splitting and projection have become entrenched parts of the couple's defensive bastion and where the couple has experienced a poor model of coupling in their families of origin.

Obstacles to interpreting the shared difficulties of a couple may arise at this point of the assessment, as it is very common for couples to present with each holding a conviction that it is the partner who is at fault and the cause of the relationship difficulty. There is often great pressure on the therapist to be drawn into a split and pressured to act in accordance with this (Morgan, 2005). Scharff and Scharff (1991) have usefully introduced a dyadic version of Fairbairn's (1944) model of endopsychic structure to depict how such splits are projected into the other partner in such situations. In this adapted version of the model it is easily seen how projective and introjective processes (via the couple link) can be used in the service of eliminating differences in the couple through what has been referred to as a "projective gridlock" (Morgan, 1995). In order to counter the pressure to collude with such splitting and projection of unwanted aspects of the couple's internal self-object relations, the therapist needs to be able to contain such projections and indeed to develop what Bion (1963) described as a "container–contained" relationship with the couple. We believe that it is only when this is achieved and "an analytic link" (Kaës, 2016) is established, with its capacity for interference, that transformative interpretations and growth become possible. It is therefore important from the outset to think about the way in which the therapist proceeds in developing this important platform for interpretive and therefore transformative work. Essential to this enterprise is the analytic stance/analytic attitude.

## The analytic stance/analytic attitude

The analytic stance or analytic attitude is basically a state of mind and a way of listening to clinical material whose development is fostered by the tripartite model of psychoanalytic training, which works with the interplay of personal analytic work, didactic learning, and supervised clinical work. It describes a state of mind that is attuned to listening to clinical material from the standpoint of both its manifest (conscious) and latent (unconscious) content. It also refers to the ability to use oneself as a therapeutic instrument, that is, one which is able to register (one's countertransference to) the emotional experience created in them by the individuals and the couple of which they are a constituent part and to use these to understand the couple's internal world and their couple link. In this regard Lemma (2016) notes that:

> The analytic attitude is about a particular way of listening: the therapist empathises with the client's subjective experience while at the same time being curious about its unconscious meaning, rather than trying to solve problems or give advice … [She continues] … Rather than being aloof, the psychoanalytic/psychodynamic therapist should be actively engaged and emotionally attuned to the client's subjective experience: they are a participant in the therapeutic process and will experience strong feelings in response to the client's communications. However, the therapist also needs to be able to stand back from the interaction with the clients so as to reflect and comment on it, thereby helping the clients gain understanding of how they relate to others. Psychoanalytic/psychodynamic work requires the therapist's ability to alternate between the temporary and partial identification of empathy and the return to the position of an observer to the interaction. (p. 7)

## The analytic setting and the frame

The analytic setting refers not only to a physical setting whose consistency and security need to be maintained, but also a virtual setting which results from the analytic stance described above, which also gives rise to behaviours that foster a sense of constancy. This extends to the physical presentation of the therapist who takes care to present herself in a manner which is predictable. The contents of the consulting room are also carefully considered with an awareness of the transference that these may evoke.

These attributes are designed to create a timeless sense of continuity. The frame is the overall boundary created by such factors. In relation to the notion of the frame, Bleger (1967) notes:

> We include within the psycho-analytic frame the role of the analyst, the set of space (atmosphere) and time factors, and part of the technique (including problems concerning the fixing and keeping of times, fees, interruptions, etc.). The frame refers to a strategy rather than to a technique. (p. 511)

The frame also contributes to the overall setting that is provided for the work, which can be compared to the operating theatre of a surgeon. The frame is an extremely complex and important concept in psychoanalysis and in couple assessment and treatment. The frame has been considered to be the repository for the most psychotic aspects of the personality of the patient (couple) (Bleger, 1967). Bleger says,

> The frame is studied as an *institution* within whose limits phenomena occur which are called "behaviours". In this sense, the frame is "dumb" but not non-existent. It makes up the non-ego of the patient, according to which the ego shapes itself. This non-ego is the "ghost world" of the patient that lies in the frame and represents a "meta-behaviour". (Bleger, 1967, p. 518)

Moreover, the frame itself involves certain limitations and boundaries; it thus provides a structure that can be thought of as an equivalent to a mind that is capable of holding psychic contents in a way that creates a sense of safety. These considerations ensure the contextual holding and containment for the psychotherapeutic work (Scharff & Scharff, 1991).

## Working with unconscious processes in the couple

In working with often complex couple presentations, the psychoanalytic psychotherapist is focused on the role of unconscious conflicts in the maintenance of disharmony or frank conflict in the couple. From the moment the referral is received the psychoanalytic psychotherapist is provided with an array of clinical data relevant to the assessment. This can include that which is conveyed (both consciously and unconsciously) by a referrer, the manner of the referral, and any difficulties that ensue when arranging to meet the couple for the first time. These extra-mural data often herald transference and countertransference reactions which will emerge later; they can thus provide vital clues concerning the internal self-object relations of each partner and the couple link.

At the point of referral, the couple therapist has to consider the approach that she will take in assessing the couple or family. Questions may arise about whether the psychoanalytic psychotherapist will see the couple separately or together or, in the case of a family, whether she will require all members to be present.

One of the chief ways that the couple therapist, like any psychoanalyst or psychoanalytic therapist, makes contact with the unconscious processes in the couple is through her countertransference or by processing experiences that have been projectively identified by the couple. These processes, as alluded to above, can begin even before the therapist has met the couple. The ability of the psychoanalytic psychotherapist, as a result of her own analysis or therapy, to receive, contain, and think about these experiences is pivotal in understanding and working with the couple's unconscious processes.

It has been increasingly acknowledged that enactments in response to powerful unconscious forces are very common when beginning therapy with couples and families. It is therefore important to think about actions that may constitute enactments, especially in terms of arrangements to which one agrees and the powerful unconscious forces that might lay behind them. This is why participation in a peer or supervision group is invaluable, as it allows the therapist to understand such potential enactments and where they have occurred to consider how they can be understood and worked with therapeutically.

In conjoint couple work a vital task in working with unconscious processes is for the therapist couple to share and reflect together after the session, analysing strong and often different reactions to the couple and the individuals within it.

## Tracking the affect

A powerful tool in the assessment of a couple is to track the affect generated by the couple as it emerges in the session. A non-analytic assessment may focus on a set format of questioning to gain relevant background information. In an analytic setting the couple therapist's focus is rather on following the direction the couple takes. The marker of this direction, with which the therapist needs to be in tune, is the affect that is manifest in the content the couple provides.

A couple may begin the session talking about the nature of their presenting difficulties and in doing so express strong affect about a particular issue. One partner, for example, might become tearful when noting that her difficulties began after the loss of the other partner's father. Instead of simply acknowledging the affect and/or proceeding with the interview, the psychoanalytic psychotherapist would want to explore this affect more deeply, perhaps commenting that it seems that there is something particularly upsetting about discussing the loss. The therapist may in this context be attempting to begin a process of bringing into consciousness the fact that there is unresolved grief that is continuing to affect the couple relationship. As such, the history is not collected in a systematic, but in an organic way. This highlights how assessment and intervention in a psychoanalytic approach are interwoven and why the assessment phase ideally extends over several interviews.

Following the affect as a technique of couple therapy also relies heavily on the notion of countertransference and the psychoanalytic psychotherapist's use of herself as a sensitive instrument which helps to access, reflect upon, experience, and make conscious the "affective centre" of the couple's presenting difficulties. When such difficulties are identified in the context of a family assessment, the play and/or affective responses of the children offer valuable material that can facilitate the understanding of the object relations and links within the family.

## The value of play in assessing couple/family difficulties

The use of children's play as a means of assessing psychopathology has a long history in psychoanalysis. Assessment of the significance of children's play and moreover its use in play therapy was exemplified by the work of Melanie Klein (1932). David and Jill Scharff (1987) have articulated the utility of play in family therapy. Ideally, this involves a co-therapist who is able to engage in the play of the children, whilst the other therapist engages verbally with parents. This can enable the therapist to point out how the behaviour or play of the children may have a correlation with an emotionally valent issue being expressed by the parents. For example, in a family session described by Scharff (2017) following a break, there was a discussion about the mother's depressed state. She had an accompanying psychosomatic headache. At this time the children in the therapy room started a sequence of play, which involved an angry attack by the play animals on an ambulance. Although much more elaborated in the actual session material, the play of the children was used to suggest that the family may have been angry with the therapist (represented by the ambulance) for leaving the family alone during the break to deal with difficult issues. Following this interpretation, informed by the children's play, the mother's mood changed and she acknowledged her anger and in doing so became aware that her headache subsided (Keogh, 2017). This example of monitoring and using the play of children in a family session highlights that the play can be considered part of the session dialogue and decoded and connected to the verbal dialogue and thus interpreted. Working with the play in this psychoanalytic manner is akin to linking latent (unconscious) and manifest (conscious) content in an attempt to make a transformative interpretation.

## Assessing the nature and role of the couple link

The link is different to an object relation and is differentiated by the fact that it is formed as a psychic space out of the *subjective reality of the other* in their relationship. As Nicolò (2016) states: "The link, which is a new element and is co-constructed, extracts different versions of the self that are re-updated in relationship to the specific link" (p. 210). There is an investment in the link as it represents "the who we are" as a couple. In the situation where the link serves to compensate for problems in the other's (or in the couple's) problems, it will be strongly defended. In terms of assessing the quality and nature of a couple link, the use of one's countertransference is central. This helps to determine the nature of the unconscious alliances that determine the way in which "the formation and processes of intersubjective links come about" (Kaës, 2016, p. 187). These could be "structuring alliances" which form the internal space, defensive alliances, which can represent a "negative pact" constituting an unconscious agreement about what is to be denied, repressed or negated within the couple, or pathological (e.g., perverse) alliances. Kaës also refers to offensive alliances that he sees as common in groups whose aim is to "cement the agreement of a group to conduct an attack, realise a project or establish supremacy over other groups" (p. 188). As Kaës points out, it is useful when assessing links to

> ... disentangle and see the relationship between the intra-psychic dimension of alliances for each person (subject of the link), the inter-psychic dimension in the psychic space of the link between the subjects of this link and *in the case of groups* their trans-psychic dimension in complex ensembles. (p. 189, italics added)

In terms of pathological links, one common link in couples who experience a difficulty in the capacity to mourn is a narcissistic link. In assessing the nature and quality of a couple link it is important to assess a number of key aspects of the couple link (Kaës, 2016). These include the consistent and specific psychic reality that the link represents, the way in which the subjects inhabit their link and the manner in which the intersection of the internal links of each of the subjects in the link results in inclusions and exclusions of psychic reality.

Such considerations are useful when assessing the link between the actual subjects in the link and the psychic reality specific to that link.

## Assessing melancholic reactions to loss in the couple

In any psychoanalytic therapy that achieves a degree of success, we assume that the analysand or patient has been able to achieve an integration of previously split-off and unrecognised aspects of himself. This usually encompasses a difficult (depressive) phase of treatment where the patient is able to face the destructiveness of his impulses towards the object. If all goes well, this leads to a phase of mourning the loss of the object, which is felt to have been destroyed, then triggering a reparative drive and the ultimate restoration of the "lost good object". The dividend of such a development is that the analysand is able to achieve a sense of his own identity as separate from the other (from the object).

Where this has not occurred, still split-off feelings towards the object can create a sense of persecution (or persecutory anxieties) as the unacceptable aspects of one's feelings towards the object are projected into the external environment, into others, and to objects in that environment. This leads to a sense of being assailed by persecutors in the external environment. These are the psychic conditions that give rise to the melancholic reaction that Freud described. This is because the individual with such a psychic constellation who experiences loss, does so in a split way through the lens of an undifferentiated self. Consequently, and as discussed previously, with a melancholic experience of loss there is an experience of a loss of the self, as one is not able to feel psychically separate from the object. In assessing a couple for indications of melancholic loss, we thus need to assess a number of specific issues. These include:

- The level of psychic development in each of the couple and their ego strengths;
- The overall developmental level of psychic functioning in the couple;
- The nature of the anxieties predominantly experienced by the couple;
- The extent to which their couple relating represents mature, individuated, reciprocal relating versus narcissistic and fused relating;
- The actual history of loss of each partner in the couple and as a couple (e.g., early parental loss, miscarriage history);
- The attachment history/style of each of the couple;
- The nature of the relationship between the individual and the couple and the lost object of attachment;
- The circumstances of the death (e.g., the death was sudden, traumatic, shame provoking);
- The degree of responsibility felt by individuals regarding the death; and
- The nature of the link, especially the presence of a narcissistic link.

Together, these factors will provide an overall indication of the extent to which the presenting problems of a couple are connected with unresolved loss and to what extent the couple or one member of the couple could be seen to be experiencing manifestations of a more complex grief reaction which is impacting on couple functioning. Such issues are best illustrated by a clinical example.

The case of Emma and Gus highlights the elements of their presentation, internal objects, and links that emerged in the assessment and informed the understanding of their grief response following the death of their daughter.

## Emma and Gus

Emma and Gus were referred to a couple therapist psychoanalytic psychotherapist by a social worker with whom they had met when their seven-year-old daughter, Bianca, was diagnosed with leukaemia. Despite treatment, Bianca died a few months later. The social worker, who had been a great support to the couple, contacted Emma about a year after the death to follow up and find out how the couple were managing. Experienced in the field of bereavement, the social worker was alert to the possibility of the couple experiencing manifestations of a complicated grief reaction. During the discussion Emma disclosed that she and Gus were not getting on well and she was anxious, as she feared that they might separate. She described how she had become very critical of her husband, even though she felt each had really supported the other during Bianca's illness and they felt very close as a couple. The social worker commented that things between Emma and her husband now seemed very strained and she wondered aloud if perhaps they were really struggling with their loss of their daughter. Emma said she didn't know, but did feel that they were in a very bad place. The social worker suggested that it might help if they spoke with a couple therapist in order to try and understand what was happening between them.

The possible connection between the development of couple difficulties and failed mourning is a connection that often eludes couples experiencing this type of difficulty. In an assessment interview it is necessary to proceed cautiously with iterative interpretations which might connect the two.

Emma discussed the idea of the referral with her husband. He was also very concerned about their marriage and immediately agreed. When they attended for the assessment interview with the couple therapist the extent of their problems became clearer. Emma, according to Gus, had become increasingly dissatisfied with her life and repeatedly stated to him that she thought her life and work were meaningless, particularly as she doubted her competency as a nurse. He also felt that she had become increasingly resentful towards him. He was upset by her anger, but could not understand what he had done to deserve such ongoing and escalating hostility, as he tried very hard to support her and help around the house. He described that she was critical of many little things he did in a way that seemed exaggerated. For example, he said she "went ballistic" when a plant they had been given died, accusing him of not taking sufficient care of it. For his part Gus felt very upset and angry about the changes in Emma, but felt that any confrontation would make her even more upset. He felt as if he was walking on eggshells. He had noted that he wanted to drink alcohol in the evenings more frequently than previously and sometimes felt incapacitated at work the next day as a result of his intoxication. In the assessment session, Gus became tearful when alluding to the fact that they had tried to conceive another child, but had not been successful. Gus felt this pressure to get pregnant and the conflict in their relationship led to their sexual relations also feeling mechanical and he had noticed that he had reduced his instigation of intimacy with Emma. She too had noted this and thought that he was not attracted to her anymore. Emma acknowledged that she felt angry, resentful, and dissatisfied with her life and uncertain about continuing their relationship and planning for a further pregnancy.

As their family histories unfolded, the therapist discovered that Emma had lost her own mother when she was 14 years old, when the family was living in the north of England. Her father, who immersed himself in work, never spoke about the death of her mother, who had died from undetected ovarian cancer. As he was often home late, Emma moved in as a weekday boarder at the school she was attending. Her father remarried when Emma was 16 and she maintained a very distant relationship with her stepmother. As a young adult Emma travelled to Australia where she met Gus. He had grown up in a remote country town, but he and his mother left for the city after his mother's decision to leave his alcoholic father when Gus was seven years old. His mother subsequently discouraged talk about Gus's father, who sought little contact with his son. Other relatives told him how his father began drinking after an accident in which a farm vehicle that he was driving rolled over, killing his father's brother, who was also in the vehicle.

It was revealed in the assessment that when Emma and Gus first lived together they had a very loving relationship. Emma was enormously supportive of Gus, as he struggled with feelings of low self-esteem. She also felt very understood and appreciated by him. Both engaged in further training and secured satisfying jobs, working hard but happily. They had all kinds of plans for a stable family life and began to build this together. It was only rarely when they were stressed that these positive perceptions of each other and their relationship would change.

As a couple therapist presented with this couple following the death of a significant attachment object (in this case their daughter), a preliminary summary is useful in working towards an overall psychodynamic formulation.

Firstly, in terms of the assessment of the mode of psychic functioning in each of the couple, the blaming evident in the relationship suggests a level of splitting and projection in the couple. This is most prominent in Emma, but Gus also shows evidence of being under the sway of a persecutory superego in the way he felt so badly about himself. Thus the couple can be seen to exhibit persecutory anxieties, which locate the couple in the paranoid–schizoid mode of functioning at this time. It would appear that under the current stressors they had regressed to this level, although they have previously been capable of a higher level of integrated functioning.

The assessment also suggests evidence (in the form of splitting and projection) of primitive anxieties. Given the nature of these anxieties and defences, it is notable that at the time of presentation there appeared to be little capacity for a mature level of individuated reciprocal functioning, but rather a narcissistic mode whereby the other becomes a self-object (that is, where the other is used to carry unwanted aspects of the self).

In such a situation, the psychoanalytic psychotherapist is interested in possible unresolved losses in the history of each of the couple. There is evidence of this in both Emma and Gus. Each had lost a parental relationship (either by death or separation) and each of these parents had also suffered a significant loss in addition to the loss of the couple relationship. This is significant in understanding their current functioning because unresolved loss in one partner makes for difficulties in responding to the experience of loss in the other. The other instead becomes a mirror reflecting difficult-to-face feelings that exist in one's self. The couple dyad in such a situation then becomes overloaded with toxic affect that cannot be easily digested and can provoke a process of decay in the relationship. In considering Gus and Emma's relationship from a psychoanalytic perspective, the loss of their daughter presented a psychic rupture which opened up traumas connected to the primal mother–baby relationship. The couple link formed by them precluded them managing this significant life event, as it had been co-constructed in order to exclude certain psychic realities which prohibit mourning.

## The psychodynamic formulation of the couple

Lemma (2016), in one of the most contemporary considerations of the psychodynamic formulation, has suggested it has a number of significant components. These include:

- Describing the problem;
- Describing the psychic cost of the problem;
- Contextualising the problem (including identifying the relevant predisposing factors);
- Describing the most dominant and recurring object relationships; and
- Identifying defences and the aims of treatment.

Such a formulation determines the unique focus of the intervention for the couple within a psychodynamic approach. In terms of describing the problem with which the couple presented, Emma saw Gus as disinterested in her and withdrawing from her emotionally and sexually, while recognising that she felt angry and critical towards him. For his part, he felt unreasonably criticised by her and disturbed that she was unhappy in her relationship with him. The emergence of critical feelings that were previously absent in the relationship offers the therapist the first clue that the loss of their daughter had resulted in a melancholic reaction. This criticism of the other represented a projected blaming, a critical attack on the self about the loss of their child. The core pain being avoided was the reality of the loss. Through the vertical link, earlier losses from the family of origin were transmitted inter-generationally and came to life following the death of their child.

The psychic cost of the problem for the couple was a breakdown of their previously happy coupledom (couple link) with an attendant risk of permanent breakdown and divorce. This entailed a distorted perception of each other as a result of a serious level of splitting and projection of unwanted emotional experience arising from the loss in each of them, especially in Emma.

In contextualising their problem, we know from her history that Emma appeared to have already carried into her marriage an unresolved loss, being that of her mother with whom she had had an ambivalent relationship. This made her particularly vulnerable to a melancholic reaction to a subsequent loss. Gus also had experienced the emotional loss of his father as a young boy, which had impacted on his sense of worthiness to be loved. This loss was reactivated by his loss of his daughter, while Emma's persistent blaming of Gus possibly resonated with unconscious childhood feelings of responsibility for his father's departure from the family. In such situations of melancholic reactions to loss the sense of blame is prevalent (Keogh & Gregory-Roberts, 2017b).

It is relevant to the couple's attraction to each other that they both had issues concerning childhood loss and trauma. The loss of their daughter appears to have over burdened their combined emotional resources, despite their wish to support and care for each other. The couple had revealed in the assessment interviews that each had experienced feelings of anxiety about loss of the other, even before the birth of their daughter.

In terms of the dominant and recurring object relations in the couple relationship, it would appear that for Gus the most dominating object relationship was one whereby Emma represented the critical mother by whom he felt blamed for the loss of his father (and in the current situation, the loss of their daughter). For Emma, Gus predominantly represented the mother she seemed to have damaged and therefore lost, whom she experienced as not wanting to be with her.

An assessment of the couple's predominant defences indicates that splitting and projection are the prominent mechanisms by which the pain of mourning is avoided. They both also engaged in a level of denial, further fostered by their extended families (family links) who could also not bear engaging with the pain of loss. The extent of these defences suggested the seriousness of their presentation, as they typify a borderline, rather than neurotic one.

In terms of the link co-created by Emma and Gus, one can perceive an essentially narcissistic type of link within the couple, which prevents the acknowledgement of differences between them. Such a narcissistic link effectively blocks the possibility of mourning and instead their internal object relations become mutually confirmed.

With all of these issues in mind, one of the main aims of the therapy could be to attempt to reframe the presenting problem by suggesting a different way of looking at their difficulties. This includes looking at unconscious aspects of their difficulties and current ways of relating to each other. The correlation of the symptomatology and the loss could be a helpful initial iterative interpretation with this couple.

The aim of the treatment may be to help them identify their feelings about the actual loss and mobilise resources in the couple to help facilitate this. The fuller description of this process will be discussed in Chapter 4.

As part of the assessment and psychodynamic formulation, the suitability of the couple for analytic work is also assessed. This involves assessing the couple's ability to make use of interpretive statements about their difficulties, and their willingness and capacity to allow the therapist to enter in, and get behind, their defensive bastion, which shields them from the psychic pain that is thought to be intolerable and not survivable. Some couples may not concur with the therapist's formulation and may not wish to engage in treatment. However, Emma and Gus developed a therapeutic alliance and showed a capacity for reflection and insight.

Once such a comprehensive assessment of the couple presenting with symptoms of unresolved loss is completed, the therapist may discuss the options available to the couple, including short-term treatment options. Then the essential step of consolidating the therapeutic alliance and beginning the valuable interpretive work can begin.

## References

Bion, W. R. (1963). *Elements of Psycho-Analysis.* London: Heinemann.

Bleger, J. (1967). Psycho-analysis of the psycho-analytic frame. *International Journal of Psycho-Analysis*, 48: 511–519.

Fairbairn, W. R. D. (1944). Endopsychic structure considered in terms of object-relationships. *International Journal of Psycho-Analysis*, 25: 70–92.

Kaës, R. (2016). Link and the transference within three interfering psychic spaces. *Couple and Family Psychoanalysis*, 6(2): 81–193.

Keogh, T. (2017). Bion's grid and the selected fact: A commentary on David Scharff's mid-phase session of family psychoanalysis. In: D. E. Scharff & E. Palacios (Eds.), *Couple and Family Psychoanalysis: A Global Perspective* (pp. 185–192). London: Karnac.

Keogh, T., & Gregory-Roberts, C. (2017a). The role of interpretation in the assessment phase of couple psychoanalysis. *Couple and Family Psychoanalysis*, 7(2): 168–180.

Keogh, T., & Gregory-Roberts, C. (2017b). A valediction forbidding mourning: Working with traumatic repetition in an older couple. In: D. E. Scharff & M. Vorchheimer (Eds.), *Clinical Dialogues on Psychoanalysis with Families and Couples* (pp. 73–83). London: Karnac.

Klein, M. (1932). The psychoanalysis of children. In: *The Writings of Melanie Klein, Vol. 2*. London: Hogarth, 1975.

Lemma, A. (2016). *Introduction to the Practice of Psychoanalytic Psychotherapy.* Hoboken, NJ: Wiley-Blackwell.

Morgan, M. (1995). *The Projective Gridlock: A Form of Projective Identification in Couple Relationships.* London: Karnac.

Morgan, M. (2005). First contacts: the therapists 'couple state of mind'as a factor in the containment of couples seen for consultations. In: F. Grier (Ed.), *Oedipus and the Couple* (pp. 17–32). London: Karnac.

Nicolò, A. M. (2016). Thinking in terms of links. *Couple and Family Psychoanalysis*, 6 (2): 206–214.

Scharff, D. (2017). Treating the family ramifications of sexual difficulty. In: D. E. Scharff & E. Palacios (Eds.), *Couple and Family Psychoanalysis: A Global Perspective* (pp. 169–182). London: Karnac.

Scharff, D. E., & J. S. Scharff (1987). *Object Relations Family Therapy*. Northvale, NJ: Aronson.

Scharff, D. E., & Scharff, J. S. (1991). *Object Relations Couple Therapy*. London: Jason Aronson.

Chapter 4

# A proposed theoretical framework and model for intervention

*Timothy Keogh and Cynthia Gregory-Roberts*

## Origins of psychoanalytic interventions with couples

Psychoanalysis, as initially articulated by Freud, acknowledged the importance of our unconscious view of others and of *our relationships* with them. This concept underpinned his notion of the transference, a central tenet of his theory. Freud's (1920) observation of his grandson's play with a cotton reel was a touching account of his deepening appreciation of the importance of our relationships with others in shaping our internal world, which became developed in his later meta-psychological writings.

These writings sowed the seeds for psychoanalysis as a theory, which proposed that our unconscious is structured by our relationship with our primary (attachment) objects, as self-object relations, and that our links with others are fundamental in shaping these internal representations. It thus also pointed to the importance of the links formed within family groups in shaping psychic life.

Despite these general theoretical developments, there was little attention paid by psychoanalysts for some time to the notion of applying their theory to address marital problems, which were considered formative in the future psychopathology of children. Flügel (1921) was an exception, devoting an entire book to the subject: *The Psycho-analytic Study of the Family*. In this work he presciently noted,

> An individual's outlook and point of view in dealing with many of the most important questions of human existence can be expressed in terms of the position he has taken up with the problems and difficulties within the relatively narrow worlds of the family. (p. 4)

Following Freud, it was later posited (e.g., Klein, 1945) that we not only internalise self-object relationships, but we internalise templates of couple relationships built up via psychic phantasies that are based on the actual couple (parental) relationships that we have experienced. These templates were seen to subsequently impact on the way we unconsciously view our future intimate relationships. These theoretical developments articulated by Klein (1945) and contemporaneously (and remarkably, in isolation) by Fairbairn (1944, 1952) occurred during the 1940s and 1950s.

Coincidently, after the Second World War in England and elsewhere, there was an increasing concern about divorce rates and marital difficulties that saw the development of organisations such as the Tavistock Marital Bureau in England, The Family Guidance Centre in New Zealand, and the Drummond Street Centre in Melbourne, Australia. These influences came together when those concerned about marital issues sought guidance from psychoanalytic theory. In England this led to the development of the Marriage Discussion Bureau at the Tavistock Institute for Human Relations in 1948. Similar developments took place in Australia and New Zealand about the same time (Keogh, 2017).

These developments stimulated theoretical developments in object relations theory applied to couples and families. Many of these emanated from Tavistock-based psychoanalysts and psychotherapists, notably Henry Dicks (1967) with his concept of the joint marital personality, John Byng-Hall (1985) who emphasised the importance of family scripts and intergenerational influences of these scripts, and Sally Box (1998) who highlighted group processes in the family as a form of defensive collusion. More contemporary contributions to an object relations-oriented approach have come from Ruszczynski (1993), Clulow (2001), and Morgan (1995), along with the contributions from David and Jill Scharff, who have written foundational textbooks on the practice of both object relations-oriented couple and family therapy (Scharff & Scharff, 1987, 1991).

Scharff and Scharff (1991) made a most useful adaptation of Fairbairn's model of endopsychic structure to the couple dyad. Using this model they showed how unwanted (split-off) aspects of the self are projected into a partner, whilst maintaining a level of conscious harmonious relating. Conflict was thus seen to erupt when events expose these projections and arguing and blaming ensue.

In terms of the other major developments in regard to couple and family psychoanalysis, Palacios (2017) notes that developments in thinking about couple and family psychoanalysis in Latin America were given their impetus by the theoretical developments of "link theory" as espoused by Pichon Rivière and Jose Bleger in Argentina in the 1960s. Berenstein (2004), Puget (2015), Kaës (2016), and more recently Losso, de Setton and Scharff (2017) who developed these ideas further.

The fuller history of the development of couple and family psychoanalytic therapy in different parts of the world has been fully outlined elsewhere (Scharff & Vorchheimer, 2017).

## An intervention framework

The approach to intervention advocated in this book has evolved out of these two main theoretical approaches to working psychoanalytically with couples and families, that is, object relations and link theory. Link theory (see Chapter 2) is based on the notion that links in couples and families shape internal object relations. The other component of the framework integrates object relations theory, as articulated by Klein (1945) and Fairbairn (1944, 1952). In particular it applies Klein's widely-known concept of psychic development from a primitive, largely un-integrated state (the paranoid–schizoid position of psychic development) to a more integrated (depressive) position which facilitates the capacity to experience oneself as separate from others, that is, free from significant projections of oneself into them.

We thus integrate link theory to enrich a previously articulated framework (Keogh & Enfield, 2013) and in doing so support the thesis that the expression of internal object relations and their modification in a couple relationship cannot be adequately appreciated without understanding the transformative potential of the couple or family link(s) (see Chapter 2).

In terms of the object relations theory component of our approach, in line with Scharff & Scharff (1987, 1991) who, following Dicks (1967) and Zinner (1976), applied Fairbairn's thinking to couples and families, our framework incorporates the idea of *how* the ego splits, as detailed in Fairbairn's model of Endopsychic structure (Fairbairn, 1944; and expanded by Scharff & Scharff, 1991) to account for these phenomena in couples. Fairbairn (1944) explained (using a theory which emphasises that individuals are motivated by their need for relationship) how the ego is split into a relationship seeking and an anti-relationship seeking ego, which relate respectively to what he refers to as *an exciting and rejecting object*. The incorporation of this schema into our framework facilitates an understanding of how, for example, partners in a couple can come to see one another, via projection, as a rejecting object to whom they feel tied, or as a tantalising/exciting object by whom they feel they can never hope to be loved (Ogden, 2010).

The overall framework we propose also accounts for more primitive anxieties in couples by incorporating the ideas of Ogden (1989) concerning autistic–contiguous anxieties as a mode of psychic experience, which occurs earlier than the paranoid–schizoid position and which involves (pre-symbolic) states of un-integration of the ego, as distinct from states of disintegration. Ogden acknowledges that his ideas were very much influenced by the writings of Tustin (1980), especially her ideas concerning the concept of psychogenic autism, as well as those of Bick (1968), Anzieu (1993), and others who highlighted the role of the skin in psychic development. Ogden described a primitive mode of psychic functioning, which he terms "autistic–contiguous". He points out that this is a mode of functioning involving primitive anxieties associated with a poorly formed psychosomatic self, which is vulnerable to states of un-integration. Moreover, he notes that this poorly formed sense of self (ego) has a tendency to merge in the relationship with the other and is associated with a lack of differentiation, and therefore boundary, with the object. He describes it as a predominantly sensory mode of psychic experience where bodily sensation (particularly at the level of the skin) creates the sense of self. Consequently, in this mode of experience, there is little sense of a "psychic skin" which provides an experience of what is inside and outside of oneself (Ogden, 1989). Anxieties related to this mode of experience may include fears of dissolving, falling into nothingness, and spilling out of oneself.

Ogden links Freud's (1923) notion that "The ego [the 'I'] is first and foremost a bodily ego" to this mode of experience. He explains how the transference relationship with a patient exhibiting such a primitive mode of functioning is characterised by the analyst being used as an autistic object (Tustin, 1980) (i.e., an object which helps the patient feel a *sense* of boundary between himself and the other). Winnicott's (1960) concept of the "psychosomatic partnership" can also be compared to this mode of experience in that it describes a relationship in which experience can be completely somatic at the same time as being completely psychological.

The proposed short-term model for intervening with couples exhibiting a melancholic reaction to loss also includes a contemporary object relations view of Oedipal anxieties, enriched with Pichon Rivière's ideas (Losso et al., 2017). In particular, we endorse Britton's idea (elaborating Freud's original concept [Freud, 1924d]) that with the resolution of Oedipal anxieties, there is an increased ability to tolerate what he calls the "third" (Britton, 1989). This notion brings with it an awareness that one's object of attachment has other relationships and creates a sense of the other or third, bringing with it demands to experience and tolerate, being both included and excluded (from coupling) (Grier, 2005). Britton (2004) suggests that the resolution of such anxieties fosters a capacity to become aware of another's point of view (essential to couple functioning) and the ability to see oneself from this vertex. This in turn fosters what has been referred to as "self-reflective functioning" (Fonagy & Target, 1997; Fonagy, 2001). When applied to couple work, this psychological development makes possible a true "psychological marriage" with another (Fisher, 1999).

We believe that Pichon Rivière's ideas concerning Oedipal issues add enormously to our understanding of couples and in particular those who have had a melancholic reaction to loss. As Losso et al. (2017) point out:

> Pichon Rivière ... re-conceptualised the dimensions of triangular links. He enlarged the conceptualisation of the Oedipus to include all triangular relations, beginning with the way a third person in the mother's mind modifies the link between mother and child, and continuing to the general principle that the presence of a third person always modifies two-person links. In this way the individual is, from the beginning, formed in a triadic structure so that the early relationship is *bicorporal and tripersonal.* Thus, while the early relationship is apparently dyadic, the third

> functions permanently and from the beginning in the mind of the mother. In a similar way, the analytic field is bicorporal, that is to say, it is between the analysand and analyst, but a third (and more) always functions in the mind of both participants and in this way these thirds expand the dimensions of the analytic relationship. (p. 131, italics added)

As Ogden (1989) has noted, psychic development (as shaped by the links that the subject forms) can be thought about in terms of modes of experience described as autistic–contiguous, paranoid–schizoid, and depressive. In each phase of psychic development the nature of the anxiety is related to "the experience of disconnectedness (disintegration) within that mode of experience" (p. 132). In particular, Ogden suggests that in the autistic–contiguous position this disconnectedness arises from what he sees as the disruption of sensory cohesion and boundedness. In the paranoid–schizoid position, he suggests that it involves persecutory anxieties (states of disintegration) associated with the splitting of the self and the object, manifest in couples who engage in endless cycles of blaming of the partner, into whom one projects the disowned aspects of himself. Moreover, in the depressive position, Ogden (1989) notes that anxieties concern a fear of having caused damage as a result of recognising destructive feelings towards the object (and a consequent need to make reparation) that disrupt whole object relations. Oedipal anxieties are especially significant in terms of a propensity towards a melancholic reaction to loss, in contrast to a capacity to mourn. Such anxieties, when not resolved, involve feelings of exclusion arising from a sense of disconnectedness linked to the awareness of one's separateness and "otherness".

Seen from this vertex, object relations evolve in *three* stages of psychic development: firstly, where the self and other are experienced in a sensory mode and the self tends to be experienced as merged with its object; secondly, a stage where difficult-to-manage aspects of the self are split off and projected into the object of attachment; and finally, a stage wherein the split-off parts of the self are integrated and the other can be seen as having an existence separate to oneself. Psychic development towards increasing separateness from the object are either facilitated or stymied by the nature of the links a person has formed. In this regard, it is important to remember that in melancholia the lost attachment object cannot be mourned because it is not experienced as separate from oneself, so it is as if a part of oneself dies with the object.

Related to this, when working with couples facing a loss, one is mindful that Pichon Rivière (Losso et al., 2017) noted that links arise out of the subject-to-subject relationship and provide the structure through which the respective sets of object relations are expressed. A pathological link (such as a narcissistic link) is thus one which prevents growth and, in the case of melancholia, maintains a pact or unconscious agreement that prevents mourning. Kaës (2016) has noted that in defensive alliances the couple can establish an unconscious pact to facilitate agreement on what aspects of their psychic disturbance are to be dealt with by being variously repressed, denied, or negated.

In a family "the symptom bearer", as referred to by Pichon Rivière (Losso et al., 2017), represents the healthiest member of the family, which is bound together by regressive links.

In families in particular, Nicolò (2016) notes,

> To think in terms of links opens up an innovative perspective regarding the comprehension of a pathology and above all normality. We can certainly say that there are challenges such as psychosis that are very difficult to understand fully if one does not consider the idea that behind these disturbances there is a specific "traumatic organisation of links" and that psychosis is not an illness of an individual person, but a problem of the whole *family* … . (p. 212, italic added)

In integrating link theory with object relations theory (which we acknowledge not all contributors to this book do explicitly), we are incorporating Pichon Rivière's notions, whose thinking was influenced by both Klein and Fairbairn. In particular we highlight that the links which the self has to its objects (internal links), are shaped by the nature of the external links formed with others, whether through the couple link or the analytic link. This means that the actual presence of the other's subjectivity causes interference in the attempts to have one's internal links confirmed within one's external links. Puget (2015) suggests that our initial links derive out of a need to resolve a sense of helplessness and are in the form of a "primitive narcissistic link mode".

In terms of internal self-object relations, Bion (1963) has previously proposed a dynamic, oscillating relationship between the paranoid–schizoid and depressive positions, which he denotes as Ps⇔D. The developmental model we have previously proposed for couples (Keogh & Enfield, 2013) expands these oscillations in Figure 4.1:

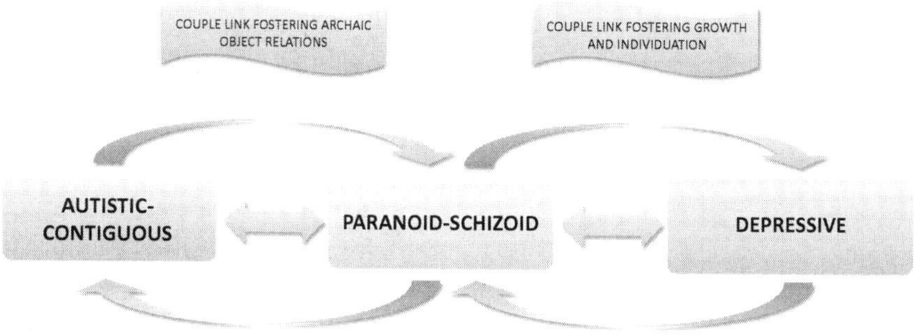


*Figure 4.1* Dynamic developmental anxieties/link theory model of couple functioning

This schema allows for an oscillation between states of merger and more individuated states of psychic functioning and the nature of associated links (especially the "primitive narcissistic link mode") and, as we have also previously noted, can also be linked to Fisher's (1999) proposed continuum of couple relating, which ranges from narcissistic coupling to a true psychological marriage.

In terms of the working-through phase of therapy, our model places emphasis on the inherent dynamism and the progressions and regressions that can occur, as well as the influence of links in shaping these, as the working-through proceeds (see Figure 4.1). There can be a series of such progressions and regressions within the overall psychic developmental pathway such that, under conditions of stress such as loss, there can be a regression to a more primitive level of functioning.

Finally, if we acknowledge that the facilitation or stymieing of psychic development is shaped by external links, we need to think about how the psychoanalytic psychotherapist can work with these links in order to create a transformation in couple functioning.

> Pichon Rivière expanded Klein's notion of internal worlds where good and bad links form the "internal group" as a psychic structure out of which the individual is constituted. He saw internal links as being in constant interaction with the external world through external links, and that such external links – that is, actual interactions with others – are both modified by internal links and in turn modify *them*. Thus, there is continual interplay between the inner world of the inner group, the familiar external world, and the wider social world. Current experience is of constant importance as interaction with the external world is in interplay with the internal world, each modifying the other over time. (Losso et al., 2017, p. 130, italic added)

We thus need to come to understand how our presence as a subject acts as an *interference* in the analytic link with the couple and how this can therefore become transformative.

Now let us examine how these theoretical concepts translate clinically as we schematically articulate our proposed short-term intervention model.

## Proposed stages of a short-term intervention with the melancholic couple

What follows is a schematic account of a short-term intervention model which incorporates these general features of our overall theoretical framework and which can be used for couples who are exhibiting features of unresolved grief.

The aim of the intervention is to help those couples who are unable to mourn the loss of a child/young adult. From a psychodynamic perspective grief and problems with mourning are indicative of underlying difficulties, which relate to a developmental failure with psychological separation and individuation.

This difficulty means that the psychic representation of self is merged with the other, leading to confusion and omnipotent attribution which can result in a phantastic view of one's capacity for destructiveness, which underpins excessive guilt.

When we meet with a couple presenting with unresolved grief we need to determine the interplay between their **presenting problems**, their loss experience, and their underpinning developmental difficulties reflected in their current **intra-psychic structure**, and the nature of their **couple link**. This interplay we refer to as the **Unresolved Grief Triad (UGT)** (see Figure 4.2). This Triad then becomes the focus of the working-through phase of treatment.

Unless the couple reveals a severely pathological level of functioning, a short-term intervention is usually indicated. An option for a particularly challenging couple, especially one who presents as a previous treatment failure, may be conjoint couple therapy. It is not possible to make these decisions, however, until one has completed an assessment, but if the short-term intervention is decided upon, then the two assessment sessions are included in the assessment/engagement phase of the short-term intervention, which usually involves 16 weekly sessions.

### *Phase one: engagement and formulation*

The first two sessions with the couple involve assessing the reasons the couple has sought help, how they construe their difficulties, and their suitability for

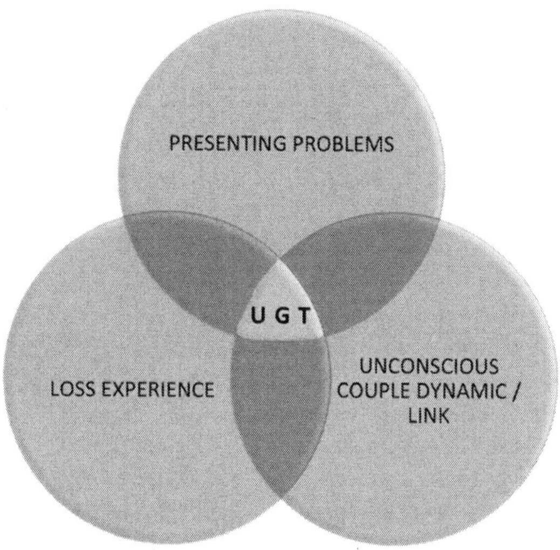


*Figure 4.2* The Unresolved Grief Triad (UGT)

psychoanalytic therapy (see also Chapter 3). This results in a psychodynamic formulation. It may be that the couple presentation is one of crisis, where the couple presents at the point of separation. In this case especially, there may be a need to use more exploratory interpretations as part of the assessment process. This is useful as a means of determining the couple's openness to seeing the presenting problem from a couple state of mind and the couple's willingness to allow the therapist to bring this third position. This is a necessary starting point to establish a contract for ongoing work (Keogh & Gregory-Roberts, 2017).

Once the couple has agreed to embark on a course of therapy and the frame that it entails, the all-important initial task is that of consolidating the *therapeutic alliance* and the associated task of building the container (in the Bionian sense) for the work. Depending on the level of the disturbance in the couple, this may be a slow process as a sense of trust and safety in the therapist(s) and process are developed. Consequently, in this phase, an emphasis is placed on empathic attunement and in building in the couple a sense of being understood. Maintaining a "couple state of mind" (Morgan, 2005) can be a demanding task, especially where one of the couple may pressure the therapist(s) to align with a negative point of view held about the partner. In these circumstances, it may be helpful to point out to the couple your need as a therapist to listen to the experience of each of the couple, rather than to be in the position of judging its correctness. In this way the therapist facilitates the development of a container–contained relationship, along with an opportunity for the therapist to convey an interest in understanding the *meaning* of what has happened, rather than judging it.

These nuances of therapist–couple interaction (the co-construction of a therapeutic link), which involve the handling of transference and the management of the therapeutic frame, can be particularly crucial in supporting couples with primitive mental states. It is also important to be aware that holding the couple in this way has a different function to that of containment, the latter of which entails a mind being present that is capable of processing their lived experience. Containment is implicit in psychic growth and involves paying attention simultaneously to the conscious and unconscious aspects of experience. Whilst the two therapeutic processes have relevance at all stages of therapy, we suggest that they are particularly important when addressing primitive anxieties. Failure to address such anxieties makes robust interpretative work less possible.

Within the initial stages of the therapy, it is also possible to *achieve some elaboration of the maternal, paternal, and couple introjects* which the couple bring to their relationship and the therapeutic relationship. This can often take the form of picking up on something that is said in the session, for example, to wonder about how issues similar to their presenting difficulties might have been managed in their families of origin. At the same time, the therapist is in a position to begin to understand something about the nature of the "vertical" and "horizontal" links that are influencing the couple relationship, as well as the nature of their couple link and its impact in terms of facilitating or stymieing growth. When working with couples who exhibit features of a melancholic reaction to grief, it is particularly important to also determine whether there is evidence of a narcissistic couple link that works against separateness in the couple (see Chapter 5).

### *Phase two: working through*

Within our short-term intervention we would assume that the couple had attended for five sessions by the time the work of the middle stage of therapy is approached. The middle stage of therapy is where the understandings that have been developed into a psychodynamic formulation of the couple's difficulties, are translated into a Unresolved Grief Triad (UGT) which focuses on the interplay of the couple's presenting difficulties, their loss experience and their unconscious couple dynamic or link. This is then worked with through the material presented from the week-to-week life of the couple. Pichon Rivière (Losso et al., 2017) describes this as "the here and now with the therapist" who become, by their actual presence, an interference to the projection of their internal objects relations which maintains an unhelpful dynamic between them.

In terms of working with loss, we are particularly interested in identifying and modifying the psychic processes that are preventing mourning from taking place. This inevitably means focusing on the splitting and projective process as it manifests in "real time" with the couple and in the transference with the psychoanalytic psychotherapist. It is also a means of being able to identify and talk about the nature of the link that has been co-constructed by the couple and its role in the growth or stymieing of psychic development.

The middle phase of the treatment involving seven sessions is therefore devoted to working through such issues. (Chapters 6 and 7 present good examples of this type of therapeutic work.)

We argue that it is helpful to refer to the grid (Table 4.1), which identities the level of developmental anxieties, the nature of the link and the necessary therapeutic focus, as a type of therapeutic compass to help locate the therapist in terms of the session material at any point of time. This can also be helpfully considered in supervision or in a peer group review, subsequent to the session. The current iteration of the grid now incorporates reference to the couple link.

### *Phase three: the termination phase*

Working towards an ending of the therapy, as an experience of loss, can itself foster the integration that is part of the overall aim of the couple work. At this point it is assumed that there has been significant work on identifying and working with the UGT and the nature of an unhealthy couple link, along

*Table 4.1* A grid depicting developmental anxiety, link and therapeutic focus

| *Developmental stage* | *Nature of anxiety* | *Countertransference/nature of link* | *Associated defences/nature of link* | *Therapeutic focus* |
|---|---|---|---|---|
| Autistic–contiguous | Fears and anxieties of dissolving, spilling/fears of falling into nothingness. | Intense and overwhelming reactions, often felt somatically/inability to think. | Defences against separateness/insistence on sameness.<br>Primitive narcissistic link. | Firstly contextual holding and then containment.<br>Less focus on interpretation. |
| Paranoid–schizoid | Anxieties related to feeling persecuted and attacked (externally or internally). | Feeling idealised or blamed/feelings of inadequacy.<br>Mutual agreement in the link. | Projection and splitting/unwillingness to accept contribution to couple difficulties.<br>Link fosters splitting/projection. | Identification of projections (and splits)/interpretation (therapist or non-therapist focused). |
| Depressive threshold/depressive | Anxieties related to feelings of despair, or the felt impossibility of repair (linked to gradually increasing levels of ego integration). | Feelings of lack of progress/sense of despair/hopelessness (and eventually) sadness/hopelessness. | Manic control, triumph and contempt finally giving way to valuing and depending on therapist (object)/more growth facilitating link. | Interpretation (assisting the tolerance) of ambivalence and focus on bringing split off feelings together. |
| Oedipal (a sub-set of both paranoid–schizoid depressive stages) | Anxieties generated by feelings of exclusion/being left out.<br>Jealousy. | Made to feel excluded/pressure to engage in enactments/forming alliances with one of the couple. | Range from primitive to more depressive modes/intolerance of otherness/ambivalence. | Interpretation of feelings of jealousy and intolerance of otherness/coupling/generational/gender differences. |

with a greater awareness of the couple's previous reliance on splitting and projection (or more primitive defences). Aided by the development of the therapeutic container, hitherto threatening emotional experience may now be felt to be more bearable (with less need to evade it or deal with it by the use of primitive psychic processes). In addition to this, the psychoanalytic psychotherapist is alert to any signs in the couple of more depressive anxieties and works with these in an attempt to stimulate the reparative urges that usually accompany them.

The therapeutic approach with a short-term couple intervention, unlike individual psychoanalytic approaches, is such that it focuses on an examination of what happens within the couple using the UGT, whilst using the transference relationship to reinforce this. Moreover, it relies greatly on the therapist's use of countertransference as a guide, whilst following the affect in the session, with the psychotherapist being more active in making connections with the couple. In the termination phase of a shorter-term therapy, there is also an emphasis on reviewing the therapy process together and a consolidation of what has become to be understood about unhelpful patterns of relating and the reasons for employing these.

## Some concluding remarks about intervention

In our experience a short-term intervention is useful for couples who have previously functioned reasonably well and whose coupling would not be described as being in the severe borderline or psychotic level of functioning.

Although the short-term model we have described (with its focus on the UGT) refers to discrete phases of intervention, in practice these somewhat overlap. These phases are not usually defined to the couple who are offered a time-specific intervention. We also indicate that we will review their progress with them at the end of this period. This allows for the possibility of the intervention being extended if required. Moreover, we also do not usually describe the first two sessions as an assessment so as not to convey, as Ogden noted, that these are sessions in which the couple could see themselves in a more passive role (Ogden, 1992).

In terms of evaluation, however, although we do not formally evaluate the outcome of the intervention, each session is evaluated post-hoc by the psychoanalytic psychotherapist by use of Bion's Grid (Bion, 1963) to determine what movement there has been in terms of the couple being able to mentalise or conceptualise their difficulties. Overall, we determine progress by evaluating the couple's psychic functioning, their reduced reliance on regressive modes of functioning, and evidence pertaining to the nature of their day-to-day life together.

In this chapter our aim has been to outline the theoretical framework underpinning our proposed short-term intervention with couples who are experiencing a melancholic reaction to loss. In particular, we have outlined how this framework has informed our approach to short-term intervention with couples who have sufficient resources to cope with the frame and the requirements of such an intervention. Part II of this book, which follows, will illustrate a range of loss experiences. The described interventions and formulations of each of these unique clinical presentations will focus on the value of a particular psychoanalytic approach to treatment, while together they highlight the richness and value of psychoanalytic ideas and concepts in working therapeutically with such couples.

## References

Anzieu, D. (1993). Autistic phenomena and the skin ego. *The Psychoanalytic Inquiry*, 13(1): 42–48.

Berenstein, I. (2004). *Devenir otro con otro*. Buenos Aires: Editorial Paidos.

Bick, E. (1968). The experience of the skin in early object relations. *International Journal of Psycho-Analysis*, 49: 484–486.

Bion, W. R. (1963). *Elements of Psycho-Analysis*. London: Heinemann.

Box, S. (1998). Group processes in family therapy: A psychodynamic approach. *Journal of Family Therapy*, 20: 123–132.

Britton, R. (1989). The missing link: Parental sexuality in the Oedipus complex. In: R. Britton, M. Feldman, & E. O'Shaughnessy (Eds.), *The Oedipus Complex Today: Clinical Implications* (pp. 83–101). London: Karnac.

Britton, R. (2004). Subjectivity, objectivity and triangular space. *The Psychoanalytic Quarterly*, 73: 47–61.

Byng-Hall, J. (1985). The Family Script: A useful bridge between theory and practice. *Journal of Family Therapy*, 7: 301–305.

Clulow, C. (2001). *Adult Attachment and Couple Psychotherapy: The 'Secure Base' in Practice and Research*. London: Routledge.

Dicks, H. V. (1967). *Marital Tensions: Clinical Studies Towards a Psychological Theory of Interaction*. London: Routledge.

Fairbairn, W. R. D. (1944). Endopsychic structure considered in terms of object-relationships. *International Journal of Psycho-Analysis*, 25: 70–92.

Fairbairn, W. R. D. (1952). *Psychoanalytic Studies of the Personality*. London: Routledge.

Fisher, J. V. (1999). *The Uninvited Guest: Emerging from Narcissism toward Marriage*. London: Karnac.

Flügel, J. C. (1921). *The Psycho-analytic Study of the Family*. London: Hogarth Press and the Institute of Psycho-Analysis.

Fonagy, P. (2001). *Attachment Theory and Psychoanalysis*. New York: Other Press.

Fonagy, P., & Target, M. (1997). Attachment and reflective function: Their role in self-organization. *Development & Psychopathology*, 9(4): 679–700.

Freud, S. (1920). Beyond the Pleasure Principle. *S.E.*, 18: 14–18.

Freud, S. (1923). The Ego and the Id. *S.E.*, 19: 19–28.

Freud, S. (1924d). The Dissolution of the Oedipus Complex. *S.E.*, 19: 171–179.

Grier, F. (2005). *Oedipus and the Couple*. London: Karnac.

Kaës, R. (2016). Link and the transference within three interfering psychic spaces. *Couple and Family Psychoanalysis*, 6(2): 81–193.

Keogh, T. (2017). Couple and family psychoanalysis in Oceania: history, influences and development. In: D. E. Scharff & E. Palacios (Eds.), *Family and Couple Psychoanalysis: A Global Perspective* (pp. 33–39). London: Karnac.

Keogh, T., & Enfield, S. (2013). From regression to recovery: Tracking developmental anxieties in couple therapy. *Couple and Family Psychoanalysis*, 3: 28–46.

Keogh, T., & Gregory-Roberts, C. (2017). The role of interpretation in the assessment phase of couple psychoanalysis. *Couple and Family Psychoanalysis*, 7(2): 168–180.

Klein, M. (1945). *Love, Guilt and Reparation*. London: The Hogarth Press.

Losso, R., de Setton, L. S., & Scharff, D. (2017). *The Linked Self in Psychoanalysis: The Pioneering Work of Enrique Pichon Rivière*. London: Karnac.

Morgan, M. (1995). *The Projective Gridlock: A Form of Projective Identification in Couple Relationships*. London: Karnac.

Morgan, M. (2005). First contacts: the therapists' couple state of mind' as a factor in the containment of couples seen for consultations. In: F. Grier (Ed.), *Oedipus and the Couple* (pp. 17–32). London: Karnac.

Nicolò, A. M. (2016). Thinking in terms of links. *Couple and Family Psychoanalysis*, 6 (2): 206–214.

Ogden, T. H. (1989). On the concept of an autistic-contiguous position. *International Journal of Psycho-Analysis*, 70: 127–140.

Ogden, T. H. (1992). Comments on transference and countertransference in the initial meeting. *Psychoanalytic Inquiry*, 12(2): 225–247.

Ogden, T. H. (2010). Why read Fairbairn? *International Journal of Psycho-Analysis*, 91: 101–118.

Palacios, E. (2017). An Argentine approach to family therapy. In: D.E. Scharff & E. Palacios (Eds.), *Family and Couple Psychoanalysis: A Global Perspective* (pp. 7–10). London: Karnac.

Puget, J. (2015). *Subjetivacion discontinua y psicoanalisis. Incertidumbre y certezas.* Buenos Aires: Lugar.

Ruszczynski, S. (Ed.) (1993). Thinking about and working with couples. In: *Psychotherapy with Couples* (pp. 197–217). London: Karnac.

Scharff, D. E., & Scharff, J. S. (1987). *Object Relations Family Therapy*. Northvale, NJ: Aronson.

Scharff, D. E., & Scharff, J. S. (1991). *Object Relations Couple Therapy*. London: Jason Aronson.

Scharff, D. E., & Vorchheimer, M. (Eds.) (2017). *Clinical Dialogues on Psychoanalysis with Families and Couples*. London: Karnac.

Tustin, F. (1980). Autistic objects. *International Review of Psychoanalysis*, 7: 27–40.

Winnicott, D. W. (1960). The theory of parent-infant relationship. In: *The Maturational Processes and the Facilitating Environment* (pp. 37–55). London: Karnac, 1990.

Zinner, J. (1976). The implications of projective identification for couple interaction. In: H. Grunebaum & J. Christ (Eds.), *Contemporary Marriage: Structure, Dynamics and Therapy* (pp. 292–308). Boston, MA: Little Brown.

# Part II

# Loss in couples and families: theory and practice

Chapter 5

# The family's use of regressive defences as an avoidance of mourning

*Anna Maria Nicolò and Stefania Tambone*

## Introduction

The family is an organism responsible for the growth of its members and for the transgenerational and intergenerational transmission of *phantasmatic* contents and models of identification. This is made possible by the family's ability to sustain pleasure and contain the suffering connected with growth, as many key moments in the life cycle, starting with the first separation, are accompanied by the need to work through psychic pain. Situations which require mourning significantly challenge the family group and each of its members in order to maintain this process of working through their psychic pain. If the family can sustain and develop a capacity to think, the passage through the successive phases of the life cycle and the consequent reorganisation of the group becomes possible and promotes new growth. However, such experiences can, in contrast, generate defences whose goal is to avoid mourning. Some of these defences are temporary, while others are pathological (Freud, 1917). In the case of families, the defences are interpersonal and transpersonal, that is, they are defences organised collectively among family members who determine family functioning and also influence group and individual functioning.

This chapter focuses on defences invoked by families to protect themselves from mourning and, in particular, which can lead to a pathological defence, identified by the Italian psychoanalyst Franco Fornari (1975) as the "paranoid working-through of mourning". This defence expresses an individual's inability to work through loss due to their resort to mechanisms characterised by a paranoid–schizoid mode of functioning. According to Melanie Klein (1984), working through losses allows individuals to preserve the value of the love-object. On the contrary, their inability to do so keeps them tied to an idealised archaic object in a deadly relationship. Such a development eventually translates into a difficulty in the capacity to think and symbolise and leads to their mental life becoming paralysed and suffocated. This state of mind is illustrated by thinking such as "If I did not agree to lose mother, I could neither imagine nor name her" (Kristeva, 1989, p. 41).

Working through loss and mourning is particularly complicated by hatred and anger, as well as by guilt about, and fear of, having damaged or destroyed the loved object. This is where the paranoid mode of working through of grief may become activated in the attempt to survive this emotional storm (Fornari, 1975). That is, in order to avoid anxiety and guilt, the tolerance of which allows the development of the depressive position (Klein, 1984), the splitting that characterises paranoid–schizoid functioning is reactivated. Everything good and vital is placed in the individuals themselves and in their love-object, and everything bad and related to death, in an external enemy.

According to Fornari (1975), this mechanism is the root cause of wars. Human beings do not acknowledge their hatred and desire to kill. Instead, they feel persecuted by the other, to whom they attribute their own hatred and desire to destroy. We can detect similar mechanisms operating in some families that present difficulties with mourning a loss, and see that these modes of mental functioning place the persecutor outside of the self of a particular family member or of the group as a whole.

## Clinical case

Key issues, which emerged over the course of a family therapy, made it possible to trace the impact of a subterranean web of un-mourned losses and the associated defences the family employed, which impeded their development. The discovery of these issues facilitated an understanding of the family's difficulties in negotiating the normal developmental transitions that were part of their family life cycle. Failed mourning processes resulted in the employment of regressive defences which immobilised, confused, alienated, and thwarted healthy separation. The discussion of the case examines the ways in which this family tried to cope with mourning processes linked to difficulties with individuation and separation and the diverse and unhelpful outcomes of their deficient working through of mourning.

## Insights from clinical work: the B Family

The B Family comprised of the parents, Nino and Maria, who were just under 60 years old, and their two sons, Michelangelo and Alessio, who were aged 25 and 21 years, respectively. The family sought help in a state of crisis. In particular, Alessio had not been coping well and had attempted suicide. The family lived in Nino's hometown, where Maria had her office, working as a freelancer. They had a number of houses, which was itself becoming a major issue for this family. They wandered like nomads between several homes, as though in a long pilgrimage in search of a mother-place that would welcome them – for a nest where they could find shelter from intrusion and where growth could be possible.

The therapeutic starting point was that of "Alessio's great crisis", which had taken place a few months earlier and alarmed the entire family. According to Alessio himself, "after years and years of being worried about my parents and my brother, it was finally my turn ... I felt I was going mad, and so I exploded." After a deep crisis, Alessio attempted suicide by throwing himself from the balcony of his own home. It was only thanks to the physical strength of his father and brother that they were able to stop him. From then on, the family system was in disarray.

Alessio's suicide attempt actually represented a desperate cry that brought the family to treatment. It cast a spotlight on the problematic family scene. With this crisis and his "explosion", he exposed a painful family situation – that of a profound discomfort that not only affected him but the entire family system. The therapist was presented with a seriously ill family with very rigid modes of psychic functioning, facing a critical situation while asking for help.

Slowly, using a varied and flexible therapeutic setting for the family, individual and couple sessions, and sessions of the fraternal subsystem, each family member was able to think of his or her own breakdown and resituate it in the context of their "link" to the family (see also Chapter 2). The eldest son, Michelangelo, had Usher's Syndrome (a rare congenital condition which causes hearing loss from birth and progressive loss of vision). He was diagnosed when he was a year-and-a-half old, but the illness worsened with the onset of puberty. Undoubtedly, this organic illness brought the focus of attention on him as the first born, with the majority of care directed toward him (with reparation as a goal) and resulting in significant neglect of Alessio's feelings.

References to the spouses' families of origin were frequent and appeared from the very beginning of the therapy. The exploration of these references made it possible to identify the family's significant relational difficulties (both among its members and toward those outside) and their inability to separate or differentiate, without automatically associating this separation with the radical, violent break of emotional links between each other. The resultant feeling was that there was significant pathology radiating out in every family "link", in every generation, and at every parental level. Initially, it was speculated that there had been an inherent deficit regarding an ability to differentiate and separate in the spouses' families of origin. Generations, roles, and genders appeared to have been blended and compacted into a single undifferentiated conglomerate, and so consequently, the boundaries of self were severely compromised.

Nino's family of origin was tied to the history of a bar that was inherited through the maternal line and which marked the family's vicissitudes and fortunes. The paternal grandparents, currently in their 80s, have three daughters and only one son, Nino, who was the second-born. The entire family system seems to have revolved around the bar and its associated dynamics of abuse, such that all the family members seem to have lived "off the mother".

Nino had worked in the bar since he was young. He talked of the ever-present difficult coexistence among family members. He referred, in particular, to the poor management of the business and the negligence, and glibness, with which the other family members approached the business, with no effort or dedication to it, but still wanting to draw profits from it. Nino, due to his passive nature, always tolerated this state of affairs until he met his wife who, in contrast, immediately noticed fraudulent practices and thefts from the business, which her husband had long refused to acknowledge.

Consequently, Nino filed a lawsuit against his relatives and switched jobs, but remained a partner in the family business, of which he is now a co-owner. His sisters continued with their dishonest management practices until a huge fine from the tax office precipitated the situation. Nino had no contact with his family of origin and blamed his wife for his estrangement. Despite the significant financial investment this decision entailed (considering that the family's situation was not at all financially comfortable), Nino and Maria appeared to be doggedly holding on to their share of the partnership, determined not to let go of it, in order not to lose their future portion of the inheritance when the mother dies.

The narrative of Maria's family history started with the mythical figure of Maria's father, a well-known jurist. Both parents were emotionally absent and distant, particularly the mother, who had "many psychological problems". The history of Maria's family was marked by a family secret. There was a grandfather who supported two families and led a double life; he had a family in America and a family in Italy, and compelled his wife to work in order to send money to the family living in America. Maria's mother suffered from an impoverished state of mind and was severely neglected by her husband, of whom she was inordinately possessive. This behaviour alienated her children.

Even though her father did not believe that women should study, Maria, like her brothers, became an established professional. In her struggle for emancipation, Maria got married at the age of 26, despite the fact that this partially slowed down her professional development. After two years of marriage she gave birth to her first child, Michelangelo, and four years later to the second, Alessio. Aged 40 she underwent a profound crisis due to an innermost sense of failure and an experience of destabilisation. This crisis, however, subsequently served to boost her career. In fact, she found an office and started working in her profession.

Maria's story about herself conveyed the image of a woman who had suffered deep and cumulative traumas and who had failed to leave behind the catastrophic image of a damaged self. She described herself as a "sacrificial victim", the bearer of a persecutory experience that overflowed and flooded the entire family functioning. It carried with it the unconscious idea that helping others implied running the highly dangerous risk of being subdued and enslaved. Thus, her anger against her sons and husband, which often appeared in the sessions, expressed an archaic rage, a rage against a primary object that failed to come to her aid. It was as if within Maria there was a lethal core that was populated by a dead mother, a cold mother that had been introjected into her own internal world. This internal object fed a sadistic and frustrating part of her that sabotaged the development of her ability to experience empathy toward herself and others.

## The impossible mourning

This family's pain thus originated in what each parent brought to the complex matrix relationships in the family group. Not only was each of them a depository of part of the pain, but also everything in these relationships seemed to be subject to destruction. Only in the presence of the therapist (as the members of the family stated many times) could thought and creativity emerge. This did not mean that each of them lacked a lively, creative side. Nevertheless, when they were together, the deathly destructive tendency prevailed; it was avoided, negated, projected, and enacted. Such a paranoid destructive dimension, from which thought was absent, maintained the unity with the object in a paradoxical dynamic of "killing while thinking one loves" (Fornari, 1975).

This family seems to have been formed out of a seemingly impossible mourning of illness and separation. Mourning was presented as something that attacked and threatened and from which one must constantly protect oneself. The transpersonal defence of a persecutory paranoid dimension was thus configured as an element that prevented any working-through of mourning. Three defences in particular seemed evident in this family. These were the use of the myth of a dead character, the maintenance of aliveness in the corpse of a family member, and a collective resorting to the paranoid working-through of mourning.

Paranoid working-through identifies the other as the guilty one and finds relief in the punishment of the other (see also Chapter 1). The other's death or punishment is thus seen to finally repay the family members for the difficulty of suffering the bereavement of loss. As Fornari (1975) states in *The Psychoanalysis of War*, what is at play is not just the anxiety caused by death, but also, in keeping with the Kleinian model, anxiety related to the death of the mother. In this way, the paranoid–schizoid position, which leaves no room for thought, emerges every time an event is experienced as threatening. The paranoid attempt at a working-through of mourning, therefore, defends the family not only against the alleged external enemy, but also against the internal one, which is placed outside.

Throughout the therapeutic process the therapist and family were offered the opportunity to access the link that connected the family members through different "points of entry". It was apparent that every family member acted both on his or her own behalf and on behalf of the entire family system. Various dynamics thus intertwined at several levels: the intrapsychic, the intersubjective, and the transpersonal levels.

## On the part of the mother, the first transpersonal defence: the myth of the dead grandfather

The mythical figure of the maternal grandfather started to take shape from the first family session. He had died more than a year earlier, but his death remained as an unelaborated, negated mourning, embedded in everyone's memory. He appeared at times as an unaffectionate, hard, but also an upright and honest man who enforced the law. At other times he was an affectionate, attentive grandfather, such as when he was the first and only one to notice his grandson Alessio's malaise, even before Alessio's collapse. In these ways he was a figure of great power that would soon become a transgenerational object. In his name, the family stuck to ritualistic celebrations in which the whole family must gather, if only in a mere sterile imitation of the ideal model of the united, cohesive family, summoned by a kind of transgenerational injunction from the dead grandfather and his mythical value of unity.

This myth, therefore, was highly "prescriptive" and, being the outcome of a group production, was unconsciously transmitted from one generation to the next and contributed to organising the family's fantasy life (Nicolò, 2014). The "thinking function" (Meltzer & Harris, 1983) was deposited in this grandfather to the extent that his death caused distress in Alessio and in the entire family. In this situation, the therapist wondered to what extent it were possible for members of families that have undergone mourning to identify not only with the dead parent, but also with the *function* or the *position* that the parent had or with which he or she had been invested. Memory, then, must keep this function (which preceded the break and the loss) intact, and thus offset the resulting "emptiness" with a new "fullness" that can maintain unaltered the functioning of the family system.

In this context, a dream brought by Alessio three months after the start of family therapy was particularly significant. The dead maternal grandfather appeared in it, and he spoke for the first time. "I dreamed that my grandfather talked to me … and it's the first time he talks to someone in dreams, because he usually just appears. He said to me, 'Leave to Giuseppe what concerns Giuseppe, and you do what concerns you'." In this dream, it is as a *third party* that the grandfather is given the floor. He is no longer a *sick father*, an object that is dominated by a crazy wife, or a *dead father*, immobilised in his functions. Rather, he is a father who speaks and uses differentiating words ("to each his own": "to Giuseppe what pertains to Giuseppe, to you what pertains to you").

The allusion to the transference is clear in this dream, but in its "polysemic dimension" (Nicolò, 2000), it represents the potential appearance of a first differentiation in the family self. Under the aegis of "to each his own", they moved toward the history of their origins, which render them unique. This dream marked the beginning of the work on this grandfather's injunctions and on the ways in which the family could work them through: what he has given, what he has taken away, what imprisons them, what they want to bury with him. This psychic evolution finally allowed them to celebrate the fantasy funeral of the dead grandfather.

## On the part of the father, the second transpersonal defence: the corpse of the living grandmother

Over time, Nino's peculiarities and his destructive dimension emerged. He neither knew how to, nor wanted to, take responsibility for the children, the family, himself, and his own body. He simply was not there engaging in a particular "passive–aggressiveness" that his wife had denounced many times. Significantly, he could not separate from his family of origin. The inheritance of the bar, the distribution of the only good thing belonging to their mother that he and his siblings had left, could not be carried out because the bar represented not just a money inheritance, but the mother herself. They could not let her die, and she would not die so long as the bar still existed. Moreover, they all sued each other so they could have a piece of her.

Mourning, in this case, seemed to constitute a deep, unelaborated core: a dynamic which also prevented the separation of the new generation in the current family, which was immersed in a repetitive logic of "cutting your nose to spite your face". Both in his new family and in the psychotherapy, the father manifested himself as the component that showed resistance to the treatment, that is, to the instrument that could promote change.

## The group fantasy of deadly separation

The myth of unity allowed the family to experience a sense of belonging and protection, but some flexibility was also necessary. Otherwise, members may have felt claustrophobically imprisoned. The experience of separation portrayed in the following material had two different levels:

1) An intrapsychic level, in which separation from an object is experienced as a loss of parts of one's own history and identity; and
2) An intersubjective level, in which separation is painfully perceived as the dispersion of the family self. The family's mode of functioning seemed to be trapped in a fantasy of "all united together" that did not allow for differentiation. As a result, a clandestine homicidal, filicidal, fantasy took shape that viewed separation as the murder of the other, or by the other. Separating, thus, meant destroying the family.

This issue emerged in all its intensity in a session wherein the family resumed therapy after the Christmas break.

> Nino starts muttering something incomprehensible. The therapist invites him to explain his point of view. With an increasingly agitated air, he expresses his opposition to this "craziness". He claims that "everyone has gone crazy here ... nobody understands anything anymore ... You're wrecking the entire family". His agitation grows and, as he expresses

> these thoughts, his body becomes more and more restless. "Go ahead … do whatever you want!" he says angrily to Michelangelo, "You want to go to Japan? Go to Japan. You want another place? … Rent a place … destroy the whole family". And then, turning to his wife, "And you, you're crazier than them … We're in dire poverty and you keep spending like crazy … we'll end up destitute". These words have an explosive effect on the two sons. Alessio starts yelling at his father, calling him the most offensive names and, in particular, asking him with insistent aggressiveness: "Say it, say why you don't want Michelangelo to leave home … say that his money is useful to you". Michelangelo, for his part, furious but resigned, tells me while looking me in the eye: "This … This is what happens when one tries to think of oneself". (Session N. 70)

In this excerpt of the session we witness the separation anxiety felt by these parents, who opposed their sons' autonomy and individuation and respond violently to it. The mother performed continuous castrations, while the father induced deep guilt. The sons' separation was impossible, for it was experienced as the loss of the narcissistically invested love-objects, a loss of part of the self, and a loss of money. The sense of imminent catastrophe often translated into a fantasy of the economic collapse of the family, for which everyone, but the ill child in particular, must provide. In this way, a link was established based on theft and an abuse of resources that recalled the pattern of functioning of the paternal family with the bar, but also of the maternal family, where the grandfather compelled his wife to support his second family, concealed in America.

## The son's illness: the uncanny event that prevents separation

There was a further important feature to this family. That is, the family illness served to maintain unity as part of a sadomasochistic dimension. This unconscious role played by disease is a double-edged sword. Michelangelo makes tyrannical use of his own disease so that the mother's attention–concern will focus on him, something that might otherwise never occur. The family, in turn, uses the patient to force everyone into stasis. Alessio, who seems to be left with the crumbs, reacts with aggression and sadism. Nevertheless, he feels that he must invent an illness, in a kind of competition to see "who is the sicker". The need to be seen was shared by the two brothers. In Michelangelo, this need had taken the organic road, and in Alessio, the psychic road.

## Moving towards the hope born from working through mourning

Psychotherapy gradually facilitated the emergence of an ability to differentiate, and hence to work through, mourning. As the treatment progressed, Michelangelo gave himself permission to show anger without fearing that it may destroy both himself and the other. In this way, he started feeling the need to begin to work through the mourning of his own illness, in contrast to his parents, who remained unable to mourn it.

The following clinical material is illustrative of this issue. There was a long period during which Michelangelo fantasised renting an entire house for himself.

> The analyst asked Michelangelo what had prevented him from becoming autonomous in terms of housing. "What a good question, doctor!" exclaims Michelangelo. "Ask them ..." and asserted that as soon as his father hears of this kind of project, he says things like, "Go ahead, by all means. Destroy the family". And the mother encourages him one day and stops him the next. The father intervened: "Well, let's hope that the war will finish eventually! (...) God help us!" The therapist emphasised that the war only ends when everyone dies, and the only way we can continue to work is if there are survivors, which will only happen if everyone does his or her share.

## Assessment of the process

Throughout the long therapeutic journey, there have been numerous threats of abandonment of the therapy in a ritualisation/repetition of the separation trauma within the sessions. It is as though there were a tendency to enact the separation from the therapist so as not to allow the separation between family members. When the sons started to seek autonomy, the couple became very frightened and reacted with violent attacks that jeopardised the continuity of the analytic work. These attacks had a twofold value; they attacked both the family self (self-sabotage) and the children (sadism).

A new fantasy was revealed whereby the therapist could become the good parent to whom Nino and Maria could entrust the children. As a result, the mother would relieve herself of her burden, and the father would continue to avoid taking charge of the children's lives. At a particularly significant junction the deficient dimension of the couple emerged. Their utter absence of sexuality (contributed to by painful intercourse [dyspareunia] in her case, and constriction of the foreskin [phimosis] in his case), was brought to light. This revelation led to the hypothesis of the breakup of the marriage as a link between a man and a woman who hated each other, but remained psychologically unable to part.

In these difficult stages, the variable setting chosen was useful for analytic work, for it enabled the redistribution of functions and allowed each family member to reclaim his or her own anxieties and emotions. The subsystem of the fraternal pair benefited from this type of setting. This facilitated the uncovering of the psychological discomfort derived from the perception of themselves as colonised by, and embedded in, the parental net. This enabled the expression of their own developmental needs of separation and autonomy, strengthened the relationship between the brothers by highlighting the lines of differentiation and allowed their gradual access to adulthood. Meanwhile, it was possible to work on the parental function of the married couple and explore the deficient and suffering couple link. Lastly, the transpersonal, transgenerational, and intrasubjective family dynamics led to the revelation of key knots in the family link on which the therapist and family could slowly work.

## Conclusions

An outcome of the therapeutic work was that a family trapped in a pathological homeostasis, comprising somatic patterns and confused states of mind, became open to differentiation and separation. Bion (1962) states that change can feel catastrophic. This was therefore a sign that the therapy was progressing – that it had shaken the psychotic functioning of the family. It appears that any therapeutic evolution cannot be devoid of pain or crises. Faced with the overflowing crises of this family, the therapist(s) were often on the verge of giving into the catastrophe of immobilisation and regression. However, it was possible to glimpse a positive and developmentally significant solution for the potential transformation of the link, a glimpse that fueled hope in the reparatory and creative capacity of the family self and of the other with whom they related.

## References

Bion, W. R. (1962). *Learning from Experience*. New York: Basic Books.

Fornari, F. (1975). *The Psychoanalysis of War*, A. Pfeifer (Trans.). Bloomington, IN: Indiana University Press.

Freud, S. (1917). Mourning and Melancholia. *S.E.*, 14: 237–258.

Klein, M. (1984). *Love, Guilt and Reparation and Other Works 1921–1945 (The Writings of Melanie Klein, Volume 1)*. New York: Free Press.

Kristeva, J. (1989). *Black Sun: Depression and Melancholia*, L. S. Roudiez (Trans.). New York: Columbia University Press.

Meltzer, D., & Harris, M. (1983). *Il ruolo educativo della famiglia*. Turin: Centro Scientifico Editore [*The Educational Role of the Family*]. London: Harris Meltzer Trust, 2013.

Nicolò, A. M. (2000). Il sogno nella psicoanalisi con la coppia e con la famiglia [Dreams in couple and family psychoanalysis]. In: A. M. Nicolò & G. Trapanese (Eds.), *Quale psicoanalisi per la coppia?* [*What Psychoanalysis for the Couple?*] (pp. 239–257). Rome: Franco Angeli, 2005.

Nicolò, A. M. (2014). Family myths and pathological links. In: A. M. Nicolò, P. Benghozi, & D. Lucarelli (Eds), *Families in Transformation* (pp. 279–291). London: Karnac.

Chapter 6

# The lamp of tragedy past: traumatic intergenerational loss and the couple[1]

*Judith Pickering*

## Introduction

The chapter begins by considering the relevance of Bion's own personal experiences as well as his theories which are relevant to understanding unmetabolised intergenerational loss.

Bion (1970), emerging from an object relations tradition, developed a theory of mind whereby the ability to tolerate frustration and the capacity to suffer psychic pain are seen to facilitate psychological growth, whilst intolerance and evasion of suffering such pain impede it. The crucial word is to "suffer", since Bion observed that there is a difference between "feeling" and "suffering" pain:

> People exist who are so intolerant of pain or frustration (or in whom pain or frustration is so intolerable) that they feel the pain but will not suffer it and so cannot be said to discover it … the patient who will not suffer pain fails to "suffer" pleasure. (Bion, 1970, p. 9)

When one cannot suffer pain, it also denudes the personality of the capacity to suffer a range of other emotional engagements with oneself and with others: including mourning the loss of another, compassion for another's suffering, or love for another. Although a "decrease in pain itself" may well be hoped for, in the "analytic experience" it should lead to an increase in the capacity for suffering (Bion, 1963, p. 62).

As described in Chapter 1, the relevance of Bion's ideas to understanding melancholia concerns the evasion of mental pain that it represents. In the couple presenting for therapy there is often a shared unconscious process resulting in a collusion in avoiding suffering such mental pain, thereby also stripping the relationship of true joy, vivacity, and fulfilment.

## Bion: mourning and melancholia

Bion experienced his own very personal experience of loss. During the First World War, as an Army officer, he was involved in a trauma of such psychological proportions that he felt that he died: his body survived, but his soul did not. "I would not go near the Amiens-Roye road for fear I should meet my ghost – I died there. For though the Soul should die, the Body lives for ever" (Bion, 1991, p. 257).

In his autobiographical writings Bion displays a pervading sense of psychic deadness accompanied by a melancholic self-hatred and guilt, which also permeated his relationships. He describes himself as hollow, an "unprepossessing mass of ineptitude" (Bion, 1985, p. 19), a body without a soul. Life was full of "frustration, futility, anger and humiliation" (Bion, 1985, p. 46).

Bion was thus not just suffering war trauma, but also many of the personality features Freud (1917) describes as belonging to the melancholic, where the nature of the primary attachment relationship and the level of regression precipitated by the loss, influence the vulnerability to a melancholic reaction.

The response of Bion to his war trauma seems to have had childhood origins in the form of a failure of containment, maternal reverie, and transmutation of "nameless dread" (Bion, 1967) on the part of his mother, which pre-disposed him to melancholia. He felt he was but "a chitinous semblance of a boy from whom the person had escaped" (Bion, 1982, p. 104), a hollow man imprisoned in an empty shell, unable to emotionally engage with others, nor with his own inner suffering.

According to Freud, mourning and melancholia were both "the reaction to the loss of a loved person, or to the loss of some abstraction which has taken the place of one, such as one's country, liberty, and ideal" (Freud, 1917, p. 243). He saw melancholia as different from mourning in that there is also a profound disturbance of self-regard (See also Chapter 1). The melancholic experiences,

> A profoundly painful dejection, cessation of interest in the outside world, loss of the capacity to love … and a lowering of the self-regard feelings to a degree that finds utterance in self-reproaches and self-revilings, and culminates in a delusional expectation of punishment. (Freud, 1917, p. 244)

Bion's personal experience is therefore akin to the antecedents and effects of a melancholic reaction that one finds in couple relationships. This theme will be taken up in relation to the clinical case material that follows concerning a couple "Aya and Joe", who illustrate the effect on the couple of un-mourned loss in the preceding generation and the concept of the "interlocking traumatic scene" (Pickering, 2006, 2008).

In terms of couple psychopathology, it is proposed that severe psychic trauma such as that experienced by Bion in the First World War, resulting in melancholic reactions to loss (whose pre-disposing origins predated the trauma in question), inhibits the capacity to find, create, and enjoy fulfilling relationships. Such relational trauma may also be transmitted to one's offspring in the form of a "malignant dowry" (Pickering, 2006), consisting of a confusion of unconscious, unresolved intergenerational traumatic matters. Consequently, the offspring may bear a terrible burden of psychological work that the parents were so unable to contend with, that they dislodged, like a bizarre object, such malignant dowries into their children. In turn, such dowries may create psychotic pockets (see also Chapter 5) because the recipient cannot metabolise another's inchoate and incomprehensible, unthinkable "beta-bits" unless they have the necessary psychological conditions of containment to comprehend, work through, and truly suffer, such traumatic matters.

Bion's war experiences were indeed traumatic and their impact on his relationships catastrophic. A "disturbance of self-regard" and embittered, cynicism, and mistrust of intimate relationship permeate Bion's autobiographical writings. When in later life love threatened to intrude in such an emotionally dead zone, Bion, at first, found himself unable to truly love.

Bion experienced multiple losses in his life including loss of his home and homeland in India, connection with his parents when sent to boarding school in England, loss of his beloved ayah, then loss of so many compatriots during the war. Painfully, Bion also experienced the loss of his first romantic love. No sooner had his lover accepted his marriage proposal than she jilted him. "It was not funny: it hurt. It still does" (Bion, 1985, p. 26).

In terms of attachment theory, Bion's attachment style at this stage of his life could be described as pre-occupied (ambivalent) which, as Stroebe, Schut and Stroebe (2005) point out, "renders a bereaved person to a pre-occupation with a lost attachment" (p. 4). The wound of rejection and loss continued to fester, as did his sardonic tone in expressing his ambivalence towards her. "The dose of venom made it certain the wound would not be … aseptically carried out, but would fester and remain open" (Bion, 1985, p. 27). He also observed that both he and she had fallen in love with a projection, a thin, two-dimensional identification, not a real person: "Two people who rush rhapsodically to the state of emotional bliss of perfect union pay in suffering for having *evaded* the toils of discovery of each other" (Bion, 1985, p. 30, italic added).

Bion then met an actress, Betty Jardine, whom he married in 1943.

He hoped Betty was:

> not deprived of the comforting lie that he was really a man and a hero, and not just an artificial representation of a man stuck up in the showcase of a universe signifying nothing and tricked out with psycho-analytic dummies intended to fool the psycho-analytic church into believing that there are real souls that require to be humanized. … "The bells of hell go ting-a-ling-a-ling" for her but not for me. The Body lives for ever. (Bion, 1985, p. 60)

In 1945, when Betty was giving birth to their first child, Parthenope, Bion did not attend the birth. He was in Normandy working with victims of shell shock. Betty died three days later from a pulmonary embolism. Receiving the call, his reaction was matter of fact and "efficient", since after all, "death is a characteristic feature of life" (Bion, 1985, p. 27). Consistent with a melancholic response, Bion blamed himself for the death. He said, "I felt I had killed her by not staying with her when her pregnancy was nearing term" (Bion, 1985, p. 26). "What killed Betty and nearly killed her baby? Physical malformation? Incompetent obstetrics? Callous or indifferent authorities? Or the revelations of the hollow drum that was being so loudly beaten by her husband's departure?" (Bion, 1985, p. 62).

The hollow drum of his departure was his lack of presence in the first place, a hollow drum with no spirit inside. That is, until a psychological miracle of restoration occurred, infusing him with a new spirit of life and love.

## Restoration of the intersubjective: Francesca, Bion, and O

If Bion was psychically dead, how did "those same dead bones" undergo rebirth (Bion, 1991, p. 60)? Bion came to be psychically reborn through the transformational power of love. In March 1951 Bion met a young widow working as a research assistant at the Tavistock Clinic whose name was Francesca. Falling in love with Francesca was a miracle, signalling restoration, and rebirth, coming into a new mode of being: "Francesca darling, you are a miracle that has happened to me, a miracle that I do not understand or ever want to understand. Enough for me that it has happened" (Bion, 1985, p. 82).

Where the world had been described as full of futility, boredom, horror, and meaninglessness, now the world is lit up with the glow of love: "I feel the one thing that can make all things possible already exists, and that is that between you and me there is already an enduring love that cannot be easily shaken even in this uncertain and painful world" (Bion, 1985, p. 82).

With Francesca's love joined with his love for her, his perception of himself also changed. He commented, "I shall be a very happy man and no one can ask for more than that … we shall have all the foundations for a really happy home, and the opportunity of sharing it and spreading it" (Bion, 1985, p. 91).

This raises the question of the respective roles of a therapeutic relationship, a couple relationship and one's own inner journey if not life itself, in bringing about insight, structural change, and healing of past trauma. Individual and couple therapy obviously play a vital role in providing a therapeutic space, a therapeutic process, and transformational relationship, in which one may uncover, confront, and work through the myriad psychological obstacles to living and loving well. However, it was not, according to Bion, his analysis that brought the healing of his soul he so desperately needed, but his own search for truth, followed by life and love with Francesca. In the period prior to meeting her, he underwent his own searingly honest soul searching, a form of self-analysis. He began to truly *suffer* pain rather than evade it. Ultimately for Bion, it was the transformational potential of a fulfilling intimate relationship itself, as well as a lifelong search for emotional truth and absolute reality, beyond knowing, that was able to bring about psychological healing, new life, creative flourishing, and true well-being.

Related to link theory as developed by Pichon Rivière (see Chapter 2), Bion was one of the first analysts to acknowledge inter-subjectivity. He recognised that emotional experience is always embedded in relationship: "An emotional experience cannot be conceived of in isolation from a relationship" (Bion, 1962, p. 42). Relational and intersubjective analytic approaches challenge earlier intrapsychic and more individualistic views of analysis, arguing that core psychic processes are inseparable from a relational matrix. Healing of relational trauma and unresolved loss, working through the many psychological obstacles to living and loving well, takes place within the crucible of relationship. Sometimes this relational crucible is analysis, sometimes couple therapy, sometimes simply life and love itself, and sometimes all three serve their respective functions.

Bion's relationship with Francesca also profoundly inspired his clinical thinking and writing from that time onwards, enabling a legacy of joy and inspiration that Francesca and the children continued to enjoy throughout their lives as well.

## Clinical case example

Let us now consider a contemporary case example of the impact of intergenerational transmission of traumatic loss on couple functioning, and the relevance of Bion's theories, in particular the selected fact, in working with these issues. The case also demonstrates how couple functioning which is at a more narcissistic level (a pre-disposing factor to melancholia) creates more challenges for the therapist in working with unresolved losses.

## The introduction agency

In the following clinical vignette, the effect of unresolved, inter-generational loss at first made its introduction as subtle notes that would gradually evolve into a coherent movement, as therapist and couple began their work of co-emergence. In this case material, the effect of unresolved (inter-generational) loss initially made its introduction as subtle notes that would gradually evolve into a coherent movement, as therapist and couple begin their work of co-construction.

The therapist's first encounter with the couple occurred when answering a referral call. A woman's clipped voice launched into a rapid-fire explanation of why she needed couple therapy.

"My name is Aya.[2] My boyfriend Joe and I have been going out for nine months, but are at a *dead end* and I don't want to waste time *flogging a dead horse*."

A week later, Aya drags a reluctant suitor into the consulting room. Before we settle in our seats, she states, somewhat imperiously, that if her boyfriend

Joe doesn't propose before the end of the session, it will simply prove she is right. Joe slumps into his chair as if wishing the very fabric might swallow him.

Rolling her eyes, Aya responds: "Just as I thought. Waste of time even coming."

Aya explains how she had met Joe through a dating agency. Previous contenders had failed to meet her selection criteria. "I was getting to the end of the road when Joe came onto the books", she explained.

The therapist suggested that perhaps the couple might give themselves a bit of breathing space to ponder what might be going on behind the scenes.

## The couple's background

In subsequent sessions, Aya explained how her family had migrated to Australia from Singapore. As an adolescent she felt a social outcast at school and so retreated into a romantic fantasy realm. She would dress like a princess, hoping for her father's attention, but interrupting him in his study, where he sat staring vacantly into space, he just bellowed at her to stop dressing in such a suggestive manner and to get back to her studies.

Meanwhile in the session, Joe, like her father, was staring out the window, as if he too were a thousand miles away. Unresponsive to Aya's prompting to "spill the beans" about his childhood, Aya filled the breach, telling me how his parents had been Lithuanian refugees and he was the youngest of three children. As a child he had suffered terrible psoriasis which made him self-conscious. His father, unable to tolerate weakness, demanded that Joe prove himself in areas of physical prowess. "Get on with it! Be a man!" was his constant refrain.

Aya's foot-stamping insistence that Joe "get on with it" and propose trip-switched him back into how he felt as a child when he was made to jump through hoops for which he did not feel ready. The expression "shot-gun wedding" floated into awareness: conjuring up the shadowy image of a shotgun at his head.

Visibly wilting, he whimpered *sotto voce*, "please, I'm not ready, give me time". Time, with its penumbra of associations with biological and Oedipal clocks, was of the essence. A catch-cry for Aya was that "time's running out, no one will ever want to marry me anyway."

Joe kept muttering under his breath: "if she would only get off my back, I could run the whole marriage and horse-drawn carriage number past her."

Aya's face crumpled. The slightest hesitancy to propose shocked Aya out of her fairy-tale expectations into a time warp relating to shame-evoking events of childhood.

Aya longed to be rescued from the grip of a lonely internal fantasy, yet her increasingly desperate attempts to liberate herself by interviewing, then dismissing, a string of potential suitors only served to cement this encryption. Seizing on Joe as a "last ditch stand", her insistent demand that he propose "now or never" tripped him into his own traumatic complex deriving from his father's bullying demands.

Underneath Aya's fantasy of being a princess-bride and Joe's of being a dashing athletic hero, both were more alike than met the eye. What manifested as vacillation on Joe's part and imperiousness on Aya's, masked feelings of inadequacy and fears of abandonment for both of them.

What had been triggered was an interlocking of two traumatic scenes. Neither Joe nor Aya realised they were in the grip of such traumatic memory systems, but experienced what was going on as if it were happening in the "here-and-now". The link between past and present only emerged much later in the analytic context.

## Malignant dowries and interlocking scenes

Due to the complex interaction of unconscious factors dictating partner choice, shared unconscious phantasies (Pincus, 1962), and mutual projective identifications, a relationship may suffer contamination from the infiltration of psychological traumata, unresolved grief, loss, disappointments, and failures of containment in the early environment. These complexes manifest as unconsciously encrypted patterns of engagement that each partner brings, like a "malignant dowry", to the marriage. The dowry box releases its contents to create an entangled destructive drama, the "interlocking traumatic scene" (Pickering, 2006, 2008). Partners unconsciously conscript each other to play allotted parts in stereotypic scenarios that encapsulate such traumatic complexes. The two scenes dovetail together to create such emotionally confused entanglement that it seems to deadlock. The interlocking mechanism has its own malignant presence, described as the "malignant third" (Pickering, 2006).

Fulfilling intimate relationships requires a constant struggle to disentangle the stalemates created by such scenes. Couple therapy aims to provide a safe environment with another mind capable of enabling containment and reflection to develop in the couple.

Bion's concept of container–contained (Bion, 1962) is highly relevant to couple work. Bion's prototype for an interpersonal container–contained relationship is that of the mother–infant where mother, through her reverie, takes in the baby's primitive psychic material, reflects upon it, retains a "balanced outlook", and transforms such "beta-elements" (undigested emotional experience) via her "alpha function" into "alpha elements", which the child then introjects as part of the development of self-containment. "Alpha function" refers to the ability to contain, metabolise, and transform primitive anxieties. A caretaker/mother processes material that has been lodged into her via projective identifications and, in and through her reverie, converts them into nascent sensory data, or alpha elements. Container–contained is an interdependent function necessary for emotional growth, for learning from experience, for transmutation of "nameless dread", grief, loss, and trauma.

## Traumatic memory

In couples, interlocking scenes may involve a varied mix of internalisations of traumatic experiences and relational disappointments, defences, shared unconscious fantasies (Pincus, 1962), and phantom presences in the relationship.

Trauma also involves shock. For example, there is a sense of shock, indignation, and profound disappointment when a child's need for recognition is not met. In the couple described, Aya's repeated disappointment at her father's failure to affirm her emergence as a young woman could be viewed as a trauma involving recurrent shock.

Another form of "shocking" experience that can resonate in a couple derives from psychic invasion by unprocessed material from one's ancestors (See also Chapter 5). Such forces may form themselves psychically into alien inner figures manifesting in dreams as witches, burglars, intruders, ghosts, uncanny presences, or "chimerical monsters" (Grotstein, 1997). These are the inter-generational phantom presences which can haunt and disrupt the couple relationship.

## Aya and Joe

It took a considerable degree of alpha function and capacity for containment in the therapist to retain a "balanced outlook" in the face of explosive eruptions from Aya and Joe in their couple therapy sessions. The repetitive rows took the form of closeness–distance struggles. The more Aya banged on the doors to Joe's internal world, the more he locked himself away. Joe blamed himself saying, "I never should have got married. I'm crap at intimacy". Aya replied, "but that's why we're in couple therapy".

Joe and Aya had each suffered failures of containment in the early environment. Unbeknown to them this was due to intergenerational transmission of trauma and loss in their parents. Joe was the only child of Lithuanian refugees who had been imprisoned in Buchenwald. Aya's cultural background was Dutch–Indonesian. During the Second World War Aya's father had been interned by the Japanese in Java. Aya described her father as morose, monotone, and emotionally unresponsive. He was haunted by nightmares of his internment, but could never speak about them. In both cases their parents never spoke of such horrors; the past was a closed book. Nevertheless, a closed book was passed down, the unread contents like "un-thought knowns" (Bollas, 1987) permeating the unconscious atmosphere with a sense of menace and foreboding.

When trauma of the past is rendered a closed book, it enters the stream of unconscious transmission. When the handing down of family and cultural stories is repressed due to pain, fear, shame, or the sense that it is unspeakable and unimaginable, it impoverishes the next generation. In place of ever vitalising myths of origin is a humming hollowness, the vaporised psychic space filled with nameless dreads (Pickering, 2012).

Aya's insecure cloying evoked in Joe memories of a disowned need to connect just as he had tried to cling to his mother. As refugees who conceived Joe on the boat from Europe, on arrival his parents put all their energies into making ends meet. His mother had also suffered a stillbirth in Buchenwald, a little girl, but she had no possibility to mourn this loss, which impacted upon her relationship with Joe. She was emotionally withdrawn, providing for his physical needs in a perfunctory way, but unable to meet any emotional need for closeness and understanding. He consequently shut down and retreated into his own world.

He continued to feel a sense of worthlessness, that he did not deserve to live, let alone be loved. As an adult, his parents were keen that he find a suitable partner and get married. At his parents' constant prompting, he signed up with an introduction agency, which is where he met Aya.

At the time they met, Joe's parents had just been placed in a nursing home. Joe worked from the family home writing history textbooks. When, after several more couple therapy sessions featuring Aya's constant prompting, they finally became engaged, Aya was adamant that he should sell his family home. "We should buy one together, to symbolise our future union as a couple", she announced in a session. Joe was appalled, as it was the symbol of all his parents had worked to achieve in the new country. In response to Aya's ever more insistent demands, he reluctantly agreed to do so. However, the same dynamics were reinvented over the styling of the house for sale.

Aya engaged a professional stylist who advised them to buy a lamp for the bedroom. Aya went shopping, but didn't want to make the final selection without Joe. Joe was reluctant to take time to do this. This proved to Aya, yet again, that he was "dragging the chains" on selling his family home.

"See", she looked accusingly at the therapist, "he doesn't really want to buy a house with me. Not sure he even wants to be with me. I'm over this!"

Joe retorted: "It's only an *el cheapo* lamp we got to sell the house. Anything you choose will be fine, love ...."

"But that's not the point!" retorted Aya.

Joe morosely muttered, "yeah right, what is the point?"

The therapist asked: "I'm wondering what the point might be for you as a couple, in choosing a lamp together?"

Joe asked Aya, "hmm, well, Aya, what is the point?"

"Well, it's not just a lamp to sell the house, it's the lamp which we'll take to the new house."

Joe saw buying a lamp as another example of Aya's relentless message that "you don't love me unless you take time off work to be with me". Aya saw the lamp as signifying the light leading them to a shared future together.

Their impasse encapsulated in the interlocking scene concerning a lamp, encompassed several relational polarities: between the autonomy of each partner as individuals and the individuation of the couple, space and closeness, intimacy, and solitude and Joe's family home as one side of the polarity representing family of origin influences, and the hope of co-creating a new marital space representing the other. The tensions between these poles was played out between them, rather than sublated to create a new third perspective transcending their various dichotomies.

The lamp as a symbol threw light on their past and on the developmental aspects of their partner choice. It also signified the future, as a soft lamp to light up their shared marital space. Joe put aside his reluctance for Aya's sake, and they went off happily to purchase it.

At the store they fought about the style of lamp. Aya wanted a small lamp with a translucent paper lampshade. Joe wanted a bright reading light so he could read in bed. Aya retorted, "bedtime is cuddle time, not study time". Their capacity to re-play the old theme with slight variations seemed relentless. So too was Aya's tendency to blame Joe and Joe's tendency to accept blame: "I'm simply crap at relationships. I should be on my own." Aya felt abject terror of abandonment and being on her own. "Nobody would ever want me, I'm just a reject." Yet such statements had an accusatory ring, which alienated Joe even further. Both felt terrible insecurity about their self-worth and right to a place in the sun.

The therapist, in her analytic reverie, pondered on how a light can be too bright, like a light in an interrogation room, and thought how a soft ambient bedside light with its mixture of illumination and softness could represent the way to bring together Bion's emotional links K (knowledge) and L (love).

But there was more to it. The therapist sat awaiting a selected fact to emerge.

## The "selected fact"

The selected fact is a term coined by the French mathematician Henri Poincaré, which for Bion refers to an "emotional experience of a sense of discovery of coherence" (Bion, 1962, p. 73) emerging out of a mass of fragmented analytic material. The selected fact signifies a "coming together, by a sudden precipitating intuition, of a mass of apparently unrelated incoherent phenomena which are thereby given coherence and meaning not previously possessed" (Bion, 1967, p. 127). It occurs as part of the process of synthesis.

## The conjoint selected fact

The concept of a "conjoint selected fact" (Pickering, 2006) has been postulated in relation to interpretations in couple therapy. It is not enough to uncover a central truth at the core of the psychic material presented by one partner. It is how this selected fact interacts with the central truth of the other partner's material, in other words there is a selected fact which serves to sublate both of the individual's selected facts, if not a series of selected facts. The word "conjoint" refers to the third entity created by the combination of the two individual selected facts. It is related to the intersubjective relational third.

The conjoint selected fact might be the discovery of the shared unconscious phantasy (Pincus, 1962) behind the couple's object choice. A shared basis for an unconscious choice may manifest in such an opposing form, that the two partners find it very difficult to see that the core of their circuitous marital scenes contains a similar aetiology, often a similar relational trauma, if not intergenerational trauma. Their reactions to an early trauma might differ, but the cause, as was the case with Joe and Aya, may be similar.

It is only when the therapist has got to the heart of what is going on: in the past and the present, in the intra-psychic system of each person and their interlocking intersubjective system, in other words a central conjoint selected fact, that sublates all these elements, that the therapist is in a position to make a mutative interpretation.

## The lamp reconsidered

Aya and Joe related how they were going to paint their bedroom, which brought to mind the unresolved issue of the bedside lamp.

Aya said, "What a scene it brought on! I kept nagging at Joe, 'why can't we do something as simple as decide on a lamp?' He kept saying, 'why bother, you don't even let me read in bed?' I retorted, 'it's not a lamp to read by, but a soft light to make love by. That's why I wanted that particular lamp with the soft translucent paper shade.' We both recognised something was being stirred up, we'd think of you and take a break, so as to tackle the issue from another angle, but as soon as one of us backed off, the other would start up again. It felt like some sinister third party was directing us!"

The "sinister third party" is a form of "malignant third" (Pickering, 2008), the hidden director of the interlocking scene. The malignant third re-instates destructive patterns, just at the junctures where change is possible. The very tools of therapeutic change can thus be turned into weapons with which to attack each other. This is precisely what Aya and Joe continued to do.

Aya lathered herself into a fury, employing psychologically pathologising terms she'd picked up in individual therapy sessions: "Joe is just a schizoid, split-off, autistic git who shies away from any form of intimacy." Joe just sulked muttering "yeah right, I know it's my fault. Should never have married me. I'm a no hoper. Better off on my own."

The image of the lamp floated back into the therapist's mind who then asked, "I wonder whether the lamp means very different things for both of you."

Aya said a lamp gave a soft romantic haze and made her feel safe and secure. Joe said the only kind of light he liked was one to read by, but Aya hated him reading in bed and hated bright lights.

Not knowing quite why, the therapist asked, "Joe, you once said something about how your parents came on a boat as refugees. Joe, what was the boat they came on?"

Joe replied, "I don't know. I knew not to ever ask such questions; it was a 'no-go zone'."

Startled by the unexpected emergence in the analytic field of the therapist's question, all three sat silently wondering its import.

Something about Joe's reluctance to buy a lamp and Aya's insistence on getting one was significant. The therapist, contemplating this, continued to feel a great deal of unease, aware that the matter had not been fully revealed. The therapist suddenly intuited why Joe did not want a lamp with a translucent shade. The consequences of this realisation were so shocking that the therapist sought to find a time and space to face it alone, in a state of analytic reverie. Here the therapist also needed to be guided by Bion's "an act of faith (F)". "F reveals and makes possible experiences that are often painful and difficult for the individual analyst and analysand to tolerate" (Bion, 1970, p. 46). The therapist eventually broke through to see what had to be seen: a lampshade made of human skin, like those made at camps such as Buchenwald. This "un-thought known" had been at first quite unthinkable, leading the therapist to protect herself by clever wrap-ups of the couple's relentless repetitions. Although these had clinical validity and were helpful, they were used to avoid if not evade facing a more difficult and terrible truth that lay behind them.

At the next session, Joe said "I asked my father about the boat. It was the SS Derna."

The SS Derna brought Jewish survivors of the Holocaust to Australia in 1948. Joe's parents' family had all perished in the war, just as their first-born had also died. His parents put all such loss behind them and refused to speak about it. Yet the sense of unspoken grief and horror haunted Joe's childhood. Like hollow drums resounding a death march, Joe's parents went through the motions of being alive whilst being psychically deadened. They were not able to foster a sense of aliveness and emotional connectedness in their child.

## Intergenerational matters and container–contained

The process of intuiting a conjoint selected fact may uncover networks of links between four layers of history behind the present issue: the relational situation in the present; the couple's relational history; family-of-origin experiences, internalisations, and mutual projective identifications manifesting in the new relationship; and intergenerational components cross-transmitted in the current relationship.

Interlocking traumatic scenes can function as the conduits for the transmission of walled-off chambers of horror deriving from trauma suffered by the ancestors. Children of survivors may be unconsciously driven to enter therapy by the need to uncover past secrets before the keys to comprehending what they carry die with their forebears. The offspring may inherit that which was too unimaginably horrific for the previous generations to have worked through. Such material involving unprocessed loss will haunt the couple dynamics of the next generation until it is uncovered, witnessed, mourned, and worked through (Pickering, 2002, 2008, 2012).

After Joe spoke the words "The Derna" something seemed to have made an imperceptible, but seismic shift. When one member of the analytic trio is finally able to see and face a hidden truth, it is as if this truth is incarnated in the room for all present to intuit and face. This forbearance mysteriously communicated itself to Joe's father, who began to speak about the unbearable memories haunting him, including the death of their first child.

The lamp had an essential symbolic meaning in their respective histories (two individual selected facts). But what lamps signified for each was very different.

"Oh my God, so the central thing for you, Aya, was that a lamp meant safety and intimacy, whereas for me, well with my history …" Joe covered his face with his hands, just murmuring "unthinkable, unthinkable, what happened to my ancestors."

"Oh Joe!" Tears streamed down Aya's cheeks and she held him as he sobbed like a little child.

Yet it was not only realising the meaning which a lamp had for each that helped uncover the truth behind their conflict but the fact that both parties could see and deeply care about both selected facts simultaneously. Aya's father had also suffered horrendous trauma while interned in Java. For Aya, a lamp that was too bright, such as Joe wanted, did not just signify her fear of his withdrawal into his internal world, but the light of interrogation. Ironically, Joe often felt interrogated by Aya. Joe's parents suffered loss that was never mourned leading to a melancholic stasis, a form of lifelessness, as if they lived one foot in the grave of those lost in the camps, including a little baby, as if they feared living when so many had died. Aya's father also never had a chance to work through the trauma of internment. Their unresolved grief in a melancholic form was passed down to their children. The shadow of the lost objects of their parents fell upon them making true intimacy, love, and aliveness impossible (Freud, 1917). The lamp signified both a memorial candle for the previously unburied dead and a light to enlighten their future. To become psychologically married both Aya and Joe had to mourn, and so suffer their parents' psychic pain and unresolved loss, bury their dead, and allow themselves to be fully alive.

## Conclusion

In the couple therapy situation with Aya and Joe, the therapist found that some key Bionian referents facilitated a transformation in a couple whose relationship had been so impacted by inter-generationally transmitted traumatic loss. Bion had himself experienced melancholic reactions to traumatic loss. His own recovery parallels the necessary therapeutic movement made by Aya and Joe in the therapeutic couple work with them. A key referent in the therapeutic couple work was the conjoint selected fact (Pickering, 2008), which was an expansion into the territory of couple therapy of Bion's psychoanalytic application of the selected fact. The conjoint selected fact could be seen to encompass shared unconscious phantasies and a complementary basis for Aya and Joe's object choices. It also encased the malignant dowries that each of the couple brought to the new relationship. In the case of Aya and Joe, an understanding of these intergenerational layers was pivotal in being able to help the couple to process the intergenerational transmission of loss and associated failed mourning that were part of the malignant dowries inhibiting growth in their relationship and transformations in and through love.

The process of intuiting the multivalent symbolic associations of the lamp for Joe and Aya also required a capacity to think the unthinkable, suffer the insufferable. This first took place through analytic reverie, which provided a container to host the realisation of the un-thought known. Through the containment of the co-constructed analytic relationship, the therapist and the couple opened the once closed book of the un-mourned dead, read its terrible contents, and began to transform melancholic evasion of impossible loss into mourning and bearing witness. Shedding its light on the past, the lamp of tragedy became a memorial candle. But a candle also signifies bringing new life and light into places of deadness and darkness. Aya and Joe began to live and love, just as Bion and Francesca had before them.

## Notes

1 This paper is based on material used in a chapter in a forthcoming book: Pickering, J., *Transformations in Love Beyond the Couple: An application of the Clinical Theory of Bion to Couple Therapy*, Routledge.

2 In the clinical examples that are used in this paper, all identifying details have been changed to protect anonymity and confidentiality.

## References

Bion, W. R. (1962). *Learning from Experience.* Northvale, NJ: Jason Aronson (reprinted, 1983).

Bion, W. R. (1963). *Elements of Psycho-Analysis.* London: Karnac.

Bion, W. R. (1967). *Second Thoughts.* London: Heinemann.

Bion, W. R. (1970). *Attention and Interpretation.* London: Tavistock.

Bion, W. R. (1982). *The Long Week-End 1897–1919.* London: Karnac.

Bion, W. R. (1985). *All My Sins Remembered; Another Part of a Life; The Other Side of Genius; Family Letters*, F. Bion (Ed.). London: Karnac, 1991).

Bion, W. R. (1991). *A Memoir of the Future.* London: Karnac.

Bollas, C. (1987). *The Shadow of the Object*. New York: Columbia University Press.

Freud, S. (1917). Mourning and Melancholia. *S.E.*, 14: 239–258.

Grotstein, J. (1997). 'Internal objects' or 'chimerical monsters': The demonic 'third forms' of the internal world. *Journal of Analytical Psychology*, 42(1): 47–81.

Pickering, J. C. (2002). Moving metaphors of self. In: R. Meares (Ed.), *The Self in Conversation* (pp. 123–143). Sydney: ANZAP.

Pickering, J. C. (2006). Who's afraid of the Wolfe couple: The interlocking traumatic scene. *Journal of Analytical Psychology*, 51(2): 251–270.

Pickering, J. C. (2008). *Being in Love: Therapeutic Pathways through Psychological Obstacles to Love*. London: Routledge.

Pickering, J. C. (2012). Bearing the unbearable: Ancestral transmission through dreams and moving metaphors in the analytic field. *Journal of Analytical Psychology*, 57(5): 576–596.

Pincus, L. (1962). *The Marital Relationship as a Focus for Casework*. London: Tavistock.

Stroebe, M., Schut, H., & Stroebe, W. (2005). Attachment in coping with bereavement: A theoretical integration. *Review of General Psychology*, 9(1): 48–66.

Chapter 7

# Some considerations regarding the impact of early parental loss on adult couple functioning

*Catriona Wrottesley*[1]

## Introduction

Some bereaved children are fortunate in having a secure relationship with their lost parent prior to their death that may afford some protection against a melancholic response. This appears not to have been the case in the female partners in the couples to be discussed. In addition, these women did not have a surviving parent who was able to share their own grief in a way that helped them to mourn; instead, their fathers were preoccupied with their own feelings and were unable to relate to those of their children. Consequently, for these women, as children, the combination of their mother's death and their father's ongoing resultant emotional incapacity represented a traumatic "double loss" (Shane & Shane, 1990) from which they never recovered. In adulthood, each woman was drawn to a partner who had similarly experienced an insufficiency of parental care (although not as a result of parental death) and who, like them, struggled with the effects of narcissistic damage and low self-esteem. In both couple relationships, each of the partners found it difficult to emotionally connect. The partner of each woman resembled an emotionally unavailable paternal object, whilst for her partner she represented a depressed or inattentive maternal object.

Arising from this are two key points that will be illustrated with the following clinical material. The first point is that the original external situation of maternal loss, together with the physical presence of an emotionally absent object (the father), was internalised through the processes of projection and introjection. This was then repeatedly replayed and reinforced in the adult couple relationship, through the same psychic processes. In this way, the past remained alive in an attempt to triumph over loss. A cycle was established that defended against change that was feared, because it was associated with catastrophic loss.

## Clinical example

Mrs X, a lawyer, lost her mother at ten years of age following a car crash. After her mother's death, Mrs X went to live with her father. She had had little opportunity to bond with him because he had divorced her mother when she was a baby. After losing her mother, Mrs X had lived with chronic anxiety, exacerbated by the absence of a containing object. She feared that any happiness or security she had achieved could suddenly be shattered or snatched away. These clinical phenomena, that is, that the disaster which Mrs X feared had, in fact, already occurred, were described in Winnicott's paper *Fear of Breakdown* (1974). After many years of therapy, Mrs X said that while she understood the phenomena, such an understanding was ineffective in allaying her present anxieties. She said, "It happened before and so of course it could happen again. A catastrophe in the past doesn't protect you from a catastrophe in the present or future. More than anything, I just want things to stay the same". In the therapist's view, Mrs X's wish for things to stay the same was a version of a survival-oriented freeze response to danger (D'Andrea, Pole, De Pierro, Freed, & Wallace, 2013; Perry, Pollard, Blakley, Baker, & Vigilante, 1995; Van der Kolk, 1994), also shared by the couple, Mr and Mrs A. Bracha (2004) identifies freeze as one of four fear responses that escalate as "a function of proximity to danger: freeze (hypervigilance) is the first, followed by flight, fight, fright (tonic immobility)" (p. 679). According to Bracha (2004), tonic immobility, a form of paralysis, was referred to in early literature as "playing dead" (p. 680).

An unfortunate consequence of these patients' wishes for "no-change" was indeed a form of paralysis, not only of self-development, but also of development within the couple relationship. Each had experienced a change that was catastrophic which had led to a chronic endeavour to maintain life as "the same" and a form of hypervigilance for potential disrupters of the status quo. This included threats from the therapy to the "closed system" (Fairbairn, 1958, p. 385) of the couple relationship and their shared unconscious world (Bannister & Pincus, 1965). These unconscious worlds consisted of shared phantasies where love, anger, or conflicts would be seen to be dangerous and therefore avoided or defended against. Such couples often fear that talking about difficulties will have disastrous consequences.

The second point relevant to the couples to be discussed further is that a woman, after losing her mother, was left in the care of a physically present, but emotionally absent father, which contributed to the installation of a lifeless internal object. This lifeless object represented *both* the dead mother (whose death was known about and yet unconsciously denied) *and* the experience of a father felt to his child to have been only half-alive. Andre Green's concept of the "dead mother" is helpful here in thinking about the installation of such an object at the centre of the ego. This obstructs the growth of the self, resulting in a developmental arrest and a potential turning away from life.

## On the brink of catastrophe

In Shane and Shane's (1990) view

> it is not the failure to mourn *per se* that is primarily pathogenic, as has been suggested in the classical child analytic literature; rather, it is the absence of an empathic self-object milieu at a time of crucial need that constitutes the chief pathogenic factor for a child who loses a parent. (p. 119)

What they refer to as an "empathic self-object milieu" is one which supplies needs vital for the development of self-esteem. Without these supplies, the child's emotional and psychological development is impacted in such a way that she may never be able to fully recover from the loss.

The term "self-object" derives from Kohut's self-psychology (1977) and neatly encapsulates the child's need for an empathic object in order to regulate feelings and establish a cohesive sense of self. The self psychology term "self-object" (Kohut & Wolf, 1978, p. 413), captures the way a young child regards his, or her, parent or caretaker as a part or an extension of himself or herself. While these parental functions, originally provided by the significant other and in an adequate caretaker environment, gradually become internalised by the child, in the absence of such an "empathic self-object milieu", these women developed feelings of low self-worth that are characteristic of melancholia. They also developed a form of shame that Cartwright (2010) suggests "emerges from a systematic undermining of the self often associated with various forms of trauma or more subtle, but undermining, patterns of relating" (p. 195). Mrs X, for instance, spoke of her feelings of shame that her mother had died. Somehow, in her mind, it became her fault. She said,

> "I felt that if I had been a different kind of child – prettier, better behaved, and more lovable, my mother would still be alive. If I had been different, my father might have taken care of me better after Mum died. Growing up, more than anything, I wanted to be part of a 'normal' family to put things right again. That's why I married straight after university and had children so young."

In adulthood, children with such a self-reproachful melancholic response to loss experience constant anxiety about "doing something wrong" or of "not managing" and fears that "people will be angry" with them.

In the external world, time moved on and these patients chronologically became adults. However, internally and emotionally they felt themselves to be children living in an adult world. It is as if time had stood still. As Bell (2006) describes

> the capacity to mourn and to bear guilt and loss are essential to the ability to fully apprehend oneself as existing in time … Where this capacity is lacking, existence in time is replaced by the construction of an illusory world in which time does not exist. Life in this illusory world is accompanied by a permanent sense of dread of being exposed to reality, felt as a catastrophic

> confrontation with a deteriorated and damaged world, a breakdown always threatening and always being evaded. (Bell, 2006, p. 803)

## The lure of the crypt

As with Mrs X, when the mother of another patient, Mrs A died, outwardly there was catastrophic loss and change. Internally there was a related catastrophic loss, which was unconsciously denied. Psychic energy was then channelled into preventing further change, now associated with catastrophe. Abraham and Torok (1972) differentiate between the idea of the introjection of the dead loved one and incorporation of it. In their view, introjection enlarges the ego when the loved other dies and the subject introjects into the self, those qualities valued in the other into the self. Incorporation, on the other hand, a more primitive psychic mechanism, is associated with a poorly differentiated sense of self; the ego takes the lost object inside and builds a wall around it in the psyche to create what Abraham and Torok (1975) term a "crypt", which they define as "a sealed-off psychic place" (p. 141). Incorporation is thus viewed as problematic, as the subject has been unable to accept the loss and there is an attempt to keep the lost object alive inside, secretly entombed: "A whole world of unconscious fantasy is created, one that leads to its own separate and concealed existence" (Abraham & Torok, 1972, p. 130). They vividly describe the psyche's refusal of the loss: "in order not to have to 'swallow' a loss, we fantasise swallowing (or having swallowed) that which has been lost, as if it were some kind of thing" (1972, p. 126).

In his memoir, *Love of Beginnings*, the French philosopher and psychoanalyst Jean-Bertrand Pontalis described how as a child, in secret, he attempted to hold onto his dead father and to the relationship they had had in life. This was made possible by a photograph taken of the two of them together, three days before his father's death.

Pontalis describes,

> A father and his son, a man standing next to a child, one hand resting on a shoulder. They're not speaking to each other, they're being photographed … it's going to represent them, to make them present together, for all time. Three days later my father died. And in order to keep my father, to hold him and hold myself with him, once again I became silent. No longer, this time, through a massive rejection of language, but in order to speak only with him in secret. Silence of death to bring the dead back to life. The only way to perpetuate the hand on the shoulder, the shoulder under the hand. (Pontalis, 1993, pp. 23–24)

Linked to this idea, it is proposed that for Mrs A and Mrs X to have fully rejoined the world of the living, including the world of relationships, would psychically equate to abandoning their mother objects and their bereaved child-selves. In this way they remained, by their mothers' sides, as will be illustrated in the session material that follows. For these patients, this secret preservation of the dead parent was deep within the self that housed the ego. As a result, the couple relationship of each of these women, who was preoccupied by the death of her mother, was deprived of a vital aspect of herself and as a consequence failed to thrive. Unconsciously, an internal struggle took place between their impulse to live and develop and a powerful anti-life impulse that pulled them towards a place in which time, loss, and the necessity and inevitability of change were denied. In this stasis, they remained tied to the experiences of the catastrophic losses of their mothers. Imprisoned in this state of developmental arrest, they had been left in a timeless experience, painfully aware that something vital was missing and unable, without help, to do anything to remedy it. Holding on to the dead mother was thus linked to a failure to achieve psychological separation and individuation compounded by a lack of a compensatory maternal function in their fathers.

## Clinical example

Mrs X described how she felt that a part of her died with her mother and in the course of the therapy this came to be understood as one means by which she unconsciously attempted to preserve their mother–child unity. This contributed to a vague but troubling sense for her that she did not fully belong in the world of the living. Although Mrs X seldom dreamt of her mother, when she did, her mother was still alive but was lost and unable to return home. Divorced, she was finally able to acknowledge that a consequence of the fact that part of her remained with her mother, meant that her couple relationship was deprived of a vital aspect of herself. Mrs X felt relieved of the painful burden of being in a relationship with an emotionally unavailable other, as she experienced her husband to be. The lifting of that burden also meant that she had greater awareness of how emotionally unavailable she herself had been and she was assailed by painful, depressive feelings of guilt about how she treated her husband. She noted,

> "I can see how tied up I was – still am – with my mother. Her death is so much a part of my identity. When I was married I really didn't have headspace for my husband, although that isn't how it felt at the time. I wanted him to take care of me. When he didn't do this in the way I wanted, I thought he was cruel. I know now how cruel he must have felt I was to him. I feel terrible about that, but I also know that at the time I couldn't help myself. I was desperate for something from him that he couldn't give me."

While Mrs X had moved beyond the hurt and bitterness she had previously felt towards her former husband and was more able to see her own contribution to their couple dynamics, her response may also be viewed as another example of a melancholic response to loss.

Green (1983) coined the term the "dead mother" for a clinical phenomenon in which, following maternal depression, "the image of a *living* (author's italics) and loving mother is transformed into a distant figure: a toneless, practically inanimate, dead parent. In reality, the mother remains alive, but she has psychically 'died' for the child" (Kohon, 1999, p. 2). Green refers to the impact on the child of a mother's depression whereby these mothers are physically alive but psychically preoccupied and therefore unavailable to their infants. For the bereaved patients discussed, the internal situation was allied, but different. Their mothers had in reality died, but their deaths were unconsciously denied. What formed in the maternally bereaved patient's mind was an *imago* that transformed the mother into "a toneless, practically inanimate, dead parent" (Kohon, 1999, p. 2). In phantasy, this mother was neither alive nor dead and it was in this condition that she was installed in her daughter's ego, leaving little room for a new love-object, as Mrs X had described. Green notes that "the subject's objects remain constantly at the limit of the ego, not wholly within, and not quite without. And with good reason, for the place is occupied in its centre, by the dead mother" (Kohon, 1999, p. 4).

The relationship of Mr and Mrs A, who came for therapy, afraid they would divorce because of unbearable feelings of coldness and distance between them, illustrates these dynamics. While Mr A's parents were still alive and Mrs A's were not, it seemed that both had internalised a lifeless unresponsive object – the "dead mother".

## Session material: Mr and Mrs A

Both Mr and Mrs A could converse with colleagues, but once they entered their home, silence descended and the emotional temperature plummeted. Each withdrew into a separate "psychic retreat" (Steiner, 1993). As devoted parents, they emerged to attend to their children, but then withdrew. Mrs A's mother had died suddenly of a brain haemorrhage when Mrs A was six years old. Within days, Mrs A presumed, she must have shut down emotionally, while outwardly she continued to function. Preoccupied with his own grief, her father could not help her. As an adult, she continued to feel like a child and longed to be cared for. Mr A was described by his mother as an undemanding baby who never cried and who played alone with his toys. It seemed that early in his life he learned there was no point in crying, as nobody came to attend to him. Mr A's mother, unhappy in her marriage, had briefly left her husband and children, before eventually returning. Mr A's parents divorced before he reached his teens.

## The therapist as a liminal figure

With Mr and Mrs A, the therapist found herself positioned as a liminal figure (liminal from the Latin word *limen* which means "a threshold"), transferentially and countertransferentially occupying positions between, and on either side, of a threshold, that is, between psychological states of aliveness and deadness. For the couple, she represented both the safe familiarity of a dead self-and-object relationship and the dreaded and hoped-for prospect of an alive self-and-object emotional connection. There were continual oscillations between these various states and ways of relating throughout the therapy.

The containing presence of the therapist and the rhythm of weekly sessions provided Mr and Mrs A with some of the reliability and support they had needed, but had not experienced as children. In the therapeutic space, they were able to receive from the therapist something of the parental care for which they had longed, while trying to engage with, and understand what, obstructed development within their relationship. First and foremost, however, they needed to make the therapist understand something of their experience. From the start of the therapy, they involved the therapist in the anxieties of their internal worlds, at the centre of which appeared to be a terror of their children being damaged, as they felt themselves to have been as children.

## Traumatic enactments

This couple lived in a world in which they experienced a sense of disaster that might befall them at any minute. At the time of the first session Mr A phoned to say he could not attend because of a work crisis, while Mrs A sent text messages from the train to say the doors had failed to open at the station and she did not know where she was heading. The therapy was punctuated by the couple's fears of snowstorms, lightning, terrorist attacks, and accidents that might prevent them getting home to their children. There was also the ever-present spectre of illness, angry authority figures, mistakes, and mishaps with irreparable consequences. In terms of the countertransference generated, the therapist was often left waiting, not knowing whether or when the couple would arrive for the session. In these ways the therapist experienced a version of the patient's childhood trauma of waiting for a mother who failed to return home. As Bollas (1999) puts it, there are those "for whom life is a trauma" (p. 94). The frame of the therapy, with its defined limits and regularity, together with the knowledge that their therapist was in the consulting room waiting with them in mind, was important to them. It gave them the sense of something stable upon which they could depend.

The way in which this couple prevented change and their formation of a lively and loving link will now be illustrated and discussed. Their unconscious logic was that it was better not to have a relationship with someone, that is to remain deprived, than to have had it, but then lost it. Mrs A's loss included losing her identity as a bereaved child, and unconsciously her place beside her mother, of whom she had no conscious memories.

## Prevention of a lively and loving link

In a further session Mrs A described an afternoon spent with friends. She had felt open, free and able to have fun. Her pleasure ended when she went home because "as usual" there was no conversation with Mr A. On exploration, it became clear that on the way home Mrs A had already begun to shut down emotionally. By the time she arrived home, she felt too disappointed and angry to talk to Mr A because she "knew" her happy feelings would vanish when she saw him. When Mr A asked Mrs A how her afternoon had been, she snapped "fine" and went silent, and he then withdrew. In this way, the earlier feelings of liveliness within Mrs A and the possibility of her enjoying something livelier with Mr A were squashed and the coldness and distance familiar to both maintained. It seemed that she held the conviction that Mr A would not be interested. Mrs A projected the uninterested and rejecting part of herself into Mr A. When she rejected his overture with a curt "fine" and he withdrew, she felt both vindicated that her conviction had been confirmed, but also rejected and disappointed. His parallel "knowing" that she would be disappointed to see him was similarly confirmed in that interaction. On this occasion, the therapist chose not to interpret their projective system. Instead the therapist said that far from thinking little of Mr A, Mrs A appeared to have considerable expectations of what he could do. She believed him capable of transforming her feelings and of making her feel "open and free". However, before she reached home, a disappointing scenario was playing in her mind and she felt angry and resentful. Mrs A's attacks on Mr A for what she perceived to be his failure to be what she wanted him to be, albeit reinforced in him by her retreating into silence, can be seen as instances of melancholic reaction to loss. While, as Freud (1917) describes, such reactions in an individual are characterised by self-reproach or self punishment, these are often seen in the couple relationship in a projected form often manifesting as accusatory or recriminatory behaviour towards a partner.

The therapist remarked that when Mrs A walked through the door, it did not sound as though the stage was set for fun. Both laughed and agreed. On this occasion, Mr and Mrs A were more available for thinking with the therapist about what each contributed to this destructive dynamic. Mr A acknowledged that his fear of Mrs A's rejection and his resentment of her attitude towards him might have made him ask in a "not very interested way". He felt that she had "that look" when she walked in. This incident was part of a larger pattern in which Mrs A's upset and anger, when Mr A disappointed her, seemed to reassure him at an unconscious level that he could control her and the level of intimacy in their relationship. In this way he reversed his early situation when, as a baby, he played alone with his toys and reportedly never cried or called out to his mother. He was now the mother in the next room who could choose when he would attend to or ignore the baby. It seemed that by means of this reversal he was trying to master the trauma of his early childhood when he lacked the means to elicit his mother's attention and care.

## The cycle of hope and disappointment

While Mrs A hoped Mr A would provide the attention and care that she had so desired to enliven her and make her feel safe, he hoped that she would turn to him with warmth and interest. Their hope, however, as shown, was most often accompanied by a defensive certainty, expressed in terms of "knowing" that the other's response would be cold, uninterested, and dismissive. Because hope and disappointment occurred virtually simultaneously in each subject's mind, the effect was like pressing the brake and accelerator together – the engine stalled. An experience had been had in the mind of the subject, causing the subject to shut down and avoid contact with the other, which then gave the other the experience of being with someone who appeared cold, uninterested, and dismissive. Any contact thereafter was suffused with cold hostility and/or fear. In this way the possibility of change in their couple dynamic was snuffed out before it could come to life.

### *Where is the parent for me?*

A major difficulty for this couple was that both, in different and yet similar ways, experienced early parental loss and Mr A's development, like Mrs A's, arrested at a particular point in childhood. He, too, was looking for a parent in relation to whom he could be a child, unconsciously repeating the painful experience of being a child with emotionally unavailable parents, and rather more consciously to finally have the maternal love and nurturing of which he felt he had been deprived. This created a regressive pull in the relationship. Neither was able to access the idealised parental care longed for from the other. Mrs A talked of her disappointment that Mr A was not "manly". She longed for a man who would scoop her up in his arms and keep her safe. Her wish was for an ideal father who could offer perfect holding and swaddling to a young baby. She demonstrated this by forming a cradle with her arms that led the therapist to wonder whether she was unconsciously expressing a longing for a parental couple with the ability to provide a form of holding that she lost too early.

In the course of the therapy with Mr and Mrs A, a lifeless aspect of their shared internal world manifested and was worked with in a way that will now be described. Gurevich writes,

> external absence is also and at the same time internal absence because it is an absence of and from the self, a dissociation. The psychic trauma of

> absence then transmutes into "something", while the absence itself becomes marked as "nothing", a nothing which in fact operates as though it were "something" with a profound and deeply intrusive impact on the vulnerable self. (Gurevich, 2008, p. 563)

It was this deeply painful something (of nothingness), characterised by coldness, silence, and distance, that Mr and Mrs A needed the therapist to understand. There were no words for "it", but it became clear that the therapist had to be in "it" with them and share the feeling this would go on forever, in order to comprehend "its" awfulness.

The couple's profound withdrawal projectively communicated to the therapist crucial aspects of their internal worlds. The therapist was to experience and contain the feelings of guilt, loss, and abandonment they found unmanageable, along with desire, rage, frustration, helplessness, and hopelessness. Their defences of dissociation and withdrawal clearly caused them enormous pain. However, so too could emotional contact with its threat of rejection and disappointment and of change. Mr A explained why he did not say "hello" and kiss or hug Mrs A when he came home. "I don't because I don't know how she'll react. If she didn't want it, I'd feel rejected and I couldn't ask her why she'd reacted that way because I'm scared she'd say it was because she doesn't love me."

### *A waking sleep*

Dissociation, an adaptive defensive response to threat, can look like a shutting down or, borrowing a descriptor from Rose (1973), a "waking sleep" (p. 593). Mr and Mrs A's unconscious drive was to prevent change and loss that were associated with catastrophe. To this end, they employed dissociative defences that mimicked death and contributed to the lifelessness of the therapy. A major challenge for this couple and for their therapist was that the emotional contact that offered the possibility of being known by another was experienced as a threat. This triggered a self-protective shutting-down that obstructed development in their capacity to relate. Such shutting down could occur at any point. Mrs A would withdraw eye contact and look down at her lap, her expression still and unreadable. Mr A would gaze into the distance, his face clear of expression. This could happen at the start of the session when they sat down. The therapist would be filled with frustration at the prospect of another hour spent trying to reach them and attempting to bring some life into what felt like a deathly space.

## Concordant countertransference

The couple's profound withdrawal created in the therapist uncomfortable and sometimes quite desperate countertransference feelings which were difficult to manage. These compelled the therapist to reflect on the meaning of the experience she was being given and of how she needed to adapt her technique to find a way to reach and work with this couple, who were at times profoundly withdrawn, seemingly overcome by something deadening. The therapist found herself offering thoughts and observations. She coaxed and prodded and waited. When these attempts failed and the therapist enquired what was happening in the silence, Mrs A would say she was in her "shell", while Mr A would say he was not thinking of anything. If the therapist enquired further about Mrs A's feeling that she needed to be in her shell, Mrs A would say it was for protection. If the therapist then asked what she might need to protect herself *from*, Mrs A would say from "prodding". It was apparent how the therapist came to "prod", which led to further withdrawal, and it could feel to the therapist as if she had no option but to settle for this cold "nothingness" and distance between her and the couple. Mr A would continue to maintain his position that he was not feeling anything. Inevitably perhaps, when despair overtook the therapist, she would find herself dissociating in what Racker (1957) terms a "concordant countertransference". In concordant countertransference or identification, based on projection and introjection, instead of an object relationship between therapist and patient(s), there is, as Racker (1957) remarks "an equation of what is one's own with what belongs to another ('this part of me is you')" (p. 164). The therapist also came to recognise her dissociation as a means of struggling to survive almost intolerable experiences of deprivation in the therapy, in which she felt that she was being starved of emotional and meaningful contact. In this way, she received a raw and excruciatingly painful intimation of what it was like for each of them growing up. At such times it felt that an unbridgeable gap had opened between Mr and Mrs A and between her and the couple. So far apart, they were nevertheless bound together in the claustrophobically oppressive atmosphere of the consulting room. Conscious of each minute that ticked by, she would feel that her mind and therapeutic capacity were under attack. Frequently, she felt she had nothing to say and there were times when she wondered whether the therapy should end. In this space, she became Green's "dead mother", a lifeless object unable to connect emotionally with her children. At other times, however, through what Racker (1957) terms "complementary identification", defined as the treatment of the therapist as "an internal (projected) object" (p. 165), the therapist identified with this projected internal object and felt herself to be a child dependent on lifeless objects for emotional connection. However, the therapist learned that when overcome by such feelings of hopelessness, she firstly had to take care of the part of herself that had been overcome by deadening projections. The therapist would try to awaken her thinking mind to maternally care for the part of her that had been overwhelmed by a sense of futility and a dread that nothing would ever change. On one occasion, she interpreted her sense that there was a conflict in the couple between the part that wanted change and had brought them to therapy, and the part that was opposed to change. In response, Mrs A became upset and said that she found the idea "strange" that the therapist would believe that significant change was possible for them, given what they had experienced as children. The following week, she told the therapist that she had broken down crying after the session and had felt so desperate that she had wanted to hurt herself. She thought the therapist was saying that she would have to forget about the "little girl" inside her, a paternal transference, and she had been very frightened of what that might mean. Initially she had sought comfort from Mr A in the form of a hug, but then wanted to be alone. This was possibly a re-enactment of her experience with her father following her mother's death. Mr A withdrew from Mrs A also during the week, but when they returned he said to the therapist that he thought she needed to have said what she did. On reflection, the therapist considered her interpretation as insufficiently processed countertransference feelings arising out of frustration and the desire to escape from claustrophobic stasis. The couple's desire for life had been projected and was being held in the therapist.

## Working through the "dead mother" countertransference

Joan Symington's paper (1985) on primitive omnipotent defences has been particularly helpful in trying to work with this couple's conflict between their need to hold themselves together in a way that prevented change and progress, and their wish for growth and change in their relationship. Symington, drawing on the work of Esther Bick, writes about how "primitive omnipotent defences … are used by the baby to hold himself together when there is no available containing object" (p. 486). Mr and Mrs A had relied on these defences to survive all of their lives and were understandably very fearful of what it might mean to relinquish them. These omnipotent defences were deployed to manage "catastrophic fear…of a state of unintegration and spilling out into space and of never being found and held together" (Symington, 1985, p.481). While the effect of their resistance to the therapy and the potential for development and change were destructive, the primary unconscious aim was not. Rather, the resistance arose out of these primitive omnipotent defences and its unconscious purpose was to hold the precarious self together. While behaviour destructive to their selves, each other, and the therapy needed to be addressed and challenged, Symington's point is that these defences are in "the service of survival" (Symington, 1985, p. 483). If destructiveness had been addressed without addressing this need for self-protection, the couple might have simply felt attacked with resultant fortification of defences. Interpretations needed to address both destructiveness and self-protection. The therapist found that when she made this link, Mr and Mrs A felt more contained and understood.

There were times, however, when words simply did not seem to reach this couple in any meaningful way. It became clear that standard psychoanalytic practice, based in words and insight-oriented interpretation, was not sufficient on its own. The therapist needed to find other ways to work with her own and the couple's shared predicament. What follows now is a brief description and discussion of some of the technical adaptations made by the therapist in the light of her growing awareness, as a result of having worked through her "dead mother" countertransference, that she must take the lead in order to stay alive and available to her couple.

## Technical considerations in working with lifelessness

At times when the couple had withdrawn, the therapist felt very dependent upon her own internal capacities and imagination to remain alive in the session. She found that when she entered a state of reverie (Ogden, 1997a, b), she could be receptive to the feelings, thoughts, and images that arose from within herself. When she felt she might have something potentially useful to say in relation to what she sensed the couple might be struggling with, she would try to put into words something of what had arisen within her.

She had come to realise that her previous attempt to provide a receptive space in the therapy, into which Mr and Mrs A might enter, may have been unconsciously experienced by them as "waiting for something to happen" and that this mimicked their own passivity in relation to initiating interaction. She had in effect joined them in the impasse, rather than offering them something different which was after all what they had sought in presenting for treatment. It seemed to the therapist that at times such as these, the couple wanted to follow the therapist, not for *her* to follow *them*. She needed a more active approach to enable something more alive between them. The therapist was to take the lead.

## Therapist as "initiator"

Bollas (1993) describes the way in which the mother will often take the lead and present an object to her infant – at first the breast or a toy. He describes this as "a specific act of intelligence" (1993, p. 402), an action replicated by Winnicott (1941) with his example of a spatula as a presented object. Bollas notes:

> The object mother is not only … a "responder", but also an initiator. The point that he makes is that her "provision" of an object – even a new one – will be felt *by the infant* to be a response to his desire or need, insofar as he lives for a few months within an illusion that those objects that show up ready for use do so as a result of his wishes. (Bollas, 1993, p. 403)

In a similar vein, Levine (1999) suggests that interpretations may also be offered in the manner of the example of Winnicott's spatula.

> In holding out the interpretation as an object of his/her own contemplation and interest, the analyst allows the patient the freedom to either join in the investigation – begin to play with and explore the interpretation on his own – or let it pass by without seeming interest. (p. 45)

It was in this manner that the therapist began to offer Mr and Mrs A an image or observation, in the same way as Winnicott offered his spatula (1941), by placing it in the space between herself and the couple for them to pick up or not. At times, she felt herself to be like Mr A as a little boy playing alone with his toys, but at other times she could be startled by the appearance of their interest when they looked up, alert and ready to play with what she had offered. The therapist then discovered the couple's warmth and playful sense of humour, whereby they could quite readily laugh with each other and with her. This spontaneity, ease, and freedom to play rarely lasted long; sometimes it dissipated by the time they reached the car following the session, while at other times it lasted a number of days, or even a week. Nevertheless, these occasions gave the therapist hope that they might eventually enjoy a greater sense of ease within their relationship and feel more connected. A hopeful sign came when they both began to say that they were no longer afraid they would divorce.

## Conclusion

The focus of this chapter was on the effect of the traumatic loss of a parent (mother) as a young child and the capacity for coupling as an adult. In particular, it addresses the traumatic "double loss" (Shane & Shane, 1990) experienced by women who lost *both* their mothers, through death before the age of 11, and who were also left with fathers who were unable to emotionally relate to their daughters. Each of them subsequently married a man who found it difficult to emotionally connect and who resembled the emotionally absent, internal parental object. In this way, the past remained alive in the present and change was feared and defended against in their relationships. The way in which the installation of a lifeless internal object, as a "dead mother", contributed to a turning away from a lively engagement in their couple relationships has been described. In the couple therapy, the lifeless internal object moved between the couple and therapist and an account was given of the therapist's working-through, of the "dead mother" countertransference, in order to find a way of working that offered the hope of something more alive within both the couple and the therapy.

## Note

1 The author is grateful to Mrs X, and also to Mr and Mrs A, who have generously given permission to write about their therapy. All identifying details are omitted or changed to preserve confidentiality.

## References

Abraham, N., & Torok, M. (1972). Mourning or melancholia: introjection versus incorporation. In: N. T. Rand (Ed. & Trans.), *The Shell and the Kernel, Volume 1* (pp. 125–138). Chicago & London: The University of Chicago Press, 1994.

Abraham, N., & Torok, M. (1975). "The lost object – me." Notes on endocyryptic identification. In: N. T. Rand (Ed. & Trans.), *The Shell and the Kernel: Renewals of Psychoanalysis, Volume 1* (pp. 139–156). Chicago, IL: University of Chicago Press, 1994.

Bannister, K., & Pincus, L. (1965). *Shared Phantasy in Marital Problems.* London: Institute of Marital Studies.

Bell, D. (2006). Existence in time: development or catastrophe. *Psychoanalytic Quarterly*, 75: 783–805.

Bollas, C. (1993). An Interview with Christopher Bollas. *Psychoanalytic Dialogues*, 3 (3): 401–430.

Bollas, C. (1999). Dead mother, dead child. In: G. Kohon (Ed.), *The Dead Mother* (pp. 87–108). London: Routledge.

Bracha, H. S. (2004). Freeze, flight, fight, fright, faint: Adaptationist perspectives on the acute stress response spectrum. *CNS Spectrums*, 9(9): 679–685.

Cartwright, D. (2010). *Containing States of Mind: Exploring Bion's 'Container Model' in Psychoanalytic Psychotherapy.* London: Routledge.

D'Andrea, W., Pole, N., De Pierro, J., Freed, S., & Wallace, D. B. (2013). Heterogeneity of defensive responses after exposure to trauma: Blunted autonomic reactivity in response to startling sounds. *International Journal of Psychophysiology*, 90(1): 80–89.

Fairbairn, W. R. D. (1958). On the nature and aims of psychoanalytical treatment. *International Journal of Psycho-Analysis*, 39: 374–385.

Freud, S. (1917). Mourning and Melancholia. *S.E.*, 14: 239–258.

Green, A. (1983). The dead mother. In: *On Private Madness* (pp. 142–173). London: Karnac, 2005.

Gurevich, H. (2008). The language of absence. *International Journal of Psychoanalysis*, 89: 561–578.

Kohon, G. (1999). Introduction. *The Dead Mother* (pp. 1–9). London: Routledge.

Kohut, H. (1977). *The Restoration of the Self.* New York: International Universities Press.

Kohut, H., & Wolf, E. S. (1978). The disorders of the self and their treatment: An outline. *The International Journal of Psychoanalysis*, 59(4), 413–425.

Levine, H. B. (1999). The ambiguity of influence: Suggestion and compliance in the analytic process. *Psychoanalytic Inquiry*, 19(1): 40–60.

Ogden, T. (1997a). Analyzing forms of aliveness and deadness. In: *Reverie And Interpretation: Sensing Something Human* (pp. 21–63). London: Karnac, 1999.

Ogden, T. (1997b). *Reverie and Interpretation: Sensing Something Human* (pp. 135–154). London: Karnac, 1999.

Perry, B. D., Pollard, R. A., Blakley, T. L., Baker, W. L., & Vigilante, D. (1995). Childhood trauma, the neurobiology of adaptation, and "use-dependent" development of the brain: How "states" become "traits". *Infant Mental Health Journal*, 16(4): 271–291.

Pontalis, J.-B. (1993). *Love of Beginnings.* London: Free Association.

Racker, H. (1957). The meanings and uses of countertransference. In: B. Wolstein (Ed.), *Essential Papers on Countertransference* (pp. 158–201). New York and London: New York University Press, 1988.

Rose, G. J. (1973). On the shores of self: Samuel Beckett's "Molloy"—irredentism and the creative impulse. *Psychoanalytic Review*, 60(4): 587–604.

Shane, E., & Shane, M. (1990). Object loss and self object loss: A consideration of self psychology's contribution to understanding mourning and the failure to mourn. *Annual of Psychoanalysis*, 18: 115–131.

Steiner, J. (1993). *Psychic Retreats: Pathological Organisations of the Personality in Psychotic, Neurotic, and Borderline Patients*. London: Routledge.

Symington, J. (1985). The survival function of primitive omnipotence. *International Journal of Psycho-Analysis*, 66(4): 481–487.

Van der Kolk, B. A. (1994). The body keeps the score: Memory and the evolving psychobiology of posttraumatic stress. *Harvard Review of Psychiatry*, 1(5): 253–265.

Winnicott, D. W. (1941). The observation of infants in a set situation. *The International Journal of Psycho-Analysis*, 22: 229–249.

Winnicott, D. W. (1974). Fear of breakdown. In: C. Winnicott, R. Shepherd, & M. Davis (Eds.), *Psychoanalytic Explorations* (pp. 87–95). Cambridge, MA: Harvard University Press, 1992.

Chapter 8

# Mourning and melancholia and the couple experience of a miscarriage

*Carl Bagnini*

## Introduction

When loss is related to the death of a person with whom there has been an attachment, a couple is usually able to share its grief in the company of supportive others. However, in the event of the loss of an unborn baby, such support is compromised by the absence of shared memories of the relationship with the deceased. In the unique circumstance of loss through a miscarriage, Casement's (2000) comment, "there are those who mourn in ways not recognized by others" (p. 1) is very apposite. In this regard it is important to acknowledge that "grief is a reaction to loss, while mourning is how we process the grief" (Leader, 2009, p. 26). Processing grief is more challenging for those couples with psychological vulnerabilities where the ego is poorly integrated.

In Chapter 1 reference was made to Freud's assertion that an integrated ego is required for mourning to be resolved, whereas in melancholia it is an un-integrated ego (with its associated undifferentiated self-object relations) that is assailed by persecutory feelings and associated guilt for having hated the lost object. The psychoanalyst or psychotherapist therefore needs to address with the couple the issues that complicate mourning the loss following miscarriage.

The therapeutic goal of accomplishing mourning can, however, be hampered by a repressed awareness of the miscarriage and associated symptoms and defences. For example, when a secret miscarriage has not been revealed, the couple is unable to link its state of mind to the intensity of the presenting conflict, chaos, or suffering. The therapist facilitates the therapeutic process by making sense of the history of both of the individuals as that history gradually unfolds, while working with the immediate affective experience of the couple in the session. When a miscarriage is ultimately acknowledged, the empty space that it creates needs to be carefully "delivered" into the therapeutic conversation. To achieve this, couple imaginings, fantasies, unmet dreams and ambivalences require sensitive exploration.

The vignettes described in this chapter illustrate the importance of the therapist's attempts to hold and contain the couple (see also Chapter 3) and to utilise his countertransference as a way of assisting the couple to connect with their unprocessed affect. The impact of inter-generationally transmitted and childhood-based trauma on mourning following a miscarriage is also examined.

## Miscarriage: a brief survey

Miscarriage, also known as spontaneous abortion and pregnancy loss, is the natural death of an embryo or foetus before it is able to survive independently. In women under the age of 35 the risk is about 10%, while it is about 45% in those over the age of 40. Risk begins to increase around the age of 30. About 80% of miscarriages occur in the first 12 weeks of pregnancy (the first trimester). The underlying cause in about half of these cases involves chromosomal abnormalities. Other conditions that can produce similar symptoms include an ectopic pregnancy and implantation bleeding. Pregnancy loss refers to the unexpected loss of an unborn baby. It can occur for any number of reasons, most of which have little or nothing to do with the behaviour of the mother or any other party.

Doctors and patients do not generally use the term "pregnancy loss" to refer to the intentional ending of an unwanted pregnancy (Danielson, 2016). Generally, pregnancy losses fall into one of four categories: miscarriage, stillbirth, birth loss, and medically-based termination. Because most pregnancy losses are random occurrences and the couple can usually go on to have a normal pregnancy, doctors do not normally complete medical testing following a single loss. However, when pregnancy loss occurs two or more times in a row doctors label it "Recurrent Pregnancy Loss" (RPL), or recurrent miscarriage, and more investigations are usually conducted. Sometimes the mother (or father) may have a treatable medical condition contributing to the losses. Regardless of the category, pregnancy losses are emotionally devastating, carrying deep psychological impacts and scars for the mother and father and support is often crucial (Raphael-Leff, 2001, 2013).

In each situation of a lost baby, couples become overwhelmed and their prenatal attachment identities as procreative partners are threatened (O'Leary & Thorwick, 2008). One result of a miscarriage is that a new pregnancy may result in the mother feeling unable to bond with the new foetus due to insufficient mourning of the prior loss.

## Couple psychotherapy following miscarriage

The psychoanalyst or psychoanalytic psychotherapist, who is well placed to assess the risk of an unresolved grief reaction, needs to be alert to a couple developing melancholic preoccupations concerning their unborn but imagined baby. This can be associated with the couple prematurely foreclosing their grieving process, paralleling the experience of their miscarriage.

For couples in whom there are psychological vulnerabilities, miscarriage and multiple miscarriages can result in an experience of the loss of an unborn baby being felt as a loss of a part of themselves. In this type of melancholic reactions the mother, for example, can lose her sense of herself as a part of a creative couple. In such instances, the mother's desperate helplessness at her inability to furnish nurturing may cause hostility that is felt towards a perceived persecuting foetus to be displaced onto their partner. Melancholia, as distinct from mourning, thus represents the darker side of loss (Bagnini, 2012). Following a miscarriage symptoms of melancholia, such as self-recrimination and a sense of impoverishment, may remain below the surface of the couple's conscious interactions. In melancholic reactions, the initial sadness felt in response to miscarriage may turn into rage and guilt and then become expressed in erratic mood swings. Initially, a couple may appear stoic or one partner may carry the emotion while the other appears relatively unaffected.

Mourning presents special difficulties for couples that have a reduced capacity for reflecting on the reality of the miscarriage and for symbolising the loss. This is because a capacity for symbolic representation is a necessary ingredient for healing. In place of an awareness of reality, powerful defences may be employed. These defences may include ignoring ambivalent feelings connected to the lost baby, manic flights from sadness, attacks on the self or the marriage, rushing into another pregnancy to produce a "replacement" child (Reid, 2007), affairs, or clinging to family members and distancing oneself from one's partner.

It is important to consider where the therapist might begin with couples whose problems are linked to unmourned loss following a miscarriage. This decision is primarily influenced by whether or not the couple identifies the problem as related to the miscarriage. Couples frequently present with other difficulties, unaware of the significance of a miscarriage as a factor influencing their difficulties.

The psychoanalyst or psychoanalytic psychotherapist aims to work with miscarriages from the *inside-out,* thinking about the symbolic meaning to the couple of the *womb* (container) and its inability to nurture and birth a baby. The *outside-in* refers to the couple's initial presentation of their relationship that is represented by the conscious concerns that brought the couple to therapy. The therapist and the couple are involved in an oscillating process that begins with the couple setting the direction that best serves their immediate needs. The therapist understands that there may be unrepresented unconscious layers to the narrative not yet in view, and that the suffering with which they present might be the result of collective developmental impasses and traumatic residues arising from the couple's individual family legacies.

A psychoanalytic approach to assessment in the event of a miscarriage involves reviewing the medical details of the course of pregnancy and of the miscarriage. It also takes into account the state of the couple relationship prior to the pregnancy and miscarriage. Focused attention is given to each partner when miscarriage is the presenting problem, as a history of losses can strongly influence the present circumstances. Individual and couple transferences are utilised as a means of recognising repetitions of relationship difficulties.

In establishing the couple therapy it is important to note any indications of the use of repression or denial (Coltart, 1987), as well as to be aware of the impact of current and past obstacles affecting the couple's development. In addition, the therapist gathers and reflects on the multiple transferences and countertransference responses as they are aroused by their anxieties, defences, and use of the therapist.

Psychoanalytically-oriented treatment is valuable to couples experiencing miscarriage in that it offers the couple adequate time, careful listening and holding in order to discover the relevant unconscious dynamics whose elucidation are crucial in order to facilitate mourning.

## Couple responses to the conception of a baby

The impact of lost pregnancies cannot be separated from the conscious and unconscious phantasies associated with conceiving a baby. These are influenced by each partner's "dream space", their individual baby-hoods, hopes, fears, and ambivalences about a future family.

When these phantasies are of a persecutory or paranoid nature they can powerfully influence the level of distress when the foetus does not develop to term. For example, a physically fit pregnant woman tearfully admitted guilt feelings in response to her hatred of the prospect of relinquishing her concept of a perfect body to the growing foetus. When the pregnancy resulted in a miscarriage she suffered strong guilt feelings concerning how these phantasies might have damaged her foetus.

It is also important to recognise the impact of the father's phantasies concerning conception when this results in a miscarriage. In one couple where there had been an intense pressure to conceive, the husband reported with frustration and anger that he felt as if sexual intercourse had been his only role. Pressures on the couple for procreation had taken a toll and when the miscarriage ensued he carried a terrible sense of failure surrounding his contribution to the conception.

For some men, the pleasure of being the only other in the relationship begrudgingly gives way to an anticipated sharing of his wife with a baby. Threats to one's narcissism and fears of giving up the exclusive dyad can surface, along with conflicts between intimacy and individual strivings that can result in complex reactions to loss. Sometimes a wife's procreative power may also be envied, even though the father should be able to join in the creative experience of the pregnancy.

## Psychic phantasies and blocked mourning

We know that following a miscarriage a focus on manifest dynamics is frequently insufficient for assisting couples. In some couples mourning is blocked due to persecutory phantasies about childbirth.

In a couple who had been in weekly therapy for 13 months, a persecutory phantasy emerged concerning displacements of earlier sibling rivalries in their family. In this couple, such unconscious phantasies which pre-dated their marriage were reactivated by the miscarriage and blocked mourning as a result of a replication of past conflicts in the current relationship. Basic assumptions in this couple, contained in their shared unconscious, facilitated a replication of past conflicted relations involving their parents and siblings. In the melancholic reaction to their miscarriage (that is, in the shared suffering in their link [see Chapter 2]), each partner reverted to child-based phantasies of persecutory babies related to their early histories. Sibling Oedipal rivalry in the husband's childhood resulted in a deep hatred towards his own father. In the wife's developmental history, it was discovered that she was the favourite child in the family, whereas other siblings were less revered. As a couple, these sibling dynamics were re-enacted in the form of a dance whereby the husband took the lead and his wife followed in a more subservient position. In this way, she could avoid the guilt related to her childhood experience of being special and protect her husband from the risk of feeling wounded. In a complementary fashion, her husband managed his rivalry with his more socially attractive wife, by keeping his jealousy in check.

In the transference-driven situation of the couple therapy, the therapist was perceived by the husband as preferring his wife, while he felt relegated to the position of a patient who was less valued. In a manner revealing the nature of her internal object relations, the wife in the couple, who had secretly enjoyed the therapist's attentiveness, managed her aroused guilt feelings by suddenly joining the husband's attacks on the therapist. In this way, she repressed how much she enjoyed being the special patient/preferred sibling. In a replication of these past persecutory relationships, the couple became united against the therapist. They united, however, not in mutuality, but in collusion, projecting their helpless incompetence and guilt into the therapist, with accusations stemming from the paranoid–schizoid realm in both of them. The therapist managed this attack on him by processing his countertransference, thereby enabling containment rather than retaliation. Their paranoid–schizoid response indicated the severity of the couple's psychopathology and their related developmental anxieties (see Chapter 4). These challenging issues needed to be faced before they could begin to mourn their lost pregnancy.

As the therapy progressed, the therapist found a moment and broke into the projective process of the couple by admitting he had realised that both were very upset, that from their points of view the treatment was failing. Working from his countertransference and linking this to their respective developmental histories, he suggested to the couple that he had missed a very troubling and painful aspect of their early experiences. He further suggested that as their therapist he had not protected them from fears of competition and guilt, instead leaving them having to protect each other. He noted that this could account for their angry mistrust of him. At that moment, the husband paused and admitted that he was fearful the treatment would fail and that he was angry with the therapist for playing favourites. Looking sheepish, he went on to ask his wife if she felt he was correct. She looked away and then at the therapist, then back to her husband, and acknowledged that she was feeling anxious about their inability to deal with feelings related to the miscarriage. She reported that the couple only spoke about the baby in the sessions. Looking at her husband she began to cry and wanted to know if he hated her for wanting the child. They went on to discuss their fear of triggering a breakdown if either partner spoke openly of what the pregnancy had evoked in them. This breakthrough, based on the therapist's countertransference, facilitated insights into the connections between their past and present traumas and the nature of their unconscious pact or their link (see Chapter 2) which fostered their mourning process.

The psychoanalyst or psychoanlytic psychotherapist needs to explore clinically relevant phantasies and dreams related to issues such as fertility, pregnancy, and the parent–child relationship. In the case of miscarriage these can be important indicators of underlying ambivalence. An important consideration is whether such ambivalence was active or dormant before the pregnancy, and whether it has been reactivated by the miscarriage. This requires the therapist to also consider whether intergenerational losses and miscarriages have been emotionally processed within the family. These issues must be factored into the clinical exploration of the couple's ability to cope with a miscarriage and also how their past histories impinge on their capacity to mourn.

## Intergenerational trauma issues and miscarriage

The coping capacity of a couple dealing with a miscarriage can be affected by intergenerational secrets related to object losses, that they may be felt but not known. In the case of a couple, Ann and Joe, repressed experiences were central to the couple's difficulties in mourning a miscarriage. Ann's mother had suffered two miscarriages which were never spoken about in the family. When Ann's mother was ten years old, her mother's untreated, post-partum depression was explained as fatigue. As an adult, after a series of painful ectopic pregnancies which were medically, but not emotionally resolved, Ann complained of excess nervous energy. She seemed to quickly recover after each miscarriage and presented an air of normality and high functioning. Ann and Joe's sexual relations resumed, now with the addition of unusually increased libido in Ann, which Joe found appealing. In the absence of other children, he also enjoyed her exclusive attention. Ann's unmetabolised and repressed anxieties about her mother's inability to function for long periods had been traumatic, resulting in her high energy, as a displaced fear of depression. The immediate circumstances of coping with miscarriages triggered these traumatic memories from her childhood. The anxiety about her mother she could not access prior to couple treatment ultimately came into conscious awareness in the sessions, thereby rendering it accessible for transformation.

Another important issue for the psychoanalyst or psychoanalytic psychotherapist to consider, in couples suffering with an unmourned loss of a miscarriage, is the effect of unresolved Oedipal issues. In the case described above, in addition to the intergenerational trauma, there were also significant Oedipal elements. The increased sexual appetite that Joe saw as a positive, actually had a manic quality which was related to an unresolved Oedipal issue related to her father, to whom Ann had turned to as a child during her mother's depression.

## The use of the psychoanalytic frame and stance

The psychoanalytic frame and stance (See also Chapter 4) provide the couple with a constant and reliable reflective space in which the unexpected can be safely contained. This creates the potential for the couple to develop an understanding of how their miscarriage has impacted on their immediate and long-standing relationship issues. Consider, for example, a couple, Maria and Fernandez, who were referred after a miscarriage which occurred in the second year of their marriage. During a flare-up of anger and a polarisation of blame in the couple, long-repressed pain surfaced in fights over their in-laws and money. The couple miscarried in the context of a marriage that was forced by an unintended pregnancy during their courtship. Moral conflict added to the couple's dilemma because they were staunchly Catholic and marriage was deemed to be the only solution to legitimise their sexual relations and pregnancy outside of marriage. Their baby was miscarried at the end of the first trimester. The wedding was imminent, and the couple felt forced to "do the right thing". They decided not to tell their families about the miscarriage. As the couple had not yet graduated from university, they relied heavily on both sets of parents for financial help. The couple's unacknowledged underbelly of unconscious guilt arose during a session in which despairingly Maria blurted, "I wish I had never been born!"

The therapist felt shaken and thought back to the unplanned pregnancy that had resulted in a miscarriage which had forced them into a premature marriage. In the context of ambivalence about depending on parents and hastening the marriage, no mourning of the lost baby was possible. The couple's unconscious melancholia, arising from the inability to integrate and process the experience of loss (Klein, 1940), produced a hardening of resentments which had not been acknowledged. As the therapist sensitively traced the couple's painful experience to the premarital pregnancy and two miscarriages, their anger softened. As a result, the couple came to realise that the miscarriage, their unacknowledged shame, mutual heartache, and ambivalence about their bond had been repressed, resulting in anger that erupted between them. Subsequently, they could acknowledge and accept their feelings, mourn the loss of their miscarriage, and thus restore their internal objects.

## The use of metaphor – a clinical vignette

Another useful feature of the analytic approach is the therapist's use of metaphor. The therapist may "dream up" images or alternate scenarios when encountering inaccessible material or impasses. Moving through such impasses requires a creative act that can be used to symbolise issues in the relationship. Metaphor enables access to repressed and unacknowledged feelings in the couple. Metaphors are used by the therapist to promote an understanding of unconscious issues in the couple that are central for new learning. The following vignette describes how such a metaphor helped a couple to connect repressed feelings to the traumatic reaction to their miscarriage.

Karin (aged 36 years) and Chuck (aged 38 years) denied emotional forces that had plagued their marriage during a succession of three miscarriages over a five-year period. The problems they presented on intake included drifting apart and preoccupations with maintaining separate lives. Each was likeable, but in a manner that conveyed "don't get too close, just be nice back". After eight months of weekly couple therapy, the premarital courtship was a focus of exploration. One form of shame appeared deeply embedded in Chuck, who had sheepishly admitted ambivalence about the prospects of fatherhood before the marriage. The therapy had addressed the sequence of three miscarriages, but neither partner was capable of amplifying any feelings of sadness or grief. The therapist hypothesised to himself about Chuck: might he be carrying a shameful sense of relief and guilt that there was no baby with whom to compete? Indeed, unacknowledged shame seemed to cast a dark shadow over the couple. Karin's shame involved believing that she was physically defective and in this way let her husband down. She had not, however, picked up his cues of relief, which made him especially devoted and attentive towards her after each miscarriage. When Karin appeared to recover, he withdrew and was sullen. She was solicitous, but silently fuming, in response to strong feelings of abandonment. During the football season, however, they both became excited anticipating each televised game, preparing food and, in doing so, recovering a mutual bonding experience by "rooting" for their team. This provoked a countertransference image in the therapist of a baby at the breast learning to feed. Concealing shame was a painful experience, stoically managed by each partner.

What was inaccessible at this point was the deep unconscious fear each of the couple carried of a perverse aggression that they considered responsible for the miscarriages. Their individual fears stemmed from childhood experiences in large families, wherein there was little consideration for the individual needs of the children. Each partner was the first-born; Chuck and Karin were both raised in families with six children. Each carried responsibility for the surrogate parenting of a succession of siblings. There were expectations in both families that from an early age the eldest child was required to look after his or her siblings. It was striking that each interpreted their role as being that of a "helper", although on close questioning it became clear that their respective roles had also evoked feelings of hatred and resentment. Hating babies was thus a shared, deeply embedded, shame-based affect in the couple.

Following the miscarriage, Chuck's unconscious relief at avoiding the responsibility of being a father was linked to this history. Whilst Karin was consciously dedicated to having a child which ultimately involved multiple miscarriages, she also carried unconscious hatred borne out of her early developmental experience involving premature responsibility for babies. The therapy gradually enabled the couple to consider the possibility that for Karin, having a child was a means of procuring redemption for the deep resentment she felt towards her parents and siblings for an emotionally impoverished childhood. The therapist also silently wondered whether the miscarriages were related to a need to violently evacuate repressed feelings about parent–sibling emotional neglect and childhood helplessness.

In a further session, the couple was uncharacteristically animated about the recent football game they had enjoyed. The usual blunted affect was replaced by a "high five" and solicitation of my interest in their football-bonded animation. The therapist felt saddened when anticipating the short life of the couple's "high". In this way, he was holding the unmourned loss that, as yet, had not been able to be brought into the therapy.

## The discovery of a football metaphor and its application

The therapist had an association during his simultaneous experience of the couple "high" about a football game, while feeling saddened by the unmourned loss of their baby. In American football, the term "miscarry" refers to the improper holding or carrying of a football that results in a fumble, a take-away, or loss of control of the ball. In psychodynamic terms, we might think of the external environment as the opposing players pursuing the ball carrier and threatening the holding capacity of the runner with the ball.

When the couple offered its "high five" reference to enjoying the football game, the football term blended into fumble–miscarry in the mind of the therapist. In a sense, a metaphor was conceived that emotionally connected the couple "high" (the manic defence against the melancholic) with the unmourned loss. The precariousness of the holding environment was applicable in significant ways for the couple as well as the footballers.

Therapeutic use of a sports metaphor may at first have appeared insensitive and strange. However, the metaphor captured the hazards of carrying a football *and* a baby in a language that they were sharing. The new meaning was evoked during a particularly strained therapy with a couple engaged in a collective psychic retreat.

When the therapist shared his spontaneous association – that the "high" was a flight from the couple "miscarrying" (not being able to "carry" the babies to birth) – the couple was able to take up the football metaphor (high as an association to defence, and miscarry as the metaphor for the hidden grief) in relation to their miscarriages. "Miscarry" was the metaphor that provided the image the couple could take in. The hidden and protected were accessed initially by the "high" (excitement and pleasure), but the "miscarry" captured the flight from grief which needed to be mourned. Consequently, they felt sufficiently safe to venture out and connect the therapist's words to the unnamed fears and underlying unresolved grief.

## Conclusions

The cases discussed have explored the influence of historically-transmitted and developmentally-derived trauma on the experience of a miscarriage. They have been presented to illustrate how the object relations therapist can aid couples dealing with unresolved grief associated with miscarriage by working with unconscious dynamics that become accessible within the therapy.

This chapter has highlighted technical measures that are available to the therapist to facilitate meaningful couple contact in such presentations. Examples of these techniques are holding and containing, the use of the therapist countertransference, interpretive flexibility, historicising with empathy and/or reverie, and the use of metaphor. Couple therapy, as a form of re-parenting that involves a moment-to-moment resonance of emotional recognition of injury, terror, and loss, was also highlighted. It is suggested that a successful couple therapy can create a new capacity to restore lost objects, made possible by attention to split-off and projected, as well as repressed, aspects of one's self and experiences.

The cases discussed show that the situation of miscarriage or repeated pregnancy loss (RPL) presents a unique form of loss that poses special challenges to the couple and the couple therapist. This is because the loss of a foetus interacts in unique and intense ways with psychic phantasies and repressed intergenerational trauma that creates a strong pull in the direction of melancholia. However, the psychoanalytic psychotherapist, in attending to the unconscious aspects of the experience, enables a working through of the intense psychic pain associated with such loss and facilitates a more adequate mourning process and the possibility that the object will be restored.

## References

Bagnini, C. (2012). *Keeping Couples in Treatment: Working from Surface to Depth*. Lanham, MD: Aronson.

Casement, P. J. (2000). Mourning and failure to mourn. *Fort Da*, 6: 20–32.

Coltart, N. (1987). Diagnosis and assessment for suitability for psycho-analytical psychotherapy. *British Journal of Psychotherapy*, 4(2): 127–134.

Danielson, K. (2016). "Miscarriage". Healthcare Center, A.D.A.M. Inc. American Accreditation Health Care Commission. Retrieved from www.urac.org

Klein, M. (1940). *Love, Guilt and Reparation and Other Works: 1921–1945. Mourning and its Relation to Manic-Depressive States*. London: Karnac.

Leader, D. (2009). *The New Black: Mourning, Melancholia and Depression*. New York: Penguin.

O'Leary, J. M., & Thorwick, C. (2008). Attachment to the unborn child and parental mental representations of pregnancy following perinatal loss. *Attachment: New Directions in Psychotherapy and Relational Psychoanalysis Journal*, 2: 292–320.

Raphael-Leff, J. (2013). Psychic "Geodes" – The Presence of Absence: 18th Enid Balint Memorial Lecture 2013. *Couple and Family Psychoanalysis*, 3(2): 137–155.

Raphael-Leff, J. (2001). *Pregnancy: The Inside Story*. London: Karnac.

Reid, M. (2007). The loss of a baby and the birth of the next infant: The mother's experience. *The Journal of Psychotherapy*, 33: 181–201.

Chapter 9

# Loss in the everyday life of couples

*Monica Vorchheimer*

## Introduction

Psychoanalytic understandings concerning melancholic reactions to loss have traditionally focused on the individual psyche. In contrast, this chapter focuses on the couple and the link between them. The "link" or *vínculo* conveys what is co-produced between two subjects who are in a relationship with each other (see Chapter 2). It is a source of unconscious meaning that stamps their relationship. It does not belong to either of the participants, but exists by virtue of their subject-to subject relationship.

Couples are challenged in everyday life with many ordinary losses, often experienced at an unconscious level, which need to be worked through in the moment. Some losses may not involve the loss of an external object as in death, but may instead entail the loss of a perceived mutual understanding between partners (the link) that creates crises which might – or might not – be triggered by actual events.

Modern love in the western world is conceptualised as the couple being united by reciprocal love. Looked at in this way, the "being together of couple-life" is rooted in an idealised representation of the togetherness, whose origin the couple can typically trace back to the experience of falling in love. They assume this representation to be shared. The need to believe in this idealised representation of the link is so powerful that partners need to believe that it is not a representation, but an actual reality. This belief – or shared illusion – functions as a form of primary narcissism (Freud, 1914), which brings together into a perfect whole (a paradise) that is otherwise experienced as disaggregated, chaotic, or heterogeneous. This is how falling in love works: as a foundational myth that creates a union of two subjectivities who share the same beliefs about their union. For this to occur, similarities are overestimated and differences are minimised in order that the couple can build up complementarities that lead to a whole set to which they both belong. It represents the creation of "a primary linkage narcissism".

The illusory quality of the narcissistic foundation of couples, based in the belief of the same representation of their link, is also supported by a further illusory assumption, that is, that the couple feels and understands each other in perfect attunement. They believe that they share everything including a past, a history, an origin, values, traditions, memories, and a sense of reciprocity. Everything is believed to be knowable between them and this is the source of their belief that they are a couple that will last forever.

The consequent loss of the idealised coupledom often underpins the presentation of couples who present for treatment, although depictions of this can be found in literature and film. *Night*, a dramatic play by Harold Pinter (1969), beautifully describes in slow motion the lovers' attempt to recover what they conceive as the origin of their love. The play's structure is rather simple, as a dialogue between a married couple aged in their forties. As the couple sit with their coffee they reminisce about when they first met and fell in love during their youth. Pinter exposes some present emotional disjunction between the characters through their dialogue about their past, which they remember differently. This difference is precisely that which gives the audience the sense that the magic of that moment is no longer part of their relationship. However, the couple continues to attempt to recover that mythical first moment of falling in love, a picture of paradise.

While seeking to recover that special momentum, the male partner in the drama recalls that the first time he held his lover was on a bridge; he recalls holding her breasts in his hands. In contrast, his partner has no recollection of the bridge, but remembers a different place where he took her hand and gently stroked it. Their memories wander along images of breasts, backs, eyes, hands, and fingers, belonging to two bodies attempting to be reunited in a unique memory. Words alternate with pauses and silences, trying to grasp the exceptionality of that moment which the couple needs to narcissistically retain.

Nevertheless, their different memories become almost a tragic divide due to the experience of not sharing the same memory and the same scenario (the same mental representation). When differences appear and spoil the magic of the moment, small details become magnified and erotic words invert into vulgarity.

Through their memories they seek coincidences, as if these coincidences will guarantee that there did exist a moment in which they felt the same, were the same, or felt their union to be whole, as a result of their complementarity.

This need to recover the shared illusion is not unique to this couple. Such illusions underpin the initial foundation of every couple; it institutes the couple itself, the sense of an "us". In ordinary life, conversations directed at maintaining the illusion are sooner or later aborted, or if they continue they lead to frustration and annoyance between the couple. In the consulting room, the therapist often witnesses the symptomatic picture of a resulting dissonance, when couples attempt to maintain such a narcissistic link.

Loss is also often thought of as related to trauma, whereby trauma and loss may overlap. Freud (1926) described several universal traumatic situations, which constitute a loss, that are present in normal development. He names castration as an example which, whether by direct or fantasised threat, constitutes the "greatest trauma of his life", or a loss for the male. He also saw the Oedipus complex itself, insofar as it is strongly connected with the castration complex, as constituting a traumatic loss situation. In the same way, the situation of weaning, the loss of faeces, and the birth of siblings also represent paradigmatic traumatic situations. The loss of the other's love, the object's love, the superego's love, are all experiences that Freud conceived as exposing the subject to trauma, the experience of helplessness or a loss of emotional potency. Freud thus argued that trauma not only involved an economic perspective, but he also implicated an intersubjective dimension to it. He described a traumatic situation such as loss as involving an unbinding of libidinal attachments with the lost object. This also presciently implied a link perspective.

In the following discussion, it is proposed that couple difficulties, which are a response to a feeling that something catastrophic and deceptive has occurred, can develop to the point whereby they pose a threat to the loss of the coupledom itself. Whilst this view derives from the author's wide clinical experience in psychoanalytic couple therapy, the current illustration is taken from the movie *45 Years*.

## Psychoanalysis and falling in love

Freud (1914) suggested that from its inception the individual psyche is disaggregated and disorganised; he remarked that at the beginning there does not exist any entity comparable to the ego. He said that the ego had to be developed. He needed this logical assumption in his theory to explain how, in this new psychic state which he named "narcissism", the initial chaos is organised. In the chaos of drives, in the new unity – the ego, there is introduced an organisation where there existed chaos. Freud felt that the primary narcissism of children described as "the paradise of his majesty the baby" as less easy to grasp by direct observation than to confirm by inference. This psychic state (narcissism), he noted, also required resolution (and for self–other differentiation to develop) before object choice, as a basis for a non-narcissistic relationship, could take place.

For the couple to be established, a similar narcissistic psychic operation is initially needed that is capable of uniting two subjects into a unity: the couple. Therefore, lovers need to represent their being-together and they need to assume that the representation of their co-created link is shared. They need to believe that paradise once existed and that in that paradise heterogeneity had built up a homogenous totality: the link, the "we". For this to happen differences have to be neglected, excluded, or only considered as part of their set complementarities. That is, what is alien is considered as not belonging to the "we".

Through this representation of the couple link, the transience of emotional certainty can be denied and instead, as with every identity, the identity of the couple is conceived of as lasting forever and as a source of security. People not only fall in love with partners, but with the narcissistic representation of their togetherness, their love. Therefore, couples do not need an actual loss to occur in order to have an experience of perceived loss in relation to their link. Insofar as illusions can only maintain a temporary hold, the occurrence of certain everyday events can become a manifestation of the loss of their shared inaugural illusion.

## Dealing with the loss of the shared illusion: mourning or melancholia?

In his essay *Mourning and Melancholia*, Freud (1917) examines the differences and similarities of mourning and melancholia, whereby he saw mourning as a normal vicissitude of loss, and melancholia as its pathological outcome. As suggested above, losses that trigger either reaction might not be an actual loss, but a representation, an abstraction, or an ideal (See also Chapter 1). Freud suggested that although there might be a reaction to an object loss, there could also be a more abstract form of loss, one wherein neither the analyst nor the patient may see clearly what has been lost. The patient might know whom he has lost, but not *what* he has lost. Related to this, Freud felt it was the unconscious dimension of the loss, that is the meaning of the loss which determines the response to loss, mourning, or melancholia.

Freud saw melancholia as involving a disturbance of self-regard and impoverishment of the ego that is absent in normal mourning processes. He saw that the ego of the melancholic is affected by a kind of a delusion of mainly moral inferiority whereby the loss impacts on ego functioning. Melancholia involves a remorse and self-reproach that is unconsciously felt to belong to the lost object the ego loves, or has loved or should have loved. In terms of couple psychopathology Freud percipiently noted,

> The woman who loudly pities her husband, to being tied to such an incapable wife as herself, is really accusing her husband of being incapable in whatever sense she may mean this. … Their complaints are really plaints in the old sense of the word. (p. 248)

Freud continued, "an object choice, an attachment of the libido to a person, had at one time existed; then, owing to a real slight or disappointment coming from this loved person, the object-relationship was shattered" (p. 249). The result is not as in mourning, whereby there is a withdrawal of the libido from the object and the displacement on a new one, but an identification with the abandoned object, resulting from the process described as the shadow of the object falling upon the ego (Freud, 1917). It is a logical need in Freud's theorisation to resort to the premise that the lost object was preceded by a narcissistic object-choice. This substitution of identification for object-choice therefore entails a regression to original narcissism.

To some extent, Freud relies on the idea that mourning will be overcome naturally or spontaneously after a certain time, insofar as it is not regarded as a pathological condition. However, in both reactions, the libido's relinquishment of its attachment to the lost object or representations has to occur gradually. The slow process of testing reality and withdrawing emotional investments is painful psychic work which, in the case of melancholic people, is harder to achieve due to unconscious ambivalence towards the lost object.

In terms of these ideas we are also indebted to Melanie Klein (1935), who termed the *depressive position* as a stage of paramount importance in psychic development (see Chapter 1). The infant's response to the awareness of the loss of the object leads to an emotional turmoil, which she considers as melancholia *in status nascendi.* Here Klein follows Freud regarding the uncertainty or indefinable feature of melancholia, which blurs the radical distinction between mourning as a normal process, and melancholia as its psychopathological outcome.

Moreover, Freud's ideas on mourning and melancholia, which follow on from his paper *On Narcissism*, are a fertile source for the understanding of how links are constituted and how discontent within couples can also be understood. The narcissistic foundation of every couple is not a mere repetition of the past, but conversely a new invention co-created by the couple.

In terms of how links are constituted and how discontent within couples can also be understood, Piera Aulagnier introduced the notion of the narcissistic contract. In articulating this concept, she argued that the group expects the subject to take up for himself what the voice of his predecessors stated in order to ensure the permanence and immutability of the group. The group – and we can replace *group* with the couple or family – guarantees transference onto the new member (the child) of recognition received by his predecessors. The child commits to the family link in order to ensure the support his narcissistic libido requires. Each newborn takes on the family burden as a carrier of continuity and reciprocity, on that condition that the group supports a place for this new member. Among the statements that support the narcissistic contract, special attention must be paid to what Aulagnier called "foundational statements" that refer to the discourse about the institution, which affirms its justification and necessity. Narcissistic contracts thus establish what has to be done and what its members are forbidden to do.

Kaës (1994) added to Aulagnier's ideas by proposing that a link imposes restrictions on the subjects who constitute it. These include constrictions regarding the renunciation or abandonment of a part of the subjects' psychic reality. Examples of these restrictions include the renunciation of instinctual aims, giving up personal ideals for the benefit of the other, restriction of beliefs, ideas, perceptive rules, and an adherence to common sentiments and ideals. These are some of the types of restrictions that are imposed when couples form a link.

Every link imposes a series of restrictions and prescribes a way of proceeding. Self-alienation processes are put to the service of (couple) link demands. This is one of the ways of managing the repressed and unrepressed issues that are required for each to maintain his or her link.

The narcissistic foundation of every couple is thus initially based in the positive identificatory dimensions of the narcissistic contract (Aulagnier, 1975). This nurtures the link ideals and, along with the necessary rejection of issues from the link, supports the belief in a shared representation. Such a link is supported by the commonality of defence mechanisms (Kaës, 1994) which excludes certain aspects of the couple relationship, by repression or disavowal, in order to keep an identity that "we *are* this" and "we *are not* this". These unconscious mechanisms determine the relationships which the subjects of a link have co-constructed between themselves and with the set of allowed issues upon which they have agreed. The world of the link is produced with what both subjects must suppress, suspend, or keep repressed which is incompatible with the relationship. This is because what is felt to be alien is felt as traumatic and not possible to be integrated or included.

As such, couples invent a shared origin, a new beginning and, in doing so, also create a new dimension of time. The individual past needs to be reshaped, insofar as that it does not belong to, or is not included in, the representation of the togetherness and therefore its significance needs to be removed.

## Loss portrayed in the film *45 Years*

These processes are well illustrated in the movie *45 Years*. The movie introduces a couple, Kate and Geoff Mercer, the week before the couple's 45th wedding anniversary. The childless couple is happily preparing for a party to celebrate the wedding anniversary, which had been thwarted five years earlier when Geoff required heart bypass surgery. This, however, is interrupted by an unexpected letter which arrives for Geoff, conveying the shattering news that the body of his first love, Katya, has been discovered, frozen and preserved, since 1962 in the glaciers of the Swiss Alps.

Suddenly, Geoff's past intrudes on the couple and the effect is disquieting. Memories flash back. Geoff says in an elliptic way that they had found her, and stresses that his wife knew about whom he is talking. The accident to which Geoff refers is decades old, prior to Kate first meeting Geoff. Although Kate knew of Katya's existence, she had not been mentioned within the couple in years. Geoff is deeply moved by the news and a buried past suddenly comes to life in his mind. He goes out for a cigarette (although they had both previously stopped smoking) straight after receiving the news, as if keeping a space of his own for his memories.

Kate realises that something is going on in his mind, something of which she is not a part, and as he says, it has tainted everything. He desires to journey to Switzerland to see the body, which causes a rift in their marriage. She tries to go on with the party planning, as if nothing had happened, but the illusion of a shared life has somehow collapsed.

The lyrics of a song by the Platters poignantly fills the room; the song refers to true love and how one knows that it is true, since some day everybody will find that all who love are blind. Certainly, all who love are blind, when blindness of differences is felt as the precondition to preserve the sense of togetherness. A certain degree of blindness maintains the illusion of completeness and contributes to the fragility of this shared illusion.

The film shows several ordinary domestic scenes of this couple. They sit in the living room reading and listening to music, as in the past. However, Kate now begins to look upset as if she is wondering if Geoff's thoughts have gone to that unshared, ghostly past. Everything has changed for this timeless and frozen couple. The emotional climate between them has changed.

Geoff unexpectedly goes to town with Kate to buy a book on climate change and its contribution to glaciers melting, reflecting his preoccupation with the news concerning Katya. Kate feels excluded and jealous while his memories are melting and recovered. Something new has entered their relationship and threatens the link between them. It is as if the past has become the present.

Reflecting on their history, Kate notes, that it was a shame not to have photos around the house, and she believes that they didn't see the point of taking pictures of themselves (remember they are a childless couple). Photographs cannot only testify to memories of the past; they can also be a material (frozen) representation of an everlasting couple. Placed on the wall, they can represent an insulation and sensory reassurance against the fleeting emotional experience of belonging to a couple.

Kate compares their naked walls to those of a friend, whose walls are full of pictures of her daughter and grandchildren. The ballroom where their anniversary party will take place is full of historic pictures, full of history, like a good marriage, as the owner of the venue notes. In response, it seems that Kate begins to question if they have a good marriage. Disillusionment has now entered their quiet house and it is as if "paradise" is lost, insofar as Kate feels that Geoff is captured by memories within which she does not belong. Now they have different pictures, but not a common one.

There is a scene where the couple engage in dancing and later in sex after an intimate conversation, sharing their losses, registering the passage of time. But no encounter lasts forever. In the middle of the night Kate wakes up and realises that Geoff has gone to the attic looking for photos of Katya in an old scrapbook. The house then seems to fill with unspoken, hidden ghosts. Kate appears calcified, frozen in an icy rage. She remains affected but silent, and that evening the couple engages in a very superficial conversation during dinner.

As the plot of the movie unfolds, the scene moves to their bed and Geoff recalls the idealised time as a young man, when he was with Katya. He airs his memories and nostalgic reflections, perhaps imagining that Kate and he would find room for these between them. However, it seems that this is not possible. Kate receives his words differently. She hears them as his concrete longings for Katya, and reacts to his idealised memories. Kate's response leads to recriminations based on the fact that Kate didn't know her. When Kate reassures Geoff that she didn't know her, the gap in their respective perceptions crystallises when she asks him whether he would have married Katya if Katya hadn't died.

A couple psychoanalyst might have helped them clarify how they were trapped in an unconscious projective process which distorted the reality of the situation. However, operating on the basis of her archaic object relations (internal links), Kate interprets his retreat as the evidence that he would have preferred Katya instead of her. He feels annoyed and unable to understand what has been evoked in her. This leads to further alienation between them whereupon he finally replies, "Yes". Appearing to be profoundly shaken, he reacts to her question literally and is unable to empathise with her pain. She would like him not to have had a past and he would have wanted her to share his past. It was as if they wished to share the experience without feeling unsettling emotions. As reproaches emerge, Kate and Geoff are no more a frozen couple. Instead, feelings of annoyance, jealousy, and, uneasiness are now parts of their link, threatening their sense of their future as a couple.

Things could have taken a different course in their relationship had they been able to clarify that his memories did not question his love towards Kate and that he could relinquish the past. Moreover, if Kate could have felt that they were not talking about Katya but about him or them, about his nostalgia of other times, of youth or ageing, it would have reframed their experience. Instead, the experience is of a complete collapse and loss of their coupledom.

The following day, she finds photo slides and slips them into the projector and discovers photos of a pregnant Katya, unveiling a disturbing secret. The absence of pictures on their walls is re-signified now in retrospect when Kate finds out that Geoff had kept Katya's pictures and that Katya had been pregnant. However, she keeps this discovery as her secret, probably interpreting this as further evidence of Geoff's false love towards her, a form of infidelity.

Notwithstanding, the party preparation goes ahead. However, Kate remains distant, except when they both engage in watching pictures of their history, which a friend has prepared. She walks along the ballroom constrained, as if watching everything from a distance, as if not belonging. There is a single moment when she seems to recover a different mood; their friend has prepared a blackboard with photos of different historic moments of their lives: their past puppy, shared friends, journeys. They both watch them joyfully, waiting for Geoff to give his anniversary speech, which they expect to bring him to tears.

In his speech Geoff said that as people get older, they seem to stop making choices, and that the choices made when young were pretty bloody important. Like the choice Kate and he made 45 years ago, that day. He goes on saying that things had not always been idyllic. Like all couples, they had their downs as well as their ups. They might all have wished to have done things differently.

As he is caught by deep emotions, he adds that he needed to say that persuading Kate to marry him was the best thing he had ever done, and he was sorry that Kate hadn't always known that. He then broke into tears declaring his love towards her, and thanking Kate for standing by him, and putting up with all his nonsenses, and wishing that long may they continue.

When the couple are invited to the floor for their anniversary dance, Kate looks sad and the final close-up isolates her amid the crush of people on the dance floor. As if she is convinced of her own convictions, a multitude of emotions plays across her face. As the credits appear on the screen the audience wonders what the aftermath of this crisis will be. The challenge for a couple psychoanalyst and such a couple would be to understand this crisis in terms of both the internal and external links.

## Discussion

Freud's premise was that in melancholia, the loss of the object is experienced through a narcissistic lens. Lovers make a narcissistic object-choice when falling in love and while having the feeling of belonging to the couple, they invest in the representation of the couple and their togetherness. That is, they not only fall in love with the other, but also with a special, magical, and supposedly shared representation of the couple. This is what gives their illusory belief its quality of exceptionality and institutes the identity of the couple.

The couple in the movie *45 Years* experience a crisis which can be seen as the effect of the disillusionment in, and consequent loss of, what had been a supposedly shared representation, that is, an illusion of an underlying passionate plenitude. The loss of this representation-object entails a loss in their link. The link in such couples can manifest itself in different ways. A typical manifestation is the type of narrative couples have about their history. When describing their origin or their lives one discovers, in the way in which they have established their link, that there is an attempt to reach an illusory unity.

Reproaches and complaints, as found in melancholia, testify to the narcissistic experience of the loss in the couple. Although these reproaches and complaints are apparently addressed to the partner, they unconsciously stand for the feeling that the idealised representation of the couple has been lost or is being lost. Although they can realise that something has been lost, they are unaware of what has been lost. When the narcissistic mechanisms cannot be maintained, the link itself is felt as being catastrophically threatened.

In the foundation of a stable modern couple, as in every couple, we find an idealised representation of the special origin of their relationship. Hence the past, which did not belong to this shared origin, had to be negated. Individual prehistory had to be coloured as irrelevant in order to provide the couple with a sense of timelessness. The representation of their being together requires a "comm-union" of desires, perhaps including the desire not to have children.

In the movie, the photo of Katya's pregnancy had been violently introduced and the couple's unconscious pact had broken down resulting in a corrosion of their intimacy. A new dimension of time was introduced into the link that required the elaboration of that which had been excluded from the existing set, in order to keep the set as an idealised one.

From this perspective, the opening moments of the film acquire new relevance: Kate was coming back home from her daily walk and comes across an ex-pupil. They exchange greetings and she asks after his children. He answers that his twins had made him wake up early. Kate replies she had forgotten (they were born) and congratulates him. We can conjecture this disavowal of the birth of the twins was connected to the couple's unconscious pact to remain childless. For this to be effective it needed to suppose a "com-union" of renouncement. The photo of a pregnant Katya, which surprises Kate, calls this into question.

Moguillansky and Seiguer (1996) suggest that the sense of belonging to the couple, grounded in a shared belief, is also structured in a triangular scene where an external other is watching the love scene (dyad) in an idealised manner. The assumption is that when this idealised emotional experience collapses, this external third is no more outside the couple, but one of the partners becomes the third, watching an idealised couple, to which he/she no longer belongs.

In considering the couple in the movie *45 Years* from a linkage perspective, their crisis would imply a focus, not on the melting of Geoff's individual frozen mourning process, but on the loss of the idealised representation of the couple itself – conceived as a narcissistic whole neglecting differences. This contributes to the feeling of a catastrophic outcome, expressed through both open and veiled reproaches and recriminations, as occurs in melancholia. Reproaches contain the desire to recover the lost, idealised, narcissistic representation of the couple; they yearn to recover the loss of the security of "paradise" whose existence feels to have been erased by the discontent. It is proposed that life in the imaginary paradise of this couple encompassed the shared wish to be childless. This paradise had to be constructed based on a commonality of such a position. But Katya's pregnancy unveils, for Kate, that this commonality was fictitious.

The film *45 Years* beautifully illustrates how disillusionment can cause a rupture to the pact the couple creates unconsciously in the initial process of falling in love. In the film disillusionment centres around a pact concerning a childless marriage, but there are many such disillusionments that couples face in everyday life which either have the potential to be worked through or to become an unresolvable crisis.

## Conclusions

Link theory adds an important explanatory concept to understanding mourning and melancholia in couples. Freud saw primary narcissism as an essential developmental stage in bringing about the necessary coherence for the formation of the ego. In the formation of a couple, narcissism also plays an important role in binding together two separate unities into a perceived "perfect" whole. This requires a particular type of link to bind the couple. In a narcissistic couple, the link and its related intersubjective perspective that the couple establishes needs to deny any differences that threaten the couple's identity. With Kate and Geoff, the couple in the movie *45 Years*, it was their predisposing, narcissistic link which led to their inability to integrate the revelation of aspects of Geoff's unprocessed history. This created a crisis of identity for the couple whereby previously excluded differences in their link dramatically intruded. In every stable link, there are moments of dis-encounter, of rupture of the illusory continuity, sameness, or complementarity which support the identity of the couple. If disillusionment can be worked through and confidence can reappear, a new stability within the couple and a reconstruction of their link becomes possible, regardless of how illusory and ephemeral this may be. Notwithstanding this, the successful resolution of a couple crisis can, however, add new strength and resilience to the link.

## References

Aulagnier, P. (1975). *The Violence of Interpretation: From Pictogram to Statement*. The New Library of Psychoanalysis. New York: Routledge, 2001.

Freud, S. (1914). On Narcissism: An Introduction. *S.E.*, 14: 67–102.

Freud, S. (1917) Mourning and Melancholia. *S.E.*, 14: 237–258.

Freud, S. (1926). Inhibitions, Symptoms and Anxiety. *S.E.*, 20: 75–176.

Kaës, R. (1994). Psychic work and unconscious alliances in therapeutic institutions. *British Journal of Psychotherapy*, 10: 361–371.

Klein, M. (1935). *Love, Guilt and Reparation and Other Works – The Writings of Melanie Klein, Volume 1* (pp. 262–289). London: Hogarth Press, 1975 (reprinted London: Karnac, 1992).

Moguillansky, R., & Seiguer, G. (1996). *La Vida Emocional de la Familia* (*The Emotional Life of Families*). Buenos Aires: Lugar Ed.

Pinter, H. (1969). *Night*. Retrieved from www.haroldpinter.org/publications/publications_byharold.shtml

# Epilogue

*Timothy Keogh and Cynthia Gregory-Roberts*

The year in which this book was written marked the hundredth anniversary of Freud's publication of *Mourning and Melancholia.* It therefore seems apposite to return to this subject, which is at the heart of our book. The overall aim of the book has been to draw attention to a specific form of suffering in couples and families – a melancholic reaction to loss – which, we propose, can be mediated by a short-term psychoanalytic intervention. In particular we have proposed a form of psychoanalytic intervention with couples and families that integrates object relations theory with link theory. In presenting these propositions we have particularly wanted to highlight the value of couple and family psychoanalysis, which has consolidated as a mode of intervention during the last decade.

As an oeuvre we have shown that as a consequence of psychological and other research, the impact and consequences of complicated and prolonged grief have become increasingly acknowledged as a significant mental health problem needing a specific diagnosis and treatment. The focus of this research, whilst largely individually focused, has also recognised that unresolved grief as it manifests in couples and families can precipitate serious psychological difficulties, which can result in family and relationship breakdown and associated economic and social impacts. Thus, we feel that attention to the plight of such couples and families is overdue.

Moreover, as we have attempted to illustrate, failure to assist such couples and families can result in an intergenerational transmission of these problems. At the broader societal level this intergenerational transmission of unresolved and particularly traumatic loss can produce escalating societal tensions and conflicts.

From a psychodynamic perspective we have argued that a predisposition to a melancholic reaction to loss is intrinsically linked to the extent to which a human being has developed a sense of himself as being psychologically separate from others. In this regard, we note that much of the recent research concerning complicated and prolonged grief has indirectly vindicated Freud's original ideas, expressed in that which many consider to be a psychoanalytic gem, that is, his paper *Mourning and Melancholia.*

In terms of object relations theory, we have outlined how the level of separation and individuation is revealed in the psychic representation of the self and other, and how these psychic representations become expressed (unconsciously) in external couple relationships. Moreover, we have suggested that the concept of the link is the co-constructed entity through which individuals in a couple dyad express their internalised templates. We have suggested that pathological links develop in a couple relationship when there is a collusion to preserve the couple's respective archaic internal object relations.

Through numerous clinical examples and vignettes we have further attempted to show the value of psychoanalytic concepts when applied clinically. These clinical examples and vignettes also point to the cross-cultural applicability of psychoanalytic theory when applied to couples and families. Part of this application includes a focused approach to assessing such reactions which requires not only general psychoanalytic competencies, but specific competencies related to the theoretical framework that has been articulated concerning unresolved grief.

Couple and family psychoanalysis has been a later development in the history of psychoanalysis. Notwithstanding this, in recent decades this field of psychoanalysis has gained a significant impetus from the formation of international committees and organisations which have fostered the global exchange of ideas amongst practitioners. The establishment of journals dedicated to couples and family psychoanalysis has also fostered the development of this area of practice. These modes of professional exchange have resulted in many practitioners being challenged by new concepts and ideas, such as link theory, which have initially been viewed as foreign (and which, in the case of link theory, was until recently only available in the form of an actual foreign language). The initial resistance to such new ideas has, however, ultimately opened a space which has allowed for a creative synthesis of new ideas to be forged in order to foster a further development of couple and family psychoanalysis. That is, it represented a process whereby being open to the other allowed a benefit which did not preclude maintaining the sense of self. This can be seen as the same challenge a couple faces when forming a creative link.

This openness to the new connects to one of the central themes of this book which is that a psychic development that does not allow for alterity, limits creativity. It is therefore a healthy psychological development for our field that such creative international dialogues have emerged. In this regard, it is also intriguing to discover that across cultures and somewhat independently, parallel theoretical developments have taken place. Indeed, if we take intersubjectivity as a common factor, it seems that couples and family psychoanalysis in all of its theoretical incarnations has increasingly pointed in the direction of the notion of a co-created entity. In this sense, whether it is Ogden's analytic third, Dicks's joint marital personality, Bion's theory of container–contained, Ferro's iteration of the concept of the analytic field or the concept of link, there has been an increasing acknowledgment in psychoanalysis and within couple and family psychoanalysis in particular, of the concept of intersubjectivity. This has involved an appreciation of a definition of intersubjectivity that implies surrendering the idea of a mind in isolation. The common assumption that intersubjectivity means "shared" or "mutual" understanding is, of course, a later development of the concept and something that is much more specific and restricted than that originally envisioned by theorists such as Husserl. His original concept was much broader in scope and did not require the achievement of a shared agreement or mutual understanding. Instead, at the interactional level, intersubjectivity for Husserl implied a perspective that was more akin to the metaphor of trading places rather than shared understanding. Moreover, the clinical examples and vignettes presented in this book place a premium on the therapist not regarding himself or the other as an "isolated mind". This allows the therapist to enter into the experience of the other either through an openness to countertransference and/or an experience of himself as part of a therapeutic link.

The clinical examples and vignettes presented by a variety of experienced psychoanalysts and psychoanalytic psychotherapists represent a range of experiences of loss including the impact of intergenerational loss of a child, parent, loss of pregnancy, and the perceived loss of a relationship. These examples also illustrate the different ways in which couple and family therapists from different cultural backgrounds approach their work and how they locate the focus of therapeutic action. This has revealed some commonalities including a strong respect for working with unconscious processes, especially transference between the couple (as the patient) and the therapist, as well as between each of the couple and the therapist. We believe that working with couples thus enriches individual therapeutic work as it enhances the understanding of the internal couple.

Returning to the central theme of this book, we are aware that whilst our focus has been on loss in couples and assisting couples to mourn, we are reminded that the development of a capacity to mourn is at the centre of all psychoanalytic interventions. To psychoanalysts and psychoanalytic psychotherapists, mourning is one of the most important of all psychoanalytic concepts in terms of psychic development. This is why Freud's seminal ideas and their elaboration, especially by Klein, are so central in the psychoanalytic literature. They have been shown to have not only an enduring relevance, but a cross-cultural one. The potency of the psychoanalytic approach with couples and families experiencing unresolved loss is that it allows for the restoration of a lost psychic object which can transform the experience of reality.

# Author Index


Abraham, K. 7, 15, 19–21, 29, 35, 105
Alvarez, A. 29–30
Anzieu, D. 62
Arizmendi, B. 3, 5
Auden, W. H. 17
Aulagnier, P. 133

Bagnini, C. 120
Bell, D. 104–105
Berenstein, I. 34, 35, 36, 37, 38, 39, 40, 61
Bick, E. 62, 113
Bion, W. R. 6, 7, 8–9, 25–26, 37, 65, 71, 86, 98; and container-contained 48, 93, 141; and intergenerational loss 87–89, 96, 99–100
Bleger, J. 49, 61
Bollas, C. 94, 108, 114
Bowlby, J. 26–28
Box, S. 61
Bracha, H. S. 103
Britton, R. 63
Byng-Hall, J. 61

Cartwright, D. 104
Casement, P. J. 118
Clulow, C. 28, 61

Dare, C. 35
de Saussure, F. 38
de Setton, L. S. 30, 61
Descartes, R. 38
Dicks, H. 35, 61, 62, 141

Enfield, S. 6, 40, 62, 65, 69

Fairbairn, W. R. D. 6, 7, 15, 21, 23–25, 47, 61, 62, 65, 103
Fisher, J. V. 66
Floyd, F. J. 4, 29
Flügel, J. C. 60
Fonagy, P. 63
Fornari, F. 77, 78, 81
Freud, S. 15, 63, 77, 99; development of psychoanalytic theory 17, 19, 38, 60; loss experienced by 18; on love 129, 130–131; meta-psychology of 21, 35, 60; on mourning/melacholia 3, 7, 15, 16, 17–19, 20, 22, 29, 35, 88, 109, 132–133, 139, 140, 142

Goethe, J. W. von 16–17
Green, A. 9, 103, 107, 112
Greenberg, J. S. 4, 29
Gregory-Roberts, C. 46, 47, 57, 68
Grotstein, J. 94
Gurevich, H. 110–111

Harris, M. 82
Heidegger, M. 38
Hong, J. 4, 29
Husserl, E. 6, 142

Jackson, S. W. 3, 16
Joseph, B. 29

Kaës, R. 6, 38, 48, 52, 61, 64–65, 133–134
Keogh, T. 6, 40, 46, 47, 51, 57, 61, 62, 65, 68, 69
Klein, M. 6, 21–23, 25, 29, 51, 124, 142; and link theory 65, 66; and object relations theory 7, 15, 21, 22–23, 35–36, 60–61, 62; and psychic development 21–22, 24, 66, 77, 81, 133
Kochanek, K. D. 4

Kohon, G. 107
Kohut, H. 38, 104
Kristensen, P. 1
Kristeva, J. 77
Kristjanson, L. J. 1
Kubler-Ross, E. 28

Lacan, J. 38–39
Leader, D. 118
Lemma, A. 4, 48, 56
Lévi-Strauss, C. 38
Levine, H. B. 114–115
Lobb, E. A. 1, 2
Losso, R. 30, 61, 63–64, 66, 69

Maciejewski, P. 1, 2
Meltzer, D. 82
Moguillansky, R. 138
Morgan, M. 7, 46–47, 61, 68

Nicolò, A. M. 52, 65, 82

O'Connor, M. F. 3, 5
Ogden, T. H. 6, 19, 21, 24–25, 26, 62–63, 64, 71, 114, 141
Owens, D. 4

Palacios, E. 5, 61
Parkes, C. 28, 30
Pickering, J. C. 88, 93, 94, 96, 97, 99, 100
Pincus, L. 35, 93, 94, 97, 103
Pontalis, J.-B. 105
Puget, J. 34, 35, 36, 37, 39, 40, 61, 65

Racker, H. 112
Rivière, P. 18, 30, 35, 37, 61, 63, 64, 65, 66, 69
Robertson, J. 27, 28
Rogers, C. H. 4, 5, 29
Rose, G. J. 111
Rosner, R. 5
Ruszczynski, S. 35, 61

Scharff, D. E. 5, 18, 24, 30, 35, 47, 49 51, 61, 62
Scharff, J. S. 18, 24, 35, 47, 49, 51, 61, 62
Schut, H. 1, 2, 89
Segal, H. 23
Seiguer, G. 138
Seltzer, M. M. 4, 29
Shane, E./Shane, M. 102, 103–104, 115
Shear, K. 27–28
Steiner, J. 107
Stroebe, M./Stroebe, W. 1, 2, 89
Symington, J. 113

Torok, M. 105
Tustin, F. 62

Vorchheimer, M. 6, 61

Weiss, R. S. 28
Winnicott, D. W. 21, 37, 63, 103, 114, 115

Zinner, J. 62

# Subject Index

Note: bold page numbers indicate tables; italic page numbers indicate figures.

accidental death 4
adolescence 42, 92
affect 56, 71, 118, 119, 126; tracking 8, 50–51
agency 17, 25, 40, 42
alcoholism 29–30, 55
alpha elements 93, 94
ambivalence 18
analytic field 64, 98, 141
analytic frame/stance/attitude 46, 48–49; linked state of mind 47; and miscarriage 124–125
analytic link 48, 65, 66
analytic reverie 96, 98, 100, 114, 127
analytic setting 46, 48–49, 50
anxieties 30, 78, 81; depressive 23, **70**, 71; developmental 5, 40, 62, **70**; and early parental loss 103; Oedipal 63–64; primitive 26, 55–56, 62–63, 68, 93; separation 1, 2, 27
assessment 7–8, 45–58; analytic setting for 46; and analytic setting/frame 48–49; and analytic stance/attitude 46, 47, 48; clinical example of 53, 54–56; and countertransference 46, 47, 49, 50, 51, 52; and couple link 52; and individual/joint couple/family sessions 50; and melancholic reactions of couple 52–53; and miscarriage 120–121; and mutative couple interpretation 47; and peer/supervision groups 50; and play 8, 51; and psychodynamic formulation 46–48, 56–58; tools in 8; and tracking affect 8, 50–51; and unconscious processes 49–50; and unresolved earlier losses 50–51, 53, 56, 57, *see also* object relations & link theories, integration of
attachment theory 2, 3, 5, 17, 26–28, 89; four attachment styles in 28
Australia 7, 61, 92, 98; death rate for indigenous people in 4
autistic–contiguous position 8, 26, 62, 64, *65*, **70**
autonomy 6, 25, 28, 84, 85–86, 95

bereavement *see* grief; mourning
beta elements 25, 89, 93
Bion concept of links 8, 25–26, 37, 96
blocked mourning 122–123
borderline disorder 4
boundaries/boundedness 26, 42, 49, 63, 64, 79

castration complex 131
child development 24; five stages of 20; Klein on 21–22
child, loss of 4–5, 15–16, 29, 142; assessment of couple following 53, 54–56; and projective/introjective processes 7, 18
childhood abuse/neglect 2, 126
child death 60–61; death rate of 4; in family experiencing loss 8, 9; narcissism of 131; and parental loss *see* parental loss, early; and play in family therapy 8, 51; reactions to loss in 29–30; of refugees 8–9, 92, 94, 95, 98–99
chuntering 29
complicated grief 1, 141; and couples *see* couples and complicated grief;

impacts of 5; and loss of child 4–5; and neuroscience 3; psychoanalytic theoretical framework for 5–6, 45; risk factors for 2; and timing of intervention 5, *see also* prolonged grief disorder
concordant countertransference 111–113
conjoint couple therapy 47, 50, 67
conjoint selected fact 8–9, 96–97, 100
container–contained 48, 68, 93, 141
containment 8, 49, 68, **70**, 71, 127; failure of 22–23, 88, 93, 94
cot death 15–16
countertransference 8, 9, 46, 47, 49, 50, 51, 52, 142; concordant 111–113; and couples following miscarriage 119, 121, 122–123, 125; and early parental loss 108, 111–112, 113–114
couple link 34–36, 39, 40, 62, 69, 129; in assessments 45, 47, 48, 50, 52, 57; developmental model of 65–66, *65*; and imposed restrictions 133–134; and love *see* love; narcissistic *see* narcissistic couple link; and shared illusion 129, 130, 132–133
couple state of mind 46–47, 68
couple therapy 6–7, 34–36, 68; and early parental loss 107–113; and intergenerational loss *see* intergenerational loss; and miscarriage *see* miscarriage; phases of 8, 34, 52–53
couples 15–30, 34–42, 45–58, 60–61, 62–69 *passim*, 94 102–115, 118–127, 129–139, 140, 141, 142
couples and complicated grief 2, 15–16, 24–25, 30; and anxious melancholic reaction 26; assessment model for *see* assessment model; and attachment styles 28; and concrete symbols 23; and defensive alliances 52, 64–65; and earlier losses 20; and interlocking traumatic scene 88; intervention approach for 5–6; and loss of parent *see* parental loss, early; manic attempts to deal with 23; and miscarriage *see* miscarriage; and projective/introjective processes 7, 18; and RPL 9; and self-object relations 45; and sexual relationship 23
cross-cultural perspective 7, 141, 142
crypt 105–106

"dead mother" concept 9, 103, 107, 112, 113–114, 115
death rates 4
denial 57, 121
depression 2–3, 20, 30, 51
depressive anxieties 23, **70**, 71
depressive position 8, 22, 23, 36, 62, **70**, 133; in developmental model 65, *65*
developmental anxieties 5, 40, 62, **70**
disillusionment 39, 135, 137
dissociation 110–111, 112
divorce 5, 57, 61, 103, 106, 107, 115
dreams 2, 82
*DSM-5* (*Diagnostic and Statistical Manual of Mental Disorders*, Fifth Revision) 2

ego 35, 132; bodily 63, *see also* self, sense of
el vinculo *see* link theory
empathic self-object milieu 104
empathy 48, 68, 81, 127
endopsychic model 24, 47, 61, 62

families and complicated grief 8; assessment model for *see* assessment model; impacts of 5; intervention approach for 6; and regressive defences *see* regression/regressive defences; and symptom bearers 65
family histories *see* personal/family histories
family therapy 8, 51, 61, 78, 82, 142
father 92, 94; emotionally absent 103, 107, 113; ideal, longing for 110; loss of 40, 50–51, 57, 102, 105
fear response 103
foetus *see* miscarriage
*45 years* (movie) 9, 131, 134–137
frozen couples 135, 136

grief 1, 118; normal process of 2; pathological *see* complicated grief; stages of 30
groups 37–38, 133
guilt/shame 24, 53, 67, 78; and couples following miscarriage 118, 121, 122, 123, 125, 126; and early parental loss 104, 106, 111; and intergenerational loss 88, 90, 92, 94

Holocaust survivors, children of 8–9, 92, 94, 95, 98–99
homicide 4
horizontal links 6, 45, 69
Humoural Theory 2

ICD-10 1
imposition 7, 34, 39, 40, 45, 46
incorporation 105
indigenous people, death rate amongst 4
individuation 23, 24, 30, 78, 84, 141; of the couple 53, *65*, 66, 67, 95
infant death *see* child, loss of
initiator, therapist as 114–115
interdependence *see* mature dependence
interference 6, 40, 42, 48, 66, 69
intergenerational loss 5, 6, 8–9, 45, 87–100, 140, 142; Bion on 87–91; and children of refugees 92, 94, 95, 98–99; clinical example of 91–93; healing of, through relationship 90–91; and interlocking traumatic scenes 88, 93, 94, 95–96, 97, 98–99; and malignant dowries 88–89, 93, 100; and memory 92, 93, 94, 95; and miscarriage 123–124, 127; and selected fact 8–9, 91, 96–97, 100
interlocking traumatic scene 88, 93, 94, 95–96, 97, 98–99
internal objects 24–25, 30, 45, 53; analyst as 40; dreams/unconscious fantasies as 39; ego's relationship with 7, 36
internal self-object links *see* self-object relations
intersubjectivity 7, 25, 26, 52, 81, 141–142; and link theory 6, 34, 38, 40, 91
intrapsychic state 9, 18, 81, 83, 91
introjection 7, 18, 35–36, 68, 81; and incorporation, compared 105; and projection 34, 37, 40, 47, 102, 112; and self-containment 93

jealousy 41, **70**, 122, 135, 136

libido 24, 35, 132, 133; detachment from objects of 3
liminal figure, therapist as 108
link theory 5–6, 7, 9, 15, 30, 34–42, 61, 141; and concept of subject 35, 36, 38–39; and couples *see* couple link; and family therapy 8; and inter-subjectivity 6, 34, 38, 39–40, 91; and object relations theory *see* object relations & link theories, integration of; and transference 40
linked frame of mind 47
links/link structures 36–38, 39, **70**, 129, 138, 141; and groups 37–38; narcissistic *see* narcissistic couple links; pathological 42, 52, 64, 141; and psychic development 66; and regressive defences 79, 86; therapeutic 46, 68, 142; vertical/horizontal 6, 8, 45, 56–57, 68–69
loss 23–26; Bion on 25–26; of child *see* child, loss of; and couple/family psychoanalysis 6–7; cross-cultural perspective on 7; Fairbairn on 23–25; infant experience of 3–4; manic attempts to deal with 23; of parent *see* parental loss, early; and postmodernism 28–29; of relationship/life stage 16–17; of shared illusion 132–134
love 89, 90–91, 129–132; in literature/film 130, 131, 134–137; loss of 130, 131, 137–139; and narcissism 129–130, 131, 132, 137
love-object 18, 20, 21, 22
loving link, prevention of 108–110

malignant dowries 88–89, 93, 100
manic states 23, 36, 120, 124
marriage 15, 54, 57, 85, 92, 120, 124; and malignant dowries 88–89, 93, 100; and marital personality 61, 141, *see also* divorce
mature dependence 24, 25
MDD (Major Depressive Disorder) 3
melancholia 2–3, 16–19, 140; Abraham on 19–21; and ambivalence 18; and avoiding pain 25, 87; Bion on 25–26, 87–91; early origins of 20–21, 88; Freud on *see Mourning and Melancholia*; and loss of self 35, 88; and malignant dowries 88–89; and miscarriage 118, 120, 122, 124–125; and mourning, compared *see under* mourning; post-Kleinian theories on 29–30; and sadism 18, 19, 20; and self-recrimination *see* self-recrimination; and shadow metaphor 19; and thirdness 63–64

memory 82, 100, 130, 133, 134; traumatic 93, 94, 124
metaphor 19, 125–127
miscarriage 4–5, 118–127, 142; and assessment 120–121; and countertransference 119, 121, 122–123, 125; couple psychotherapy following 119–121; and defences 120; and fear of fatherhood 125; and guilt/shame 118, 121, 125, 126; impact on couples of 119, 120; and intergenerational issues 123–124, 127; and metaphor 125–127; and Oedipal/sibling issues 122–123, 124, 126; and persecutory phantasies/blocked mourning 122–123; and personal histories 119, 121, 122–124, 126; and phantasies of conception 121; and psychoanalytic frame/stance 124–125; rates 5, 119; RPL 5, 9, 119, 127; and sense of self 120; undisclosed 118
mortality 4, 15–17, 45, 53-58 *passim*, 78, 81, 82, 90, 102–115, 118, 129–139,
mother, loss of 9, 55, 57, 81, 103–104, 105, 106–107, 109–110, 115
mother–baby relationship 21–22, 24–25, 56, 114; and container-contained 93; links in 37
mourning 1, 20, 118; avoidance of *see* regression/regressive defences; blocked 122–123; and culture 7, 18; incapacity for 3, 4; Klein on 21–23; as loss of object 18; and melancholia, compared 3, 17, 18, 20, 22, 23, 27, 35, 88, 120, 132–134; phases of 27, 52–53; and timing of intervention 5
*Mourning and Melancholia* (Freud) 7, 16, 17–19, 20, 22, 35, 88, 109, 132–133, 139, 140, 142
mutative couple interpretation 47

nameless dread 25, 88, 93, 94
narcissism 4, 9, 29, 39, 53, 102; and early parental loss 102; and melancholia 16–17, 18, 19, 21, 35, 64, 91, 133; relinquishment of 23
narcissistic contract 133–134
narcissistic couple link 9, 39, 52, 53, 55–56, 57, 64, 65, 66, 69, **70**, 91; and *45 Years* 138, 139; and falling in love 129–130, 131, 132, 133
*Night* (Pinter) 130

object, good/bad 21–23, 25, 53
object relations theory 3, 15, 21, 23–25, 30, 141; and Oedipal anxieties 63; and splitting 7, 21–22, 52–53; and three stages of psychic development 64, *see also* internal objects; self-object relations
object relations/link theories, integration of 5–6, 30, 34, 35–36, 39, 45, 51, 62, 65, 140; clinical demonstration of 40–42; and subject/subjectivity 35, 36, 38–39, 40; and therapeutic relationship 46
object, restoration of lost 30, 53
Oedipus situation 22, 63–64, **70**, 122, 124, 131
omnipotent defences 113
*On Narcissism* (Freud) 18, 35, 133
*On Transience* (Freud) 3
oral stage 20

pain, feeling/suffering 87
paranoid-schizoid position 8, 21–22, 23, 55, 62, 64, **70**; in developmental model 65, *65*; and regressive defences 77, 78, 81
parental loss, early 4, 9, 55, 57, 102–115; and anxiety 103, 104, 107; clinical examples of 102–103, 104, 105–111; and couple relationships 102, 106, 108–111, 112; and crypt/incorporation 105–106; and "dead mother" concept 9, 103, 107, 112, 113–114, 115; and dissociation 110–111; as double loss 102, 115; and empathic self-object milieu 104; and fear response 103; and guilt/shame 104, 106, 111; and obstruction of growth of self 103, 104–105, 107, 109; and therapeutic relationship 108, 111–115; and therapist as initiator 114–115; and therapist as liminal figure 108
parents: alcoholic/depressed 29–30; and loss of children *see* child, loss of; as templates of self-object relations 60–61
PCBD (Persistent Complex Bereavement Disorder) 2
peer group review 50, 69
persecutory anxieties 23, 25, 53, 55
personal/family histories 50–51, 55, 57, 79–80, 92–93; and miscarriage 119, 121, 122–124, 126

phantasies, unconscious 36, 93, 100; of childbirth 122–123; of conceiving baby 121; of infant 21, 22
phobic responses 26
Pinter, Harold 130
play in family therapy 8, 51
Polybus 2
post-Kleinian theories 29–30, 35
postmodernism 28–29
pregnancy loss *see* miscarriage
primitive mental states 6, 26
projection 24; and introjection 34, 37, 40, 47, 102, 112
projective gridlock 7, 47
projective identification 23, 25
prolonged grief disorder 1–2; diagnostic category for 2
psychic development 8, 23–24, 25, 26, 69; and external links 66; and paranoid-schizoid/depressive positions 21–22, 23, 62; and sense of self 3, 4, 25; three stages of 64
psychic phantasies 40, 60–61, 122–123, 127
psychic retreat 107, 127
psychoanalysis 3–4, 9–10, 141–142; couple/family *see* couple/family psychoanalysis; and cross-cultural perspective 7, 141, 142; Freud's development of 17, 19; link concept in 37, 141–142
psychoanalytic frame/stance *see* analytic frame/stance/attitude
psychoanalytic theoretical framework 5–7, 30, 60–72, 141; background to 60–61; short-term intervention in *see* short-term intervention model, *see also* object relations & link theories, integration of
psychodynamic formulation 8, 20, 30, 46–48, 56–58, 68
psychogenic autism 62
psychosis/psychotic functioning 8, 20, 49, 65, 71, 86
psychosomatic self 62–63

Recurrent Pregnancy Loss (RPL) 5, 9, 119, 127
reflective couple interpretation 47
refugees, children of 92, 94, 95, 98–99
regression/regressive defences 77–86, 120; clinical example of 78–86; and dead mother 81; and family histories 79–80; and family illness 79, 84; and links 79, 86; and myth of unity of family 82, 83; and paranoid-schizoid position 77, 78, 81; and sadism 84, 85; and separation anxiety 83–84, 85; three manifestations of 81; and working through mourning 84–86
relationships 39–40, 91; attachment 27–28, 88; human need for 7, 21, 23–24, 60, 62; object 24, 36, 37, 45, 56, 60, 132; therapist–patient *see* therapeutic relationship/alliance
reparation 9, 36, 64, 79
restoration of the object 30, 53, 142
reverie: analytic 96, 98, 100, 114, 127; maternal 88, 93
RPL (Recurrent Pregnancy Loss) 5, 9, 119, 127

sadism 18, 19, 20, 84, 85
selected fact 8–9, 91, 96–97, 100
self, psychosomatic 62–63
self, sense of 3, 4, 25, 28, 53, 62–63; and miscarriage 120
self-esteem 55, 102, 104
self-object relations 6, 7, 9, 34, 35, 45, 46, 50, 65–66, 118; and early parental loss 104; narcissistic 56; and templates of parental relationships 60–61; and therapy 47–48
self-psychology 104
self-reproach/-punishment 1, 6, 16, 18, 20, 21, 45, 55, 88, 109, 132; perverse pleasure in 29; projection of 109
separation anxiety/distress 1, 2, 27
shadow metaphor 19
shame *see* guilt/shame
shared illusion 129, 130, 132–133
shock 92, 94, 98
short-term intervention model 66–71; aim of 66–67; evaluation in 71; phase one (engagement/formulation) 67–69; phase two (working through) 69; phase three (termination) 8, 69–71; and links, vertical/horizontal 68–69; therapeutic alliance in 68; and Unresolved Grief Triad (UGT) 67, *67*, 69, 71; use of grid in 69, **70**
sibling rivalry 122–123, 131
skin, psychic 26, 62–63

splitting/projection process 7, 16, 18, 21–22, 24, 47, 55, 57, 69, **70**, 71
*status nascendi* 133
subject-subject link *see* link theory
subject/subjectivity 35, 36, 38–39, 52, 65; as doing with others 40, *see also* intersubjectivity
suicidal ideation 1, 6, 19
suicide/attempted suicide 4, 78, 79
superego 17, 18, 45, 55, 131
symbol formation 23

Tavistock Clinic (London) 27, 28, 61, 90
termination phase 8, 69–71
therapeutic relationship/alliance 7, 8, 40, 46, 58, 68, 142; and analytic reverie 96, 98, 100, 114, 127; and continuity/predictability 48–49, 108; and couples following miscarriage *see* miscarriage; and early parental loss 108, 111–115; therapist as initiator in 114–115; therapist as liminal figure in 108, *see also* analytic stance/attitude; countertransference
thirdness/malignant third 37, 63–64, 93, 97, 141
*Totem and Taboo* (Freud) 18
tracking affect 8, 50–51
transference 37, 38, 40, 47, 49, 60, 82, 122, 142, *see also* countertransference
transformation 6, 47, 48, 51, 62, 66, 86; and love 90–91, 99–100
transgenerational objects 77, 82, 86
transitional objects/phenomena 37
transpersonal defences/dynamics 30, 77, 81, 82–83, 86, *see also* regression/regressive defences
trauma 27, 28, 30, 80, 110–111, 130–131; childhood 9, 56, 108, 119, 131; and double loss 102, 115; and malignant dowries 88–89, 93, 100; and war 87–88, *see also* interlocking traumatic scene
traumatic enactments 108–109
traumatic memory 93, 94, 124

unconscious 17, 39, 60, 93, *see also* transference
unresolved grief 1, 5, 9, 45–58, 66, 91, 93, 99, 119, 127, 142,
Unresolved Grief Triad (UGT) 67, *67*, 69, 71

vertical links 6, 8, 45, 56–57, 69

working through 8, 22–23, 66, 69, 89, 115; and anger/guilt 78; and grid 69, **70**; and regressive defences 84–86